ACCOUNTING FOR MANAGEMENT

ACCOUNTING FOR MANAGEMENT

Bhavna Bahuguna

CENTRUM PRESS
NEW DELHI-110002 (INDIA)

CENTRUM PRESS
H.O.: 4360/4, Ansari Road, Daryaganj,
New Delhi-110002 (India)
Tel: 23278000, 23261597, 23255577, 23286875

B.O.: No. 1015, Ist Main Road, BSK IIIrd Stage,
IIIrd Phase, IIIrd Block, Bangalore-560085 (INDIA)
Tel: 080-41723429

Email: centrumpress@gmail.com
Visit us at: www.centrumpress.com

Accounting for Management

First Edition, 2011

ISBN 978-93-80921-22-8

PRINTED IN INDIA

Printed at Mehra Offset Press, Delhi.

Contents

Preface — *vii*

1. Accounting: An Introduction — 1
2. Branches of Accounting — 13
3. Cost Management — 29
4. Financial Analysis — 91
5. Emerging Dimensions in Accounting — 121
6. Cost Accounting — 156
7. Cost Control Techniques — 169
8. Key Concepts of Accountancy — 198
9. Financial Accounting — 227
10. Accounting for Public Sector — 272

Index — 295

Preface

Management accounting is concerned with the provisions and use of accounting information to managers within organizations, to provide them with the basis to make informed business decisions that will allow them to be better equipped in their management and control functions.

Management Accounting is "the process of identification, measurement, accumulation, analysis, preparation, interpretation and communication of information used by management to plan, evaluate and control within an entity and to assure appropriate use of and accountability for its resources. Management accounting also comprises the preparation of financial reports for non-management groups such as shareholders, creditors, regulatory agencies and tax authorities".

We hope that the discussion made in this book will help the readers to understand and learnt about the different aspects of Accounting for Management.

Author

Preface

1

Accounting: An Introduction

ACCOUNTING

Accounting is the language of business. It is a standard set of rules for measuring a firm's financial performance.

Assessing a company's financial performance is important for many groups, including:

- The firm's officers (managers and employees)
- Investors (current and potential shareholders)
- Lenders (banks)
- General public Standard financial statements serve as a yardstick of communicating financial erformance to the general public.

For example, monthly sales volumes released by McDonald's Corp. provide both its managers and the general public with an opportunity to assess the company's financial performance across major geographic segments.

IMPORTANCE OF ACCOUNTING

Making Corporate Decisions

Suppose a telecom company is looking to acquire a regional company to boost its presence in that region. There are several potential targets that fit the bill. How does this company determine which of these targets, if any, would make a good acquisition candidate?

Making Investment Decisions

A mutual fund is looking to invest in several diverse

technology companies—Microsoft, Oracle, and Intel. How does this mutual fund determine in which of these targets it should make an investment?

Accounting Facilitates Corporate and Investment Decisions

A major part of corporate and investment decisions relies on analyzing all of the companies' financial information. Accounting, the standard language by which such financial information can be assessed and compared, is fundamental to making these decisions.

USES OF ACCOUNTING

Accounting is used by a variety of organizations, from the federal government to nonprofit organizations to small businesses to corporations. As suggested, be discussing accounting rules as they pertain to publicly traded companies.

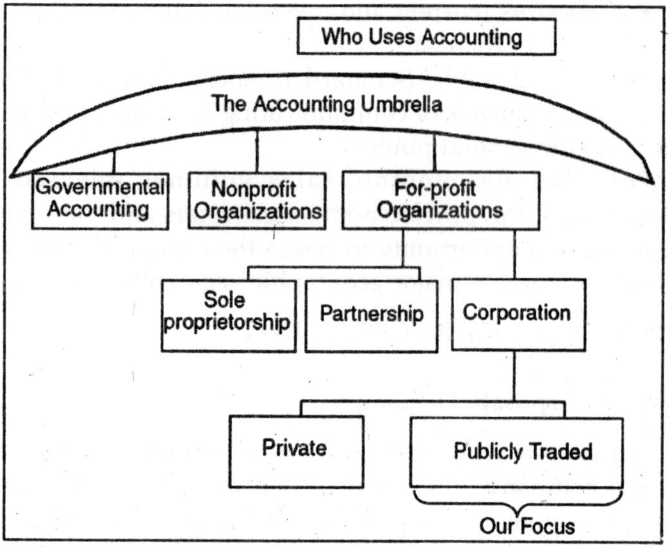

ACCOUNTING INFORMATION SYSTEM

Accounting information system is a system of records, usually computer based, which combines accounting principles and concepts with the benefits of an information system and which is used to analyse and record business transactions for the purpose to prepare financial statements and provide accounting data to its users. Some accounting information systems are still manual, i.e. accounting records are made with a pen, paper and manual entries into accounting books.

How are Such Systems Used? These systems can be customised to meet the needs of a business. For example, information technology professionals responsible for business processes and information technology professionals responsible for the accounting information system can work together to develop and implement such a system so that it automatically gets information from other sources already in use by the business. Also, the systems can be set up to feature certain functions that are important to the business and eliminate functions minor to the business. Information can be automatically fed, or manually fed into a business accounting information system at whatever pace and however often it is necessary.

What are the Benefits of Using Accounting Information System? Businesses use accounting information systems to make their accounting activities easier, quicker, and more accurate, since accounting records are analysed and financial statements are prepared within the system, which allows to safe time of employees and avoid mistakes.

Since many accounting information systems are equipped with error-reducing mechanisms and gather information regarding transactions electronically and automatically, data entry and computing errors are rare.

Also since such systems are often automatically populated with transaction information, many accounting processes are less cumbersome and time-consuming when using such system.

Of course implementation of such system requires investment and time to be spent on the implementation, however future benefits are much higher that the expenses incurred. Also to consider whether business needs accounting information system and what kind of system is required thorough analysis of business and accounting processes has to be made to determine precise requirements.

ACCOUNTING CONCEPTS

THE 5 BASIC ACCOUNTS

Basic accounting rules group all finance related things into 5 fundamental types of "accounts".

That is, everything that accounting deals with can be placed into one of these 5 accounts:

1. *Assets*: Things you own.
2. *Liabilities*: Things you owe.
3. *Equity*: Overall net worth.
4. *Income*: Increases the value of your accounts.
5. *Expenses*: Decreases the value of your accounts.

It is clear that it is possible to categorize your financial world into these 5 groups. For example, the cash in your bank account is an asset, your mortgage is a liability, your paycheck is income, and the cost of dinner last night is an expense.

THE ACCOUNTING EQUATION

With the 5 basic accounts defined, what is the relationship between them? How does one type of account affect the others? Firstly, equity is defined by assets and liability. That is, your net worth is calculated by subtracting your liabilities from your assets:

$$\text{Assets} - \text{Liabilities} = \text{Equity}$$

Furthermore, you can increase your equity through income, and decrease equity through expenses. This makes sense of course, when you receive a paycheck you become "richer" and when you pay for dinner you become "poorer". This is expressed mathematically in what is known as the Accounting Equation:

$$\text{Assets} - \text{Liabilities} = \text{Equity} + (\text{Income} - \text{Expenses})$$

This equation must always be balanced, a condition that can only be satisfied if you enter values to multiple accounts. For example: if you receive money in the form of income you must see an equal increase in your assets. As another example, you could have an increase in assets if you have a parallel increase in liabilities.

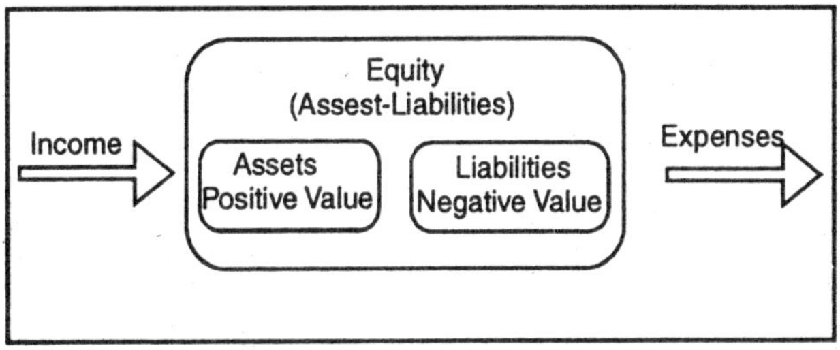

A graphical view of the relationship between the 5 basic accounts. Net worth (equity) increases through income and decreases through expenses. The arrows represent the movement of value.

DOUBLE ENTRY

The accounting equation is the very heart of a double entry accounting system. For every change in value of one account in the Accounting Equation, there must be a balancing change in another. This concept is known as the Principle of Balance, and is of fundamental importance for understanding GnuCash and other double entry accounting systems. When you work with GnuCash, you will always be concerned with at least 2 accounts, to keep the Accounting Equation balanced.

Double entry accounting serves two purposes. The first is to create an accounting trail, money always has to come from somewhere and go to somewhere. Additionally, double entry accounting historically served to double check the math of an accountant. Because the numbers are entered into multiple accounts simultaneously, there are multiple places to check to make sure the totals match. Of course, with the advent of computers, the chances of a mathematical problem are low, but it is good to know that the concept still exists!

Double entry accounting has been around since the late 15th century, when it was described by an Italian friar, Luca Pacioli. Traditional double entry accounting involves recording each transaction in a book called a ledger, then copying each part of the transaction to separate books called journals. This method is still used in businesses today as a way to avoid entry errors and to track the source of those errors. GnuCash simplifies this traditional accounting by copying part of each transaction for you, so it may not catch some of the entry errors that would show up in traditional accounting. But it will flag transactions that are not balanced, and it will let you know when an account name is missing.

CONVENTIONS OF ACCOUNTING

RELEVANCE

The convention of relevance emphasizes the fact that only such information should be made available by accounting as is relevant and useful for achieving its objectives. For example, business is interested in knowing as to what has been total labour cost? It is not interested in knowing how much employees spend and what they save.

OBJECTIVITY

The convention of objectivity emphasizes that accounting information should be measured and expressed by the standards which are commonly acceptable. For example, stock of goods lying unsold at the end of the year should be valued as its cost price not at a higher price even if it is likely to be sold at higher price in future. Reason is that no one can be sure about the price which will prevail in future.

FEASIBILITY

The convention of feasibility emphasizes that the time, labour and cost of analyzing accounting information should be compared vis-à-vis benefit arising out of it. For example, the cost of 'oiling and greasing' the machinery is so small that its break-up per unit produced will be meaningless and will amount to wastage of labour and time of the accounting staff.

PRINCIPLES OF ACCOUNTING

In order to manage a business effectively from the financial perspective, it is always important to measure:

- How many assets there are;
- How much profit is being generated;
- When the cash is coming in, and
- How it is being spent.

Accounting is nothing more than the measurement of these processes to reflect what has happened to a business over a relevant period of time. The asset piece is measured by the *Balance Sheet*, whilst the profit and cash pieces are measured by the *Income Statement/Profit and Loss Account* and the *Cash Flow Statement* respectively.

A good financial analyst should be aware of these simple facts, which are essential for any financial modeling exercise. Also read the Glossary of Accounting Terms for a run-down on the key terms and terminology used in accounting.

THE INCOME STATEMENT/PROFIT AND LOSS ACCOUNT

The income statement/profit and loss account measures the sales made and the costs incurred over a particular time period. For external reporting this is usually for a year but internally most businesses will prepare their income statement/ profit and loss account on a weekly or a monthly basis.

The income statement/profit and loss account captures a sale when the product or service is delivered to the customer. Cash may or may not change hands at this stage.

Costs are recorded in the income statement/profit and loss account to reflect the costs of making the sales during that time period. This is called the matching or accruals concept. This concept states that the costs recorded must match to the sales made in the relevant time period. Although the jargon in an income statement/profit and loss account may vary (especially from country to country) the costs are always deducted from sales in order of how closely they relate to the sale itself.

The order that cost deduction appears is therefore:

- Cost of product sold
- Sales, general and administration costs
- Interest expense
- Tax expense

After costs are deducted from sales, we are left with the bottom line profit (also known as the net income or profit after tax) which belongs to the shareholders, and consequently is reflected as part of shareholders' equity on the balance sheet.

BALANCE SHEET

The balance sheet shows the position that the business is in at the end of the relevant time period. It shows the assets the business has, its liabilities, and the amount of equity belonging to the shareholders. The reason it is called the balance sheet is because total assets must equal liabilities and shareholders' equity:

Assets = Liabilities + Shareholders' Equity

The 2 sides of this equation must always equal or balance.

The liabilities and equity shows where the business gets its funds and the assets shows how those funds have been used.

The assets is generally divided into 2 sub-sections, showing the short term and long term assets. In this context, a long term item is one whose life in the business is expected to be longer than 1 year.

Examples of long term or fixed assets include:

- Property
- Plant and machinery
- Financial investments that are to be held for the long term
- Patents
- Licenses

Short term assets are those whose lives are shorter than 1 year and include:

- Inventories or stock
- Account recievables/debtors (when credit is given to customers)
- Cash
- Financial investments that are to be held for the short term only (i.e. less than 1 year)

Liabilities are also broken down into short and long term items.

Short term liabilities include:

- Accounts payable/creditors (when credit is taken from suppliers)
- Income taxes payable
- Short term borrowings (where the repayment date is within 1 year)

Long term liabilities include borrowings where the repayment date is longer than 1 year from the balance sheet date.

Shareholders' equity is made up of 2 key pieces. The capital piece represents the shares bought by the investors when the business was set up. This represents the cash that was physically given to the business by the investors, i.e. shareholders. The 2nd (and often more significant) piece is retained earnings/profit and loss reserve. This is the cumulative profit earned that has not been paid to the owners in dividends but has been re-invested in the future growth of the business instead.

CASH FLOW STATEMENT

The final area is the cash flow statement. This shows how cash has been generated and used over the relevant time period.

Most cash flow statement styles will present the flows of cash using 3 main categories:

1. Operating cash flows
2. Investing cash flows
3. Financing cash flows

Operating cash flows will include the flows from the core operations of the business and is driven by trading. Investing cash flows deal with any investments in the future of the business. Any new plant and equipment would be included. And finally the financing deals with any investments made by shareholders and any dividends paid to them.

ROLE OF ACCOUNTANT IN AN ORGANIZATION

Accounting can be defined as the process of collecting,

recording, presenting and analyzing/interpreting financial information for the users of financial statement.

Accountant can also be describe as a person who has undergone a formal or professional training in the process of accounting and who belongs to at least one of the recognized professional accountancy bodies such as Institute of Chartered Accountants of Nigeria (ICAN), Association of Chartered Accountant (ACA), Institute of Chartered Accountant (ICA) etc. Accounting systems take economic events and transactions that have occurred and process the data in those transactions into information that is helpful to managers and other users, such as sales representatives and production supervisors.

Accounting systems provide information such as financial statements (the income statement, balance sheet and statement of cash flows) and performance reports (such as the cost of operating a plant or providing a service).

Managers use accounting information:

- To administer each of the activity or functional areas for which they are responsible and;
- To coordinate those activities or functions within the framework of the organization as a whole

MANAGEMENT ACCOUNTING, FINANCIAL ACCOUNTING AND COST ACCOUNTING

Management Accounting

Management accounting and financial accounting have different goals. Management Accounting measures, and reports financial and non-financial information that helps managers make decisions to fulfill the goals of an organization. Managers use management accounting information to choose, communicate and implement strategy. They also use management accounting information to coordinate product design, production and marketing decisions. Management accounting focuses on internal reporting.

Financial Accounting

Financial Accounting focuses on reporting to external

parties. It measures and records business transactions and provides financial statements that are based on generally accepted accounting principles (GAAP). Managers are responsible for the financial statements issued to investors, government regulators and other parties outside the organization.

Executive compensation is often directly affected by the numbers in these financial statements. It is not difficult to see that managers are interested in both management accounting and financial accounting.

Cost Accounting

Cost Accounting provides information for management accounting and financial accounting. Cost accounting measures and reports financial and non-financial information relating to the cost of acquiring or utilizing resources in an organization. Cost accounting includes those parts of both management accounting and financial accounting in which cost information is collected or analysed.

Report such as balance sheets, income statements and statements of cash flow are common both in management and financial accounting. Most companies adhere to, or only mildly depart from, GAAP for their basic internal financial statements. Why? Because accrual accounting provides a uniform way to measure an organization's financial performance for internal and external purposes.

However, management accounting is more wide-ranging than financial accounting's emphasis on financial statements. Management accounting embraces more extensively such topics as the development and implementation of strategies and policies, budgeting, special studies and forecasts, influence on employee behaviour, and non-financial as well as financial information

The accountant's roles in the organization can be analyses:

- Preparation and presentations of timely accurate financial/accounting reports to management
- Identification of areas of inefficiency and wastages of resources in industries

- Treasury functions: Accountant also plays the role of treasury functions in such a way that they raise finance, cash management etc
- Setting up effective system of internal and accounting controls
- Preparation of feasibility reports: These reports assist management in assessing the viability/profitability or otherwise of proposed capital expenditure such as opening of a new factory or branch
- Investigation of the performance/operations of competing business organizations to assist management in policy formulation
- Investigation of frauds within the organization: Accountant plays the role of investigation of frauds within the organization
- Accountant assists the organization to avoid-rather than evade tax by using his knowledge of the tax laws

An accountant plays uncountable roles in organization to mention few.

2

Branches of Accounting

FINANCIAL ACCOUNTING

The purpose of accounting is to provide the information that is needed for sound economic decision making. The main purpose of financial accounting is to prepare financial reports that provide information about a firm's performance to external parties such as investors, creditors, and tax authorities.

Managerial accounting contrasts with financial accounting in that managerial accounting is for internal decision making and does not have to follow any rules issued by standard-setting bodies.

Financial accounting, on the other hand, is performed just as to Generally Accepted Accounting Principles (GAAP) guidelines.

CPA'S

The primary accounting professional association in the U.S. is the American Institute of Certified Public Accountants (AICPA). The AICPA prepares the Uniform CPA Examination, which must be completed in order to become a certified public accountant. To be eligible to become a CPA, one needs an undergraduate degree in any major with 150 credit hours of course work. Of these 150 credit hours, a minimum of 36 credit hours must be in accounting. Only about 10% of those taking the CPA exam pass it the first time.

ACCOUNTING STANDARDS

In order that financial statements report financial

performance fairly and consistently, they are prepared just as to widely accepted accounting standards. These standards are referred to as Generally Accepted Accounting Principles, or simply GAAP. Generally Accepted Accounting Principles are those that have "substantial authoritative support".

ACCRUAL VS. CASH METHOD

Many small businesses utilize an accounting system that recognizes revenue and expenses on a cash basis, meaning that neither revenue nor expenses are recognized until the cash associated with them actually is received. Most larger businesses, however, use the accrual method.

Under the accrual method, revenues and expenses are recorded just as to when they are earned and incurred, not necessarily when the cash is received or paid. For example, under the accrual method revenue is recognized when customers are invoiced, regardless of when payment is received. Similarly, an expense is recognized when the bill is received, not when payment is made.

Under accrual accounting, even though employees may be paid in the next accounting period for work performed near the end of the present accounting period, the expense still is recorded in the current period since the current period is when the expense was incurred.

UNDERLYING ASSUMPTIONS, PRINCIPLES AND CONVENTIONS

Financial accounting relies on the following underlying concepts:

- *Assumptions*: Separate entity assumption, going-concern assumption, stable monetary unit assumption, fixed time period assumption.
- *Principles*: Historical cost principle, matching principle, revenue recognition principle, full disclosure principle.
- *Modifying conventions*: Materiality, cost-benefit, conservatism convention, industry practices convention.

FINANCIAL STATEMENTS

Businesses have two primary objectives:

1. Earn a profit
2. Remain solvent

Solvency represents the ability of the business to pay its bills and service its debt.

The four financial statements are reports that allow interested parties to evaluate the profitability and solvency of a business.

These reports include the following financial statements:

- Balance Sheet
- Income Statement
- Statement of Owner's Equity
- Statement of Cash Flows

These four financial statements are the final product of the accountant's analysis of the transactions of a business. A large amount of effort goes into the preparation of the financial statements.

The process begins with bookkeeping, which is just one step in the accounting process. Bookkeeping is the actual recording of the company's transactions, without any analysis of the information.

Accountants evaluate and analyse the information, making sense out of the numbers.

For the reports to be useful, they must be:

- Understandable
- Timely
- Relevant
- Fair and Objective

DOUBLE ENTRY ACCOUNTING

Financial accounting is based on double-entry bookkeeping procedures in which each transaction is recorded in opposite columns of the accounts affected by the exchange. Double entry accounting is a significant improvement over simple and more error-prone single-entry bookkeeping systems.

FUNDAMENTAL ACCOUNTING MODEL

The balance sheet is based on the following fundamental accounting equation:

Assets = Liabilities + Equity

This model has been used since the 18th century. It essentially states that a business owes all of its assets to either creditors or owners, where the assets of a business are its resources, and the creditors and owners are the sources of those resources.

TRANSACTIONS

To record transactions, one must:

- Identify an event that affects the entity financially.
- Measure the event in monetary terms.
- Determine which accounts the transaction affects.
- Determine whether the transaction increases or decreases the balances in those accounts.
- Record the transaction in the ledgers.

Most larger business accounting systems utilize the double entry method. Under double entry, instead of recording a transaction in only a single account, the transaction is recorded in two accounts.

THE ACCOUNTING PROCESS

Once a business transaction occurs, a sequence of activities begins to identify and analyse the transaction, make the journal entries, etc. Because this process repeats over transactions and accounting periods, it is referred to as the accounting cycle.

MANAGEMENT ACCOUNTING

Management accounting is the internal business building role of accounting and finance professionals who work inside organizations.

These professionals are involved in designing and evaluating business processes, budgeting and forecasting, implementing and monitoring internal controls, and analyzing, synthesizing, and aggregating information—to help drive economic value.

The role of management accounting differs from that of public accounting, since management accountants work at the "beginning" of the value chain, supporting decision making, planning and control, while audit and tax functions involve checking the work after the fact. Management accountants are valued business partners, directly supporting an organization's strategic goals. With a renewed emphasis on good internal controls and sound financial reporting, the role of the management accountant is more important than ever.

It obviously takes more people to "do" the work than it does to "check" the work. In fact, of the five million finance function professionals in the U.S., more than 90% work inside organizations as management accountants and finance professionals.

Some common job titles for management accountants in organizations of all sizes and structure include:

- Staff Accountant
- Cost Accountant
- Senior Accountant
- Corporate or Division Planner
- Financial Analyst
- Budget Analyst
- Internal Auditor
- Finance Manager
- Controller
- Vice President, Finance
- Treasurer
- Chief Financial Officer (CFO)
- Chief Executive Officer (CEO)

TRADITIONAL VS. INNOVATIVE PRACTICES

In the late 1980s, accounting practitioners and educators were heavily criticized on the grounds that management accounting practices had changed little over the preceding 60 years, despite radical changes in the business environment.

Professional accounting institutes, perhaps fearing that management accountants would increasingly be seen as superfluous in business organizations, subsequently devoted considerable resources to the development of a more innovative skills set for management accountants.

The distinction between 'traditional' and 'innovative' management accounting practices can be emphasized by reference to cost control techniques. Cost accounting is a central method in management accounting, and traditionally, management accountants' principal technique was variance analysis, which is a systematic approach to the comparison of the actual and budgeted costs of the raw materials and labour used during a production period.

While some form of variance analysis is still used by most manufacturing firms, it nowadays tends to be used in conjunction with innovative techniques such as life cycle cost analysis and activity-based costing, which are designed with specific aspects of the modern business environment in mind. Life-cycle costing recognizes that managers' ability to influence the cost of manufacturing a product is at its greatest when the product is still at the design stage of its product life-cycle (i.e., before the design has been finalized and production commenced), since small changes to the product design may lead to significant savings in the cost of manufacturing the products.

Activity-based costing (ABC) recognizes that, in modern factories, most manufacturing costs are determined by the amount of 'activities' (e.g., the number of production runs per month, and the amount of production equipment idle time) and that the key to effective cost control is therefore optimizing the efficiency of these activities. Activity-based accounting is also known as Cause and Effect accounting.

Both lifecycle costing and activity-based costing recognize that, in the typical modern factory, the avoidance of disruptive events (such as machine breakdowns and quality control failures) is of far greater importance than reducing the costs of raw materials. Activity-based costing also deemphasizes direct labour as a cost driver and concentrates instead on activities that drive costs, such as the provision of a service or the production of a product component.

ROLE WITHIN A CORPORATION

Consistent with other roles in today's corporation, management accountants have a dual reporting relationship. As a strategic partner and provider of decision based financial and operational information, management accountants are responsible for managing the business team and at the same time having to report relationships and responsibilities to the corporation's finance organization.

The activities management accountants provide inclusive of forecasting and planning, performing variance analysis, reviewing and monitoring costs inherent in the business are ones that have dual accountability to both finance and the business team. Examples of tasks where accountability may be more meaningful to the business management team vs. the corporate finance department are the development of new product costing, operations research, business driver metrics, sales management scorecarding, and client profitability analysis.

Conversely, the preparation of certain financial reports, reconciliations of the financial data to source systems, risk and regulatory reporting will be more useful to the corporate finance team as they are charged with aggregating certain financial information from all segments of the corporation. One widely held view of the progression of the accounting and finance career path is that financial accounting is a stepping stone to management accounting. Consistent with the notion of value creation, management accountants help drive the success of the business while strict financial accounting is more of a compliance and historical endeavor.

In corporations that derive much of their profits from the information economy, such as banks, publishing houses, telecommunications companies and defence contractors, IT costs are a significant source of uncontrollable spending, which in size is often the greatest corporate cost after total compensation costs and property related costs. A function of management accounting in such organizations is to work closely with the IT department to provide IT Cost Transparency.

An Alternative View

A very rarely expressed alternative view of management accounting is that it is neither a neutral or benign influence in organizations, rather a mechanism for management control through surveillance.

This view locates management accounting specifically in the context of management control theory. Stated differently, Management Accounting information is the mechanism which can be used by managers as a vehicle for the overview of the whole internal structure of the organization to facilitate their control functions within an organization.

SPECIFIC CONCEPTS

Grenzplankostenrechnung (GPK)

Grenzplankostenrechnung (GPK) is a German costing methodology, developed in the late 1940s and 1950s, designed to provide a consistent and accurate application of how managerial costs are calculated and assigned to a product or service. The term Grenzplankostenrechnung, often referred to as GPK, has best been translated as either Marginal Planned Cost Accounting or Flexible Analytic Cost Planning and Accounting.

Lean Accounting (Accounting for Lean Enterprise)

In the mid to late 1990s several books were written about accounting in the lean enterprise. The term lean accounting was coined during that period. These books contest that traditional accounting methods are better suited for mass production and do not support or measure good business practices in just in time manufacturing and services.

The movement reached a tipping point during the 2005 Lean Accounting Summit in Dearborn, MI. 320 individuals attended and discussed the merits of a new approach to accounting in the lean enterprise. 520 individuals attended the 2nd annual conference in 2006.

Resource Consumption Accounting (RCA)

Resource Consumption Accounting is formally defined as a dynamic, fully integrated, principle-based, and comprehensive management accounting approach that provides managers with decision support information for enterprise optimization.

RCA emerged as a management accounting approach around 2000 and was subsequently developed at CAM–I the Consortium for Advanced Manufacturing–International, in a Cost Management.

After spending the next seven years carefully refining and validating the approach through practical case studies and other research, a group of interested academics and practitioners established the RCA Institute to introduce RCA to the marketplace and raise the standard of management accounting knowledge by encouraging disciplined practices.

Throughput Accounting

The most significant, recent direction in managerial accounting is throughput accounting; which recognizes the interdependencies of modern production processes. For any given product, customer or supplier, it is a tool to measure the contribution per unit of constrained resource.

Transfer Pricing

Management accounting is an applied discipline used in various industries. The specific functions and principles followed can vary based on the industry. Management accounting principles in banking are specialized but do have some common fundamental concepts used whether the industry is manufacturing based or service oriented. For example, transfer pricing is a concept used in manufacturing but is also applied in banking.

It is a fundamental principle used in assigning value and revenue attribution to the various business units. Essentially, transfer pricing in banking is the method of assigning the interest rate risk of the bank to the various funding sources and uses of the enterprise.

Thus, the bank's corporate treasury department will assign funding charges to the business units for their use of the bank's resources when they make loans to clients. The treasury department will also assign funding credit to business units who bring in deposits (resources) to the bank.

Although the funds transfer pricing process is primarily applicable to the loans and deposits of the various banking units, this proactive is applied to all assets and liabilities of the business segment.

Once transfer pricing is applied and any other management accounting entries or adjustments are posted to the ledger (which are usually memo accounts and are not included in the legal entity results), the business units are able to produce segment financial results which are used by both internal and external users to evaluate performance.

RESOURCES AND CONTINUOUS LEARNING

There are a variety of ways to keep current and continue to build one's knowledge base in the field of management accounting. Certified Management Accountants (CMAs) are required to achieve continuing education hours every year, similar to a Certified Public Accountant. A company may also have research and training materials available for use in a corporate owned library. This is more common in "Fortune 500" companies who have the resources to fund this type of training medium.

Cost Management and the Institute of Management Accounting(IMA) site are sources which includes Management Accounting Quarterly and Strategic Finance publications. Indeed, management accounting is needed in an organization.

MANAGEMENT ACCOUNTING TASKS/SERVICES PROVIDED

The primary tasks/services performed by management accountants.

The degree of complexity relative to these activities are dependent on the experience level and abilities of any one individual:

- Variance Analysis
- Rate and Volume Analysis
- Business Metrics Development
- Price Modeling
- Product Profitability
- Geographic vs. Industry or Client Segment Reporting
- Sales Management Scorecards
- Cost Analysis
- Cost Benefit Analysis
- Cost-Volume-Profit Analysis
- Life cycle cost analysis
- Client Profitability Analysis
- IT Cost Transparency
- Capital Budgeting
- Buy vs. Lease Analysis
- Strategic Planning
- Strategic Management Advise
- Internal Financial Presentation and Communication
- Sales and Financial Forecasting
- Annual Budgeting
- Cost Allocation
- Resource Allocation and Utilization

THE ACCOUNTING CYCLE

The accounting process is a series of activities that begins with a transaction and ends with the closing of the books.

Because this process is repeated each reporting period, it is referred to as the accounting cycle and includes these major steps:

- Identify the transaction or other recognizable event.
- Prepare the transaction's source document such as a purchase order or invoice.

- Analyse and classify the transaction. This step involves quantifying the transaction in monetary terms (e.g. dollars and cents), identifying the accounts that are affected and whether those accounts are to be debited or credited.
- Record the transaction by making entries in the appropriate journal, such as the sales journal, purchase journal, cash receipt or disbursement journal, or the general journal. Such entries are made in chronological order.
- Post general journal entries to the ledger accounts. The steps are performed throughout the accounting period as transactions occur or in periodic batch processes. The following steps are performed at the end of the accounting period:
- Prepare the trial balance to make sure that debits equal credits. The trial balance is a listing of all of the ledger accounts, with debits in the left column and credits in the right column.

  At this point no adjusting entries have been made. The actual sum of each column is not meaningful; what is important is that the sums be equal. Note that while out-of-balance columns indicate a recording error, balanced columns do not guarantee that there are no errors.

  For example, not recording a transaction or recording it in the wrong account would not cause an imbalance.
- Correct any discrepancies in the trial balance. If the columns are not in balance, look for math errors, posting errors, and recording errors.

  Posting errors include:

  - Posting of the wrong amount,
  - Omitting a posting,
  - Posting in the wrong column, or
  - Posting more than once.

- Prepare adjusting entries to record accrued, deferred, and estimated amounts.
- Post adjusting entries to the ledger accounts.
- Prepare the adjusted trial balance. This step is similar to the preparation of the unadjusted trial balance, but this time the adjusting entries are included. Correct any errors that may be found.
- Prepare the financial statements.
    - *Income statement*: Prepared from the revenue, expenses, gains, and losses.
    - *Balance sheet*: Prepared from the assets, liabilities, and equity accounts.
    - *Statement of retained earnings*: prepared from net income and dividend information.
    - *Cash flow statement*: Derived from the other financial statements using either the direct or indirect method.
- Prepare closing journal entries that close temporary accounts such as revenues, expenses, gains, and losses. These accounts are closed to a temporary income summary account, from which the balance is transferred to the retained earnings account (capital). Any dividend or withdrawal accounts also are closed to capital.
- Post closing entries to the ledger accounts.
- Prepare the after-closing trial balance to make sure that debits equal credits. At this point, only the permanent accounts appear since the temporary ones have been closed. Correct any errors.
- Prepare reversing journal entries (optional). Reversing journal entries often are used when there has been an accrual or deferral that was recorded as an adjusting entry on the last day of the accounting period. By reversing the adjusting entry, one avoids double counting the amount when the transaction occurs in the next period. A reversing journal entry is recorded on the first day of the new period.

Instead of preparing the financial statements before the closing journal entries, it is possible to prepare them afterwards, using a temporary income summary account to collect the balances of the temporary ledger accounts (revenues, expenses, gains, losses, etc.) when they are closed. The temporary income summary account then would be closed when preparing the financial statements.

Steps in The Accounting Cycle

Identify the Transaction
Identify the event as a transaction
and generate the source document.

↓

Analyse the Transaction
Determine the transaction amount,
which accounts are affected,
and in which direction.

↓

Journal Entries
The transaction is recorded in the
journal as a debit and a credit.

↓

Post to Ledger
The journal entries are transferred
to the appropriate T-accounts
in the ledger.

↓

Trial Balance
A trial balance is calculated
to verify that the sum of the debits
is equal to the sum of the credits.

↓

Adjusting Entries
Adjusting entries are made for
accrued and deferred items.

The entries are journalized and
posted to the T-accounts
in the ledger.

↓

Adjusted
Trial Balance
A new trial balance is calculated
after making the adjusting entries.

↓

Financial Statements
The financial statements
are prepared.

↓

Closing Entries
Transfer the balances of the
temporary accounts
(e.g. revenues and expenses)
to owner's equity.

↓

After-Closing
Trial Balance
A final trial balance is
calculated after the closing
entries are made.

PREPARATION OF FINANCIAL STATEMENTS

Businesses create financial statements at the end of each month, quarter and fiscal year. These financial statements tell the story of how well the business has done over a certain period of time.

That time period being a month, quarter or year. These financial statements are analysed and reviewed for management reasons and decision-making reasons. Financial statements are created using the information from ledger accounts. One statement uses and builds on the information of another.

INCOME STATEMENT

The income statements are usually the first financial statement to be created. The information is drawn from the ledger accounts and formed into the income statement. The income statement reports the revenues, expenses and resulting net income or loss. This statement only shows the results for the period that it was created for. The ledger accounts that are used in the creation of the financial statement are the revenue accounts, expense accounts and capital gains or losses accounts.

STATEMENT OF RETAINED EARNINGS

The next statement to be created is the statement of retained earnings. This statement uses information directly from the financial statement. This statement shows the earnings retained by operations. In order to build this statement, you must take the beginning retained earnings from the previous period as well as the net income from this current period. This statement also takes into account the dividends paid out during the accounting period. The dividends paid out are subtracted from retained earnings.

BALANCE SHEET

The next statement to be created is the balance sheet. The balance sheet is meant to report on a companies financial health at a given period in time.

This statement has three parts:

1. Assets,
2. Liabilities and
3. Owners equity.

This statement simply reports the balances of these accounts and tallies the results. If the balance sheets shows more assets than liabilities, the business is headed in the right direction.

3

Cost Management

DEFINITION OF COST

In business, retail, and accounting, a cost is the value of money that has been used up to produce something, and hence is not available for use anymore. In economics, a cost is an alternative that is given up as a result of a decision. In business, the cost may be one of acquisition, in which case the amount of money expended to acquire it is counted as cost.

In this case, money is the input that is gone in order to acquire the thing. This acquisition cost may be the sum of the cost of production as incurred by the original producer, and further costs of transaction as incurred by the acquirer over and above the price paid to the producer. Usually, the price also includes a mark-up for profit over the cost of production. Costs are often further described based on their timing or their applicability.

ACCOUNTING VS OPPORTUNITY COSTS

In accounting, costs are the monetary value of expenditures for supplies, services, labour, products, equipment and other items purchased for use by a business or other accounting entity. It is the amount denoted on invoices as the price and recorded in bookkeeping records as an expense or asset cost basis.

Opportunity cost, also referred to as economic cost is the value of the best alternative that was not chosen in order to pursue the current endeavour—i.e, what could have been accomplished with the resources expended in the undertaking.

It represents opportunities forgone. In theoretical economics, cost used without qualification often means opportunity cost.

COMPARING PRIVATE, EXTERNAL, SOCIAL AND PSYCHIC COSTS

When a transaction takes place, it typically involves both private costs and external costs. Private costs are the costs that the buyer of a good or service pays the seller. This can also be described as the costs internal to the firm's production function.

External costs, in contrast, are the costs that people other than the buyer are forced to pay as a result of the transaction. The bearers of such costs can be either particular individuals or society at large.

Note that external costs are often both non-monetary and problematic to quantify for comparison with monetary values. They include things like pollution, things that society will likely have to pay for in some way or at some time in the future, but that are not included in transaction prices.

Social costs are the sum of private costs and external costs. For example, the manufacturing cost of a car reflects the private cost for the manufacturer. The polluted waters or polluted air also created as part of the process of producing the car is an external cost borne by those who are affected by the pollution or who value unpolluted air or water.

Because the manufacturer does not pay for this external cost and does not include this cost in the price of the car, they are said to be external to the market pricing mechanism. The air pollution from driving the car is also an externality produced by the car user in the process of using his good.

The driver does not compensate for the environmental damage caused by using the car. A psychic cost is a subset of social costs that specifically represent the costs of added stress or losses to quality of life.

COST ESTIMATES AND COST OVERRUN

When developing a business plan for a new company, product, or project, planners typically make cost estimates in order to assess whether revenues/benefits will cover costs. This is done in both business and government. Costs are often underestimated resulting in cost overrun during implementation.

Main causes of cost underestimation and overrun are optimism bias and strategic misrepresentation. Reference class forecasting was developed to curb optimism bias and strategic misrepresentation and arrive at more accurate cost estimates. Cost Plus, is where the Price = Cost plus or minus X%, where x is the percentage of built in overhead or profit margin.

COST MANAGEMENT

Cost management is the process by which companies control and plan the costs of doing business. Individual projects should have customised cost management plans, and companies as a whole also integrate cost management into their overall business model. There is no single accepted definition for this term, because it has such broad applications and possible strategies. When properly implemented, cost management will translate into reduced costs of production for products and services, as well as increased value being delivered to the customer.

For a company's management to be effective overall, cost management must be an integral feature of it. It is easiest to understand this concept if it is explained in the context of a single project. For instance, before a project is started, the anticipated costs should be identified and measured. These expenses should then be approved before any purchasing occurs. During the process of completing a project, all incurred costs should be noted and kept in a record of some kind, to help ensure that the costs are controlled and kept in line with initial expectations, to the extent that this is possible.

Taking this approach to cost management will help a company determine whether they accurately estimated expenses at first, and will help them more closely predict expenses in the future. Any overspending can also be monitored in this way, and either eliminated in future projects or specifically approved if the expense was necessary. Cost management cannot be used in isolation; projects must be organized and tailored with this strategy in mind.

Starting a project with cost management in mind will help to avoid certain pitfalls that may be present otherwise. If the objectives of the project are not clearly defined at first, or are changed during the course of the project, cost over-runs will be more likely. If costs are not fully researched before the project, they may be underestimated, thereby inflating the expectation of the project's success unrealistically. Construction projects are subject to their own particular challenges; these can include constraints in the form of laws and regulations that must be planned around.

If the project is completely and clearly defined, this will facilitate effective management of the costs it will incur. Effective cost management strategies will help a team deliver a finished project within the allocated budget, while also making it as valuable as possible to the company. There is always the possibility of unexpected costs, but preparation in the form of cost management will likely make them much easier to deal with when they occur.

COST BEHAVIOUR

The most important building block of both microeconomic analysis and cost accounting is the characterization of how costs change as output volume changes. Output volume can refer to production, sales, or any other principle activity that is appropriate for the organization under consideration. The following discussion examines the volume of production in a factory, but the same principles apply regardless of the type of organization and the appropriate measure of activity. Costs can be variable, fixed, or mixed.

VARIABLE COSTS

Variable costs vary in a linear fashion with the production level. However, when stated on a per unit basis, variable costs remain constant across all production levels within the relevant range. The following two charts depict this relationship between variable costs and output volume.

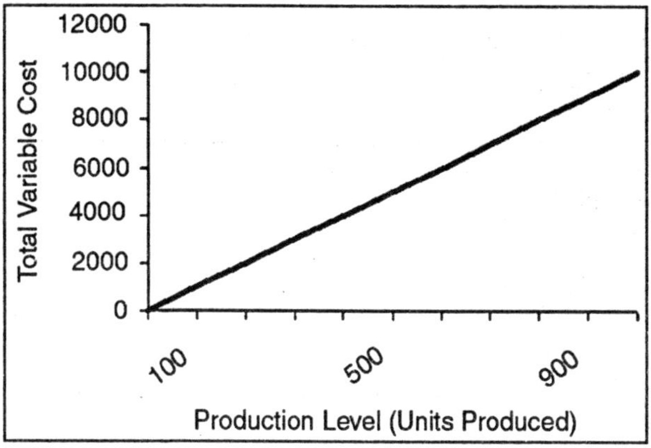

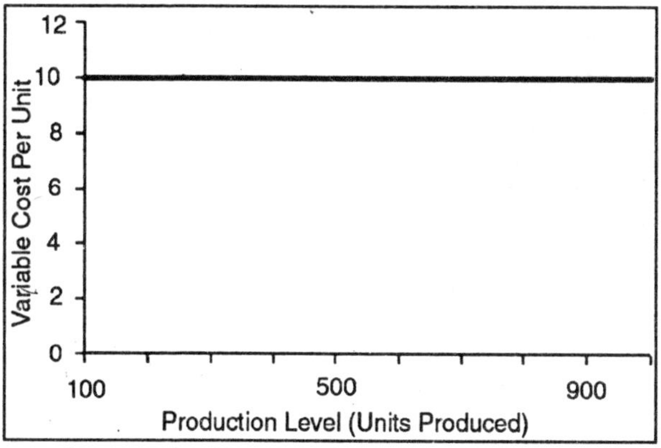

A good example of a variable cost is materials. If one pair of pants requires $10 of fabric, then every pair of pants requires $10 of fabric, no matter how many pairs are made. The fabric cost is $10 per unit at every level of production. If one pair is made, the total fabric cost is $10; if two pairs are made, the total fabric cost is $20; and if 1,000 pairs are made, the total fabric cost is $10,000. Hence, the total cost is increasing and linear in the production level.

FIXED COSTS

Fixed costs do not vary with the production level. Total fixed costs remain the same, within the relevant range. However, the fixed cost per unit decreases as production increases, because the same fixed costs are spread over more units. The following two charts depict this relationship between fixed costs and output volume.

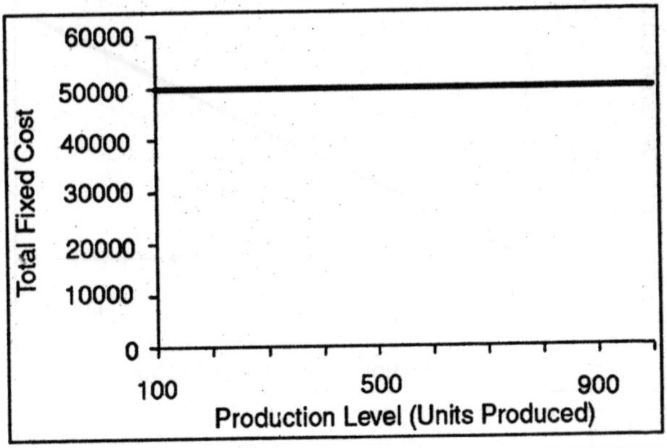

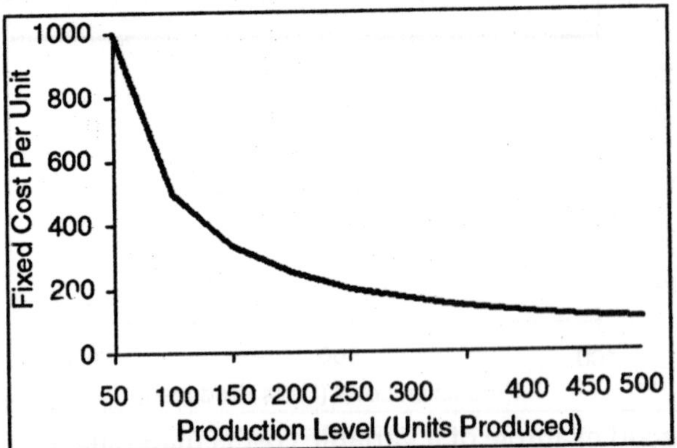

In this example, fixed costs are $50,000. The first chart shows that fixed costs remain $50,000 at all production levels from 100 units to 1,000 units. The second chart shows that the fixed cost per unit decreases as production increases. Hence, when 100 units are manufactured, the fixed cost per unit is $500 ($50,000 ÷ 100). When 500 units are manufactured, the fixed cost per unit is $100 ($50,000 ÷ 500).

RELEVANT RANGE

The relevant range is the range of activity over which these relationships are valid. For example, if the factory is operating at capacity, increasing production requires additional investment in fixed costs to expand the facility or to lease or build another factory. Alternatively, production might be reduced below a threshold at which point one of the company's factories is no longer needed, and the fixed costs associated with that factory can be avoided. With respect to variable costs, the company might qualify for a volume discount on fabric purchases above some production level.

The relevant range for characterizing fabric as a variable cost ends at that production level, because the fabric cost per unit of output is different when the factory produces above that threshold than when the factory produces below that threshold.

MIXED COSTS

If, within a relevant range, a cost is neither fixed nor variable, it is called semi-variable or mixed. Following are two common examples of mixed costs.

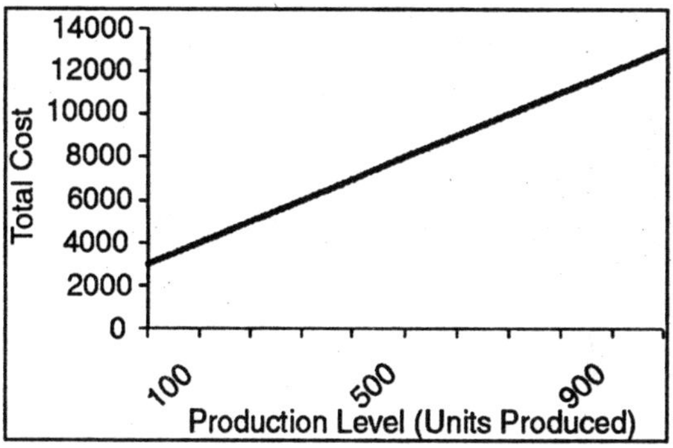

In this example, although the total cost line increases in production, it does not pass through the origin because there is a fixed cost component. An example of a cost that fits this description is electricity. A fixed amount of electricity is required to run the factory air conditioning, computers and lights.

There is also a variable cost component related to running the machines on the factory floor. The fixed component in this example is \$3,000 per month. The variable cost component is \$10 per unit of output. Hence, at a production level of 500 units, the total electric cost is \$8,000 [\$3,000 + (\$10 × 500)].

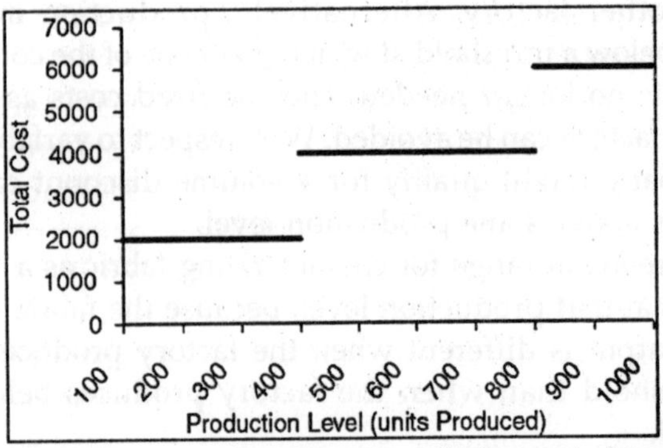

The mixed cost in the chart is called a step function. An example of such cost behaviour would be the total salary expense for shift supervisors. If the factory runs one shift, only one shift supervisor is required. In order for the factory to produce above the maximum capacity of a single shift, the factory must add a second shift and hire a second shift supervisor, so that total shift supervisor salary expense doubles. If the factory runs three shifts, three shift supervisors are required.

COST BEHAVIOUR ASSUMPTIONS IN MANAGEMENT ACCOUNTING VERSUS MICROECONOMICS

Microeconomic analysis usually assumes decreasing marginal costs of production, sometimes followed by increasing marginal costs of production beyond a certain production level. Hence, economists' graphs of the total cost of production and the average per-unit cost of production show smooth, curved functions.

Management accountants usually assume the linear relationships depicted in the graphs. Linearity is a more accurate description of many situations encountered by management accountants than the economists' curves, and even when linearity constitutes a simplifying assumption it is almost always sufficiently descriptive for the task at hand.

BASIC COST MANAGEMENT CONCEPTS

Multi-product firms have to account for costs that can be

tied to a product, direct costs. They also have to account for indirect costs not directly measurable. A 'cost object' can be a product, service, process or any items which management requires cost information. The way that costs are assigned depends on their nature. A direct costs is easily traceable with a high degree of accuracy and indirect, or overhead, cost cannot be easily identifiable with a particular object.

Product costs are costs allocated to a product; this is not just physical products. All other costs are period costs. Such costs are expenses to the income statement in the period they are incurred. Product costs are recognised as an expense in the income statement only when the product is sold. Prior to sale the cost of products is shown as an asset due to the accrual principle.

The stages in the allocation of overheads to products are as follows:

- Identify overhead costs collected from production and service cost centres and apportion as appropriate and possible.
- Once identified allocate to production departments.
- Allocate overheads to a single product by dividing the number of products into the total overhead. The resulting sum can then be applied as cost to the product.

Total Overheads of a Production Costs Centre ($s)/Level of Activity (units). Predetermined overhead absorption rates are estimates of future expenditures. Estimates are used becuase some overhead costs are not known for some time until afterthey have incurred.

Normal costing is where the cost object is determined using the actual costs for the direct the direct costs and a predetermined rate for the allocation of indirect costs.

Functional-based cost accounting classifies all costs as either fixed or variable in relation to changes in the volume of units produced.

Activity-based costing tries to capture changes in technology by apportioning oveheads to product costs taking into account activity and transactions that drive the cost. An activity cost pool is where the costs of an activity under the ABC system are accumulated. Drives are factors that cause changes in the use of resources. The focus in ABC is managing activities instead of costs.

Absorption costing is where the cost of inventories is determined in order to include an appropriate share of variable and fixed costs. Fixed costs are allocated on the basis of normal operating capacity. In variable costing, only the production costs are used.

Using absorption costsing, production overhead costs are included as a product cost whereas in variable costing they are treated as a period cost. This leads to different values of inventory and therefore different net profit figures.

The difference in profits derived from the application of the two methods can be reconciled by the following:

Fixed Overhead Absorption Rate * Movement of Inventories in a period = Difference in Profits

ACTIVITY BASED COSTING

Activity Based Costing is an accounting technique that allows an organization to determine the actual cost associated with each product and service produced by the organization without regard to the organizational structure. It is developed to provide more-accurate ways of assigning the costs of indirect and support resources to activities, bushiness processes, products, services, and customers.

ABC systems recognize that many organizational resources are required not for physical production of units of product but to provide a broad array of support activities that enable a variety of products and services to be produced for a diverse group of customers. The goal of ABC is not to allocate common costs to products. The goal is to measure and then price out all the resources used for activities that support the production and delivery of products and services to customers.

CONCEPT OF ACTIVITY-BASED-COSTING

Activity Based Costing is an accounting technique that allows an organization to determine the actual cost associated with each product and service produced by the organization without regard to the organizational structure. It is developed to provide more-accurate ways of assigning the costs of indirect and support resources to activities, bushiness processes, products, services, and customers.

ABC systems recognize that many organizational resources are required not for physical production of units of product but to provide a broad array of support activities that enable a variety of products and services to be produced for a diverse group of customers. The goal of ABC is not to allocate common costs to products. The goal is to measure and then price out all the resources used for activities that support the production and delivery of products and services to customers.

An organization performs activities to do its business. These activities define the kind of business you are in: a ship owner has an activity to unpack boats; an accounting firm prepares tax returns; a manufacturer produces products; a council delivers services; a university teaches students. All activities consume resources. It is the consumption of these resources that adds to overhead costs.

The basis of Activity Based Costing is: look at the activities required to produce the cost of the product or service. The activities consume resources and the cost of these can be calculated.

The amount of activity required for each product and service is determined, hence the real cost can be determined:

- The activity is the work that is done.
- The resource is what the activity uses to do the work e.g. people, equipment, and services. Resources cost money.
- The cost of the activity depends on the quantity of resources used to accomplish the activity.
- The cost driver for an activity is the factor that influences the amount of the resources that will be consumed by this activity.

  Example: The activity is delivering goods. The costs of this activity include the truck drivers' wages, fuel, depreciation of the truck, insurance, etc. The quantities of the resources that will be consumed by this activity are influenced by the number of deliveries made per year. Hence the cost driver could be the number of deliveries. A cost driver is designed to allocate the delivery activity cost pool to the cost objects.

- The activity driver measures how much of the activity is used by the cost object.
  Example: Product A is delivered once a month, whereas product B is delivered once a week. Products A and B require a different number of deliveries, hence the cost of the delivery activity should be assigned to each product on the basis of the number of deliveries each uses.
- The cost object is whatever it is you wish to cost. It could be a product, service, process, job or customer.

While traditional costing arbitrarily allocates overhead costs, ABC traces overhead costs by looking at the activities that each product and service calls upon. With ABC the products consume the activities. It is the activities that cost money. If there were no activities, no resources would be consumed. It is the activities that you do that define your business.

USE OF ACTIVITY-BASED-COSTING

Activity-Based-Costing is necessary for the following reasons:

- Understand TRUE profitability of your customers, products, or services
- Quantify the cost of non-value added activities such as errors and reworks
- Identify opportunities to reduce costs and/or increase efficiency
- Obtain actionable information to negotiate price increases for unprofitable clients
- Understand why profitability may be mediocre despite good strategic fundamentals
- Stratify overhead costs so they can be managed more effectively

HOW DOES ABC WORK?

The first stage in an initial ABC study is to develop a fundamental understanding of the Resources and Activities of an organization.

The Resources are then mapped to the Activities, thereby quantifying the cost of performing each of these Activities. These costs are traced to Cost Objects providing tremendous insight into where an organization is making and losing money.

ABC MODEL

The objective of an ABC implementation is to relate all of the costs of doing business to products, services, or customers.

Developing the initial model consists of the following five steps:

1. Identify the Resources of an organization
2. Determine Activities that are supported by Resources
3. Define Cost Objects
4. Develop Resource Drivers to link Resources to Activities
5. Develop Cost Drivers to link Activities to Cost Objects

Step 1: Identify Resources

Resources represent the expenditures of an organization. Examples include production labour, sales and marketing labour, occupancy and utilities, equipment, and supplies. These are the same costs that are represented in a traditional accounting view; unlike traditional accounting, ABC links these costs to products, customers, or services.

Step 2: Identify Activities

Activities represent the work performed in an organization.

ABC Activities for the sales department in a typical organization might include:

- Making sales calls to existing customers
- Making sales calls to potential customers
- Making customer service calls

- Training product representatives
- Evaluating products and improving product knowledge
- Distributing samples
- Attending trade shows and other events

Traditional accounting will often break the cost of the sales department into salaries, benefits, allocated rent, supplies, and so on. Unlike traditional accounting, which reports what the costs are, ABC accounts for these costs based on what activities caused them to occur.

By determining the actual activities that occur in various departments, such as accounting, customer service, and sales, it is then possible to more accurately relate these costs to customers, products, and services.

Step 3: Identify Cost Objects

ABC provides profitability by one or more cost object, usually represented by products, customers, and/or services. Cost Object profitability is utilized to identify money losing customers, to validate separate divisions or business units, or to measure the performance of individual projects, jobs, or contracts.

Defining the outputs to be viewed is an important step in a successful ABC implementation.

Step 4: Determine Resource Drivers

Resource Drivers provide the link between the expenditures of an organization and the Activities performed within the organization.

For example, the total salary of a customer service representative would likely be allocated to the Activities performed based on the amount of time spent performing the Activity. If 50% of her time is spent performing the activity, taking orders for existing customers, 50% of her salary would be allocated to this Activity.

Step 5: Determine Cost Drivers

Determination of Cost Drivers completes the last stage of

the model. Cost Drivers trace, or link, the cost of performing certain Activities to Cost Objects. For example, taking orders for existing customers may be linked to specific customers based on the number of orders taken, if each order takes approximately the same amount of time. If order taking time varies based on the customer, this cost may be linked based on another driver or multiple drivers.

OPERATING COST

Operating costs are the recurring expenses which are related to the operation of a business, or to the operation of a device, component, piece of equipment or facility.

BUSINESS OPERATING COSTS

For a commercial enterprise, operating costs fall into two broad categories:

1. Fixed costs, which are the same whether the operation is closed or running at 100% capacity
2. Variable costs, which may increase depending on whether more production is done, and how it is done (producing 100 items of product might require 10 days of normal time or take 7 days if overtime is used. It may be more or less expensive to use overtime production depending on whether faster production means the product can be more profitable).

Business Overhead Costs

Overhead costs for a business are the cost of resources used by an organization just to maintain its existence. Overhead costs are usually measured in monetary terms, but non-monetary overhead is possible in the form of time required to accomplish tasks.

Examples of overhead costs include:

- Payment of rent on the office space a business occupies
- Cost of electricity for the office lights
- Some office personnel wages

Non-overhead costs are incremental costs, such as the cost of raw materials used in the goods a business sells.

Operating Cost is calculated by Cost of goods sold + Operating Expenses. Operating Expenses consist of:. Administrative and office expenses like rent, salaries, to staff, insurance, directors fees etc. Selling and distribution expenses like advertisement, salaries of salesmen.

EQUIPMENT OPERATING COSTS

In the case of a device, component, piece of equipment or facility, it is the regular, usual and customary recurring costs of operating the equipment. This does not include the capital cost of constructing or purchasing the equipment.

Operating costs are incurred by all equipment — unless the equipment has no cost to operate, requires no personnel or space and never wears out. In some cases, equipment may appear to have low or no operating cost because either the cost is not recognized or is being absorbed in whole or part by the cost of something else.

Equipment operating costs may include:

- Salaries or Wages of personnel
- Advertising
- Raw materials
- License or equivalent fees imposed by a government
- Real estate expenses, including
  - Rent or Lease payments
  - Office space
  - Furniture and equipment
  - Investment value of the funds used to purchase the land, if it is owned instead of rented or leased
  - Property taxes and equivalent assessments
  - Operations taxes, such as fees assessed on transportation carriers for use of highways
- Fuel costs such as power for operations, fuel for production

- Public Utilities such as telephone service, Internet connectivity, etc.
- Maintenance of equipment
- Office supplies and consumables
- Insurance
- Depreciation of equipment and eventual replacement costs
- Damage due to uninsured losses, accident, sabotage, negligence, terrorism and routine wear and tear.
- Taxes on production or operation
- Income taxes

Some of these are not applicable in all instances.

For example:

- A solar panel placed on one's home for use in generating electric power generally has only capital costs; once it's running there are no personnel costs, utility costs or depreciation and it uses no extra land so it has no real operating costs; however there may need to be taken into account costs of replacement if damaged.
- An automobile or any other item purchased for personal use has no salary cost because the owner does not charge themselves for operating the device.
- An item which is leased may have some or all of these costs included as part of the purchase price.

It might be questionable to assert that the cost of ten extra people on the sales force are an incremental cost or an overhead cost, since the wages for these people are both overhead and incremental. The staff needed to keep the shop operational are mostly considered as overhead.

OVERHEAD COST

In business, overhead, overhead cost or overhead expense refers to an ongoing expense of operating a business. The term overhead is usually used to group expenses that are necessary to the continued functioning of the business, but cannot be immediately associated with the products/services being offered.

Overhead expenses are all costs on the income statement except for direct labour,direct materials and direct expenses. Overhead expenses include accounting fees, advertising, depreciation, insurance, interest, legal fees, rent, repairs, supplies, taxes, telephone bills, travel and utilities costs.

Overhead can be classified under four headings:

1. Functional classification
2. Classification on the nature of expenditure
3. Element-wise classification
4. Classification on behaviour of expenditure

TARGET COSTING

As a totally new product and its industry develops, it starts to compete based on its new technology, concept, and/ or service.

Competitors emerge and the basis for competition evolves to other areas such as cycle time, quality, or reliability. As an industry becomes mature, the basis of competition typically moves to price.

Profit margins shrink. Companies begin focusing on cost reduction. However, the cost structure for existing products is largely locked in and cost reduction activities have limited impact.

As companies begin to realise that the majority of a product's costs are committed based on decisions made during the development of a product, the focus shifts to actions that can be taken during the product development phase.

Until recently, engineers have focused on satisfying a customer's requirements. Most development personnel have viewed a product's cost as a dependent variable that is the result of the decisions made about a products functions, features and performance capabilities. Because a product's costs are often not assessed until later in the development cycle, it is common for product costs to be higher than desired. This process is represented in Figure.

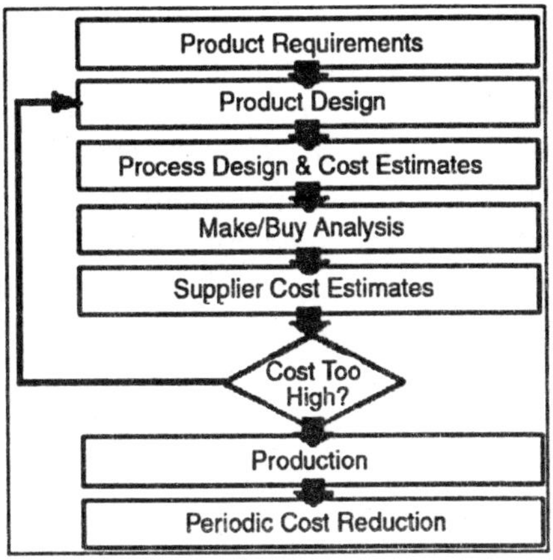

Fig. Traditional Cost Management Approach

Target costing represents a fundamentally different approach.

It is based on three premises:

1. Orienting products to customer affordability or market-driven pricing,
2. Treating product cost as an independent variable during the definition of a product's requirements, and
3. Proactively working to achieve target cost during product and process development. This target costing approach is represented in Figure.

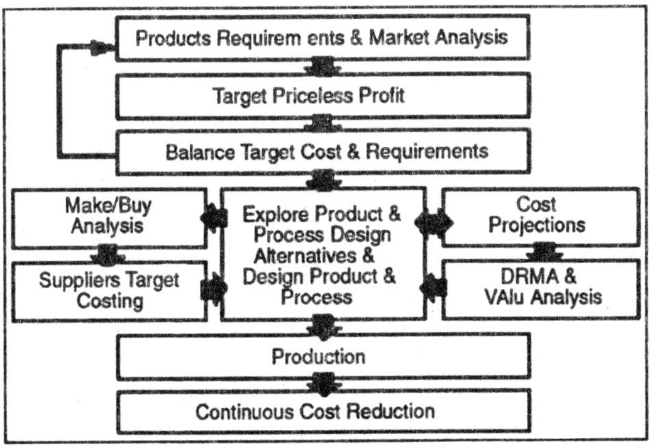

Fig. Target Cost Concept

Target costing builds upon a design-to-cost (DTC) approach with the focus on market-driven target prices as a basis for establishing target costs. The target costing concept is similar to the cost as an independent variable (CAIV) approach used by the U.S. Department of Defence and to the price-to-win philosophy used by a number of companies pursuing contracts involving development under contract.

The following ten steps are required to install a comprehensive target costing approach within an organization:

1. *Re-orient culture and attitudes*: The first and most challenging step is re-orient thinking toward market-driven pricing and prioritized customer needs rather than just technical requirements as a basis for product development. This is a fundamental change from the attitude in most organizations where cost is the result of the design rather than the influencer of the design and that pricing is derived from building up a estimate of the cost of manufacturing a product.
2. *Establish a market-driven target price*: A target price needs to be established based upon market factors such as the company position in the market place (market share), business and market penetration strategy, competition and competitive price response, targeted market niche or price point, and elasticity of demand. If the company is responding to a request for proposal/quotation, the target price is based on analysis of the price to win considering customer affordability and competitive analysis.
3. *Determine the target cost*: Once the target price is established, a worksheet is used to calculate the target cost by subtracting the standard profit margin, warranty reserves, and any uncontrollable corporate allocations. If a bid includes non-recurring development costs, these are also subtracted. The target cost is allocated down to lower level assemblies of subsystems in a manner consistent with the structure of teams or individual designer responsibilities.

Table. Target Cost Calculation Worksheet

Sign	Price/Cost Element	Esti-mate Factor	% Factor	Per Unit	Amount
	Manufacturer's suggested retail price				$495.00
–	Standard dealer margin $(148.50)		30%	$ –	
=	Cost to retailer				$346.50
–	Shipping/distribution cost to retailer		0%	$15.00	$(15.00)
=	Selling Price to retailer				$ 331.50
–	Distribution cost/mark-up		15%	$–	$ (49.73)
–	Shipping/Logistics cost to distribution centre		0%	$ 17.00	$ (17.00)
=	Manufacturer's selling price				$ 264.78
–	Profit margin		8%	$ –	$ (21.18)
–	Warranty cost		2%	$ –	$ (5.30)
–	Corporate allocations		10%	$–	$ (26.48)
–	Business unit selling, general and Administrative		12%	$ –	$ (31.77)
	Non-recurring Development cost	1200000			
	Estimated production volume	200000			
–	Allocated non-recurring devalopment cost			$ 600	$ (6.00)
=	Business unit target cost				$ 174.05
–	Overhead		45%	$ –	$ (78.32)
=	Direct Target cost (labour and material)				$ 95.73

4. *Balance target cost with requirements*: Before the target cost is finalized, it must be considered in conjunction with product requirements. The greatest opportunity to control a product's costs is through proper setting of requirements or specifications. This requires a careful understanding of the voice of the customer, use of conjoint analysis to understand the value that customers place on particular product capabilities, and use of techniques such as quality function deployment to help make these tradeoff's among various product requirements including target cost.
5. *Establish a target costing process and a team-based organization*: A well-defined process is required that integrates activities and tasks to support to support target costing. This process needs to be based on early and proactive consideration of target costs and incorporate tools and methodologies described subsequently.

   Further, a team-based organization is required that integrates essential disciplines such as marketing, engineering, manufacturing, purchasing, and finance. Responsibilities to support target costing need to be clearly defined.
6. *Brainstorm and analyse alternatives*: The second most significant opportunity to achieve cost reduction is through consideration of multiple concept and design alternatives for both the product and its manufacturing and support processes at each stage of the development cycle. These opportunities can be achieved when there is out-of-the-box or creative consideration of alternatives coupled with structured analysis and decision-making methods.
7. *Establish product cost models to support decision-making*: Product cost models and cost tables provide the tools to evaluate the implications of concept and design alternatives. In the early stages of development, these models are based on parametric estimating or analogy techniques. Further on in the development

cycle as the product and process become more defined, these models are based on industrial engineering or bottom-up estimating techniques. The models need to be comprehensive to address all of the proposed materials, fabrication processes, and assembly process and need to be validated to insure reasonable accuracy. A target cost worksheet can be used to capture the various elements of product cost, compare alternatives, as well as track changing estimates against target cost over the development cycle.

8. *Use tools to reduce costs*: Use of tools and methodologies related to design for manufacturability and assembly, design for inspection and test, modularity and part standardization, and value analysis or function analysis. These methodologies will consist of guidelines, databases, training, procedures, and supporting analytic tools.
9. *Reduce indirect cost application*: Since a significant portion of a product's costs are indirect, these costs must also be addressed. The enterprise must examine these costs, re-engineer indirect business processes, and minimize non-value-added costs. But in addition to these steps, development personnel generally lack an understanding of the relationship of these costs to the product and process design decisions that they make. Use of activity-based costing and an understanding of the organization's cost drivers can provide a basis for understanding how design decisions impact indirect costs and, as a result, allow their avoidance.
10. *Measure results and maintain management focus*: Current estimated costs need to be tracked against target cost throughout development and the rate of closure monitored. Management needs to focus attention of target cost achievement during design reviews and phase-gate reviews to communicate the importance of target costing to the organization.

KAIZEN COSTING

The process of continual cost reduction that occurs after a product design has been completed and is now in production. Cost reduction techniques can include working with suppliers to reduce the costs in their processes, implementing less costly re-designs of the product, or reducing waste costs.

THE VALUE CHAIN

To better understand the activities through which a firm develops a competitive advantage and creates shareholder value, it is useful to separate the business system into a series of value-generating activities referred to as the value chain. In his 1985 book Competitive Advantage, Michael Porter introduced a generic value chain model that comprises a sequence of activities found to be common to a wide range of firms. Porter identified primary and support activities as shown in the following diagram:

Table. Porter's Generic Value Chain

Inbound Logistics	>	Operations	>	Outbound Logistics	>	Marketing & Sales	>	Service	>	MARGIN
Firm Infrastructure										
HR Management										
Technology Development										
Procurement										

The goal of these activities is to offer the customer a level of value that exceeds the cost of the activities, thereby resulting in a profit margin.

The primary value chain activities are:

- *Inbound Logistics*: The receiving and warehousing of raw materials, and their distribution to manufacturing as they are required.

- Operations: the processes of transforming inputs into finished products and services.
- *Outbound Logistics*: The warehousing and distribution of finished goods.
- *Marketing and Sales*: The identification of customer needs and the generation of sales.
- *Service*: The support of customers after the products and services are sold to them.

These primary activities are supported by:

- *The infrastructure of the firm*: Organizational structure, control systems, company culture, etc.
- *Human resource management*: Employee recruiting, hiring, training, development, and compensation.
- *Technology development*: Technologies to support value-creating activities.
- *Procurement*: Purchasing inputs such as materials, supplies, and equipment.

The firm's margin or profit then depends on its effectiveness in performing these activities efficiently, so that the amount that the customer is willing to pay for the products exceeds the cost of the activities in the value chain. It is in these activities that a firm has the opportunity to generate superior value. A competitive advantage may be achieved by reconfiguring the value chain to provide lower cost or better differentiation.

The value chain model is a useful analysis tool for defining a firm's core competencies and the activities in which it can pursue a competitive advantage as follows:

- *Cost advantage*: By better understanding costs and squeezing them out of the value-adding activities.
- *Differentiation*: By focusing on those activities associated with core competencies and capabilities in order to perform them better than do competitors.

COST ADVANTAGE AND THE VALUE CHAIN

A firm may create a cost advantage either by reducing the cost of individual value chain activities or by reconfiguring the value chain.

Once the value chain is defined, a cost analysis can be performed by assigning costs to the value chain activities. The costs obtained from the accounting report may need to be modified in order to allocate them properly to the value creating activities.

Porter identified 10 cost drivers related to value chain activities:

1. Economies of scale
2. Learning
3. Capacity utilization
4. Linkages among activities
5. Interrelationships among business units
6. Degree of vertical integration
7. Timing of market entry
8. Firm's policy of cost or differentiation
9. Geographic location
10. Institutional factors

A firm develops a cost advantage by controlling these drivers better than do the competitors.

A cost advantage also can be pursued by reconfiguring the value chain. Reconfiguration means structural changes such a new production process, new distribution channels, or a different sales approach. For example, FedEx structurally redefined express freight service by acquiring its own planes and implementing a hub and spoke system.

DIFFERENTIATION AND THE VALUE CHAIN

A differentiation advantage can arise from any part of the value chain. For example, procurement of inputs that are unique and not widely available to competitors can create differentiation, as can distribution channels that offer high service levels.

Differentiation stems from uniqueness. A differentiation advantage may be achieved either by changing individual value chain activities to increase uniqueness in the final product or by reconfiguring the value chain.

Porter identified several drivers of uniqueness:

- Policies and decisions
- Linkages among activities

- Timing
- Location
- Interrelationships
- Learning
- Integration
- Scale
- Institutional factors

Many of these also serve as cost drivers. Differentiation often results in greater costs, resulting in tradeoffs between cost and differentiation.

There are several ways in which a firm can reconfigure its value chain in order to create uniqueness. It can forward integrate in order to perform functions that once were performed by its customers. It can backward integrate in order to have more control over its inputs. It may implement new process technologies or utilize new distribution channels. Ultimately, the firm may need to be creative in order to develop a novel value chain configuration that increases product differentiation.

TECHNOLOGY AND THE VALUE CHAIN

Because technology is employed to some degree in every value creating activity, changes in technology can impact competitive advantage by incrementally changing the activities themselves or by making possible new configurations of the value chain.

Various technologies are used in both primary value activities and support activities:

- *Inbound Logistics Technologies*:
  - Transportation
  - Material handling
  - Material storage
  - Communications
  - Testing
  - Information systems
- *Operations Technologies*:
  - Process
  - Materials

  - Machine tools
  - Material handling
  - Packaging
  - Maintenance
  - Testing
  - Building design and operation
  - Information systems
- *Outbound Logistics Technologies*:
  - Transportation
  - Material handling
  - Packaging
  - Communications
  - Information systems
- *Marketing and Sales Technologies*:
  - Media
  - Audio/video
  - Communications
  - Information systems
- *Service Technologies*:
  - Testing
  - Communications
  - Information systems

Note that many of these technologies are used across the value chain. For example, information systems are seen in every activity. Similar technologies are used in support activities. In addition, technologies related to training, computer-aided design, and software development frequently are employed in support activities.

To the extent that these technologies affect cost drivers or uniqueness, they can lead to a competitive advantage.

LINKAGES BETWEEN VALUE CHAIN ACTIVITIES

Value chain activities are not isolated from one another. Rather, one value chain activity often affects the cost or performance of other ones. Linkages may exist between primary activities and also between primary and support activities.

Consider the case in which the design of a product is changed in order to reduce manufacturing costs. Suppose that inadvertantly the new product design results in increased service costs; the cost reduction could be less than anticipated and even worse, there could be a net cost increase.

Sometimes however, the firm may be able to reduce cost in one activity and consequently enjoy a cost reduction in another, such as when a design change simultaneously reduces manufacturing costs and improves reliability so that the service costs also are reduced. Through such improvements the firm has the potential to develop a competitive advantage.

ANALYZING BUSINESS UNIT INTERRELATIONSHIPS

Interrelationships among business units form the basis for a horizontal strategy. Such business unit interrelationships can be identified by a value chain analysis.

Tangible interrelationships offer direct opportunities to create a synergy among business units. For example, if multiple business units require a particular raw material, the procurement of that material can be shared among the business units. This sharing of the procurement activity can result in cost reduction. Such interrelationships may exist simultaneously in multiple value chain activities.

Unfortunately, attempts to achieve synergy from the interrelationships among different business units often fall short of expectations due to unanticipated drawbacks. The cost of coordination, the cost of reduced flexibility, and organizational practicalities should be analysed when devising a strategy to reap the benefits of the synergies.

OUTSOURCING VALUE CHAIN ACTIVITIES

A firm may specialize in one or more value chain activities and outsource the rest. The extent to which a firm performs upstream and downstream activities is described by its degree of vertical integration.

A thorough value chain analysis can illuminate the business system to facilitate outsourcing decisions. To decide which activities to outsource, managers must understand the firm's strengths and weaknesses in each activity, both in terms of cost and ability to differentiate.

Managers may consider the foilowing when selecting activities to outsource:

- Whether the activity can be performed cheaper or better by suppliers.
- Whether the activity is one of the firm's core competencies from which stems a cost advantage or product differentiation.
- The risk of performing the activity in-house. If the activity relies on fast-changing technology or the product is sold in a rapidly-changing market, it may be advantageous to outsource the activity in order to maintain flexibility and avoid the risk of investing in specialized assets.
- Whether the outsourcing of an activity can result in business process improvements such as reduced lead time, higher flexibility, reduced inventory, etc.

THE VALUE CHAIN SYSTEM

A firm may specialize in one or more value chain activities and outsource the rest. The extent to which a firm performs upstream and downstream activities is described by its degree of vertical integration.

A thorough value chain analysis can illuminate the business system to facilitate outsourcing decisions. To decide which activities to outsource, managers must understand the firm's strengths and weaknesses in each activity, both in terms of cost and ability to differentiate.

Managers may consider the following when selecting activities to outsource:

- Whether the activity can be performed cheaper or better by suppliers.
- Whether the activity is one of the firm's core competencies from which stems a cost advantage or product differentiation.
- The risk of performing the activity in-house. If the

activity relies on fast-changing technology or the product is sold in a rapidly-changing market, it may be advantageous to outsource the activity in order to maintain flexibility and avoid the risk of investing in specialized assets.

- Whether the outsourcing of an activity can result in business process improvements such as reduced lead time, higher flexibility, reduced inventory, etc.

A firm's value chain is part of a larger system that includes the value chains of upstream suppliers and downstream channels and customers. Porter calls this series of value chains the value system, shown conceptually below:

Table. The Value System

... →	Supplier Value Chain	→	Firm Value Chain	→	Channel Value Chain	→	Buyer Value Chain

Linkages exist not only in a firm's value chain, but also between value chains. While a firm exhibiting a high degree of vertical integration is poised to better coordinate upstream and downstream activities, a firm having a lesser degree of vertical integration nonetheless can forge agreements with suppliers and channel partners to achieve better coordination. For example, an auto manufacturer may have its suppliers set up facilities in close proximity in order to minimize transport costs and reduce parts inventories. Clearly, a firm's success in developing and sustaining a competitive advantage depends not only on its own value chain, but on its ability to manage the value system of which it is a part.

LIFE-CYCLE COST ANALYSIS

ENERGY EFFICIENCY AND LIFE-CYCLE COST ANALYSIS

Life-cycle cost (LCC) analysis is the most rational, objective method for selecting the optimum HVAC system for a laboratory facility. Through LCC analysis, all factors that influence total system cost can be identified and quantified. Subjective factors such as fuel cost adjustments, component reliability, and maintenance costs are also included. LCC analysis can be used to assess the economic consequences of any decision by comparing two or more alternatives.

Annual Cost Comparison

Review of the annual cost of space conditioning for a laboratory or cleanroom shows the high impact of energy costs. A Class 10,000 cleanroom system costs five to 10 times as much to operate annually as the conditioning system for the facility's office spaces; a Class 100 laboratory cleanroom system will cost 50 times as much.

In either case, however, the contributions to total cost are:

- Energy costs, contributing 65 to 75 per cent;
- Capital costs, i.e. interest plus depreciation, contributing 15 to 25 per cent; and
- Maintenance costs, contributing 10 per cent.

A life-cycle cost analysis does not need to be extremely complex to yield reasonably accurate figures for first and operational costs. A modified LCC, similar to a simple payback, does not account for inflation or cost of money; this modified LCC can give an order-of-magnitude appraisal to help determine whether or not to add an EEM to a system.

If LCC computations are easily understood, the analysis is more likely to be used by design teams and accepted by researchers/owners. One approach to simplifying life-cycle cost analysis is to convert facility operating costs to an equivalent annual expense per fume hood. This number can serve as a common denominator for comparing the composite performances of various system designs and for examining the sensitivity of each design alteration. The energy engineer should concentrate on determining realistic values for the most sensitive design factors before selecting the HVAC system type.

LCC Factors

LCC factors that influence a laboratory's HVAC system design can be broken into three categories: design factors, economic factors, and performance factors. Sometimes other factors must be considered; for example, a functional-use factor may be developed based on efficiency studies of personnel in the operations of different laboratory systems or components. Because laboratory personnel LCCs are very high, the more functional a design or system is, the more LCC savings are possible. An example is the workspace flexibility and reduced costs of space planning that can be afforded by a raised floor system.

JUST-IN-TIME

Just-in-time (JIT) is an inventory strategy that strives to improve a business's return on investment by reducing in-process inventory and associated carrying costs. To meet JIT objectives, the process relies on signals or Kanban between different points in the process, which tell production when to make the next part. Kanban are usually 'tickets' but can be simple visual signals, such as the presence or absence of a part on a shelf. Implemented correctly, JIT can improve a manufacturing organization's return on investment, quality, and efficiency.

Quick notice that stock depletion requires personnel to order new stock is critical to the inventory reduction at the centre of JIT. This saves warehouse space and costs. However, the complete mechanism for making this work is often misunderstood.

For instance, its effective application cannot be independent of other key components of a lean manufacturing system or it can "...end up with the opposite of the desired result.". In recent years manufacturers have continued to try to hone forecasting methods, however some research demonstrates that basing JIT on the presumption of stability is inherently flawed.

ACTIVITY-BASED MANAGEMENT

Activity-based management (ABM) is a method of identifying and evaluating activities that a business performs using activity-based costing to carry out a value chain analysis or a re-engineering initiative to improve strategic and operational decisions in an organization. Activity-based costing establishes relationships between overhead costs and activities so that overhead costs can be more precisely allocated to products, services, or customer segments. Activity-based management focuses on managing activities to reduce costs and improve customer value.

Kaplan and Cooper. Cost and effect: Using integrated cost systems to drive profitability and performance. Boston: Harvard Business School Press.) divide ABM into operational and strategic:

Operational ABM is about "doing things right", using ABC information to improve efficiency. Those activities which add value to the product can be identified and improved. Activities that don't add value are the ones that need to be reduced to cut costs without reducing product value.

Strategic ABM is about "doing the right things", using ABC information to decide which products to develop and which activities to use. This can also be used for customer profitability analysis, identifying which customers are the most profitable and focusing on them more.

A risk with ABM is that some activities have an implicit value, not necessarily reflected in a financial value added to any product. For instance a particularly pleasant workplace can help attract and retain the best staff, but may not be identified as adding value in operational ABM. A customer that represents a loss based on committed activities, but that opens up leads in a new market, may be identified as a low value customer by a strategic ABM process.

Managers should interpret these values and use ABM as a "common, yet neutral, ground ... this provides the basis for negotiation". ABM can give middle managers an understanding of costs to other teams to help them make decisions that benefit the whole organisation, not just their activities' bottom line.

COST-VOLUME-PROFIT ANALYSIS

Cost-volume-profit (CVP) analysis expands the use of information provided by breakeven analysis. A critical part of CVP analysis is the point where total revenues equal total costs (both fixed and variable costs). At this breakeven point (BEP), a company will experience no income or loss. This BEP can be an initial examination that precedes more detailed CVP analyses.

Cost-volume-profit analysis employs the same basic assumptions as in breakeven analysis.

The assumptions underlying CVP analysis are:

- The behaviour of both costs and revenues in linear throughout the relevant range of activity.
- Costs can be classified accurately as either fixed or variable.
- Changes in activity are the only factors that affect costs.
- All units produced are sold.
- When a company sells more than one type of product, the sales mix will remain constant.

INTERNAL RATE OF RETURN

The Internal Rate of Return (IRR) is the discount rate that generates a zero net present value for a series of future cash flows. This essentially means that IRR is the rate of return that makes the sum of present value of future cash flows and the final market value of a project equal its current market value.

Internal Rate of Return provides a simple 'hurdle rate', whereby any project should be avoided if the cost of capital exceeds this rate. Usually a financial calculator has to be used to calculate this IRR, though it can also be mathematically calculated using the following formula:

$$CF_0 + \frac{CF}{(1+r)} + \frac{CF_2}{(1-r)^2} + \frac{CF_3}{(1+r)^3} + \frac{CF_n}{(1+r)^n} = 0$$

In the formula, CF is the Cash Flow generated in the specific period. IRR, denoted by 'r' is to be calculated by employing trial and error method.

Internal Rate of Return is the flip side of Net Present Value (NPV), where NPV is the discounted value of a stream of cash flows, generated from an investment. IRR thus computes the break-even rate of return showing the discount rate.

A simple decision-making criteria can be stated to accept a project if its Internal Rate of Return exceeds the cost of capital and rejected if this IRR is less than the cost of capital. However, it should be kept in mind that the use of IRR may result in a number of complexities such as a project with multiple IRRs or no IRR. Moreover, IRR neglects the size of the project and assumes that cash flows are reinvested at a constant rate.

The Modified Internal Rate of Return (MIRR) is an other financial measure used to determine the attractiveness of an investment.

In IRR calculations, positive cash flows are assumed to be 'paid' instantly to the investor who can use them immediately to reinvest on a new project. But in reality, the positive cash flows are not paid instantly to the investors, but rather kept by the 'project management entity' until the end of the project.

The Modified Internal Rate of Return assumes that the positive cash flows are immediately re-invested until the end of the project. To make these calculations, it is common practice to use the weighted average cost of capital as interest rate on the positive cash flows.

ASPECTS OF DECISION-MAKING

AVERAGE COST

In economics, average cost is equal to total cost divided by the number of goods produced. It is also equal to the sum of average variable costs plus average fixed costs. Average costs may be dependent on the time period considered. Average costs affect the supply curve and are a fundamental component of supply and demand.

$$AC = \frac{TC}{Q}$$

Average cost is distinct from the price, and depends on the interaction with demand through elasticity of demand and elasticity of supply. In cases of perfect competition, price may be lower than average cost due to marginal cost pricing.

Average cost will vary in relation to the quantity produced unless fixed costs are zero and variable costs constant. A cost curve can be plotted, with cost on the y-axis and quantity on the x-axis. Marginal costs are often shown on these graphs, with marginal cost representing the cost of the last unit produced at each point; marginal costs are the first derivative of total or variable costs.

A typical average cost curve will have a U-shape, because fixed costs are all incurred before any production takes place and marginal costs are typically increasing, because of diminishing marginal productivity. In this "typical" case, for low levels of production there are economies of scale: marginal costs are below average costs, so average costs are decreasing as quantity increases.

An increasing marginal cost curve will intersect a U-shaped average cost curve at its minimum, after which point the average cost curve begins to slope upward. This is indicative of diseconomies of scale. For further increases in production beyond this minimum, marginal cost is above average costs, so average costs are increasing as quantity increases.

An example of this typical case would be a factory designed to produce a specific quantity of widgets per period: a certain production level, average cost is higher due to under-utilised equipment, while above that level, production bottlenecks increase the average cost.

Relationship to Marginal Cost

When average cost is declining as output increases, marginal cost is less than average cost. When average cost is rising, marginal cost is greater than average cost. When average cost is neither rising nor falling marginal cost equals average cost.

Other special cases for average cost and marginal cost appear frequently:

- *Constant marginal cost/high fixed costs*: Each additional unit of production is produced at constant additional expense per unit. The average cost curve slopes down continuously, approaching marginal cost. An example may be hydroelectric generation, which has no fuel expense, limited maintenance expenses and a high up-front fixed cost. Industries where fixed marginal costs obtain, such as electrical transmission networks, may meet the conditions for a natural monopoly, because once capacity is built, the marginal cost to the incumbent of serving an additional customer is always lower than the average cost for a potential competitor. The high fixed capital costs are a barrier to entry.

- *Minimum efficient scale/maximum efficient scale*: Marginal or average costs may be non-linear, or have discontinuities. Average cost curves may therefore only be shown over a limited scale of production for a given technology. For example, a nuclear plant wo'·ld be extremely inefficient for production in small quantities; similarly, its maximum output for any given time period may essentially be fixed, and production above that level may be technically impossible, dangerous or extremely costly. The long run elasticity of supply will be higher, as new plants could be built and brought on-line.
- *Low or zero fixed costs/constant marginal cost*: Since there is no economy of scale, average cost will be close to or equal to marginal cost. Examples may include buying and selling of commodities etc...

Relationship Between AC, AFC, AVC and MC

- The Average Fixed Cost curve starts from a height and goes on declining continuously as production increases.
- The Average Variable Cost curve, Average Cost curve and the Marginal Cost curve start from a height, reach the minimum points, then rise sharply and continuously.
- Marginal Cost curve is the determining curve, while the rest are determined curves.

- The movement in the Marginal Cost curve determines the movement and direction of the other curves.
- The Average Fixed Cost curve nears the Average Cost curve initially and then moves away from it. The Average Variable Cost Curve is never parallel or intersects the Average Cost curve due to the existence of the Average Fixed Cost in all units of production.
- The Marginal Cost curve always passes through the minimum points of the Average Variable Cost and Average Cost curves, though the Average Variable Cost curve attains the minimum point prior to that of the Average Cost curve.

AVERAGE FIXED COST

Average fixed cost is an economics term used to describe the total fixed costs divided by the quantity (Q) of units produced.

$$AFC = \frac{TFC}{Q}$$

Average fixed cost is a per-unit measure of fixed costs. As the total number of goods produced increases, the average fixed cost decreases because the same amount of fixed costs are being spread over a larger number of units.

Average variable cost plus average fixed cost equals average total cost.

$$ATC = AVC + AFC$$

AVERAGE VARIABLE COST

Average variable cost (AVC) is an economics term to describe a firm's variable costs divided by the quantity (Q) of total units of output. It is a cost that a firm must generate from its business if it must continue business because firm must incur it whether it makes profit or not.

$$AVC = \frac{TVC}{Q}$$

Where:

- TVC = Total Variable Cost
- AVC = Average Variable Cost
- Q = Quantity of Units Produced

Average variable cost plus average fixed cost equals average total cost:

$$AVC + AFC = ATC.$$

COST-MINIMIZATION ANALYSIS

Cost-minimization is the simplest of the pharmacoeconomics tools and is applied when comparing two drugs of equal efficacy and equal tolerability

Therapeutic equivalence must be referenced by the author conducting the study and should have been done prior to the cost-minimization work.

Since equal efficacy and equal tolerability is already demonstrated, there is no requirement to find a common efficacy denominator as would be the case when conducting a cost-effectiveness study.

The author is not precluded from doing so through the use of "cost/cure" or "cost/year of life gained". If efficacy and tolerability is demonstrated, however, then a simple comparison of "cost/course of treatment" can suffice for the purpose of comparing two or more therapeutically equivalent treatment alternatives.

However when doing so you do run the risk of confusing possible target markets due to the issue of severity of possible deaths occurring. This was the case in New York in 2004 with the well known case 'Murpheys Law' which is now a well known case study for cost minisation. This was all due to severe cost cutting leading to 'Murpheys' death due to a large back lash from his employees resulting in his death! Cost minimisation should be carefully considered before being implomented.

When conducting a cost-minimization study, the author needs to measure all costs inherent to the delivery of the therapeutic intervention and that are relevant to the pharmacoeconomic perspective.

COST/BENEFIT ANALYSIS

You may have been intensely creative in generating solutions to a problem, and rigorous in your selection of the best one available. However, this solution may still not be worth implementing, as you may invest a lot of time and money in solving a problem that is not worthy of this effort.

Cost Benefit Analysis or CBA is a relatively* simple and widely used technique for deciding whether to make a change. As its name suggests, you simply add up the value of the benefits of a course of action, and subtract the costs associated with it.

Costs are either one-off, or may be ongoing. Benefits are most often received over time. We build this effect of time into our analysis by calculating a payback period. This is the time it takes for the benefits of a change to repay its costs. Many companies look for payback on projects over a specified period of time e.g. three years.

How to Use the Tool

In its simple form, cost-benefit analysis is carried out using only financial costs and financial benefits. For example, a simple cost benefit ratio for a road plan would measure the cost of building the road, and subtract this from the economic benefit of improving transport links. It would not measure either the cost of environmental damage or the benefit of quicker and easier travel to work.

A more sophisticated approach to building a cost benefit models is to try to put a financial value on intangible costs and benefits. This can be highly subjective - is, for example, a historic water meadow worth $25,000, or is it worth $500,000 because if its environmental impcrtance? What is the value of stress-free travel to work in the morning?

These are all questions that people have to answer, and answers that people have to defend. The version of the cost benefit approach we explain here is necessarily simple. Where large sums of money are involved project evaluation can become an extremely complex and sophisticated art. The fundamentals of this are explained in Principles of Corporate

Finance by Richard Brealey and Stewart Myers - this is something of an authority on the subject.

Example

A sales director is deciding whether to implement a new computer-based contact management and sales processing system.

His department has only a few computers, and his salespeople are not computer literate. He is aware that computerized sales forces are able to contact more customers and give a higher quality of reliability and service to those customers. They are more able to meet commitments, and can work more efficiently with fulfillment and delivery staff.

His financial cost/benefit analysis is shown:

Costs:

- 10 network-ready PCs with supporting software @ $2,450 each
- 1 server @ $3,500
- 3 printers @ $1,200 each
- Cabling and Installation @ $4,600
- Sales Support Software @ $15,000

Training costs:

- Computer introduction - 8 people @ $400 each
- Keyboard skills - 8 people @ $400 each
- Sales Support System - 12 people @ $700 each

Other costs:

- Lost time: 40 man days @ $200/day
- Lost sales through disruption: estimate: $20,000
- Lost sales through inefficiency during first months: estimate: $20,000

Benefits:

- Tripling of mail shot capacity: estimate: $40,000/year
- Ability to sustain telesales campaigns: estimate: $20,000/year
- Improved efficiency and reliability of follow-up: estimate: $50,000/year
- Improved customer service and retention: estimate: $30,000/year

- Improved accuracy of customer information: estimate: $10,000/year
- More ability to manage sales effort: $30,000/year

COST-EFFECTIVENESS ANALYSIS

Cost-effectiveness analysis (CEA) is a technique for selecting among competing wants wherever resources are limited. Developed in the military, CEA was first applied to health care in the mid-1960s and was introduced with enthusiasm to clinicians by Weinstein and Stason in 1977:

"If these approaches were to become widely understood and accepted by the key decision makers in the health-care sector, including the physician, important health benefits or cost savings might be realised."

Regardless of whether this hope was realised, CEA has since become a common feature in medical literature.

THE BASICS OF CEA

CEA is a technique for comparing the relative value of various clinical strategies. In its most common form, a new strategy is compared with current practice in the calculation of the cost-effectiveness ratio:

$$\text{CE ratio} = \frac{\text{cost}_{\text{new strategy}} - \text{cost}_{\text{current practice}}}{\text{effect}_{\text{new strategy}} - \text{effect}_{\text{current practice}}}$$

The result might be considered as the "price" of the additional outcome purchased by switching from current practice to the new strategy. If the price is low enough, the new strategy is considered "cost-effective."

It's important to carefully consider exactly what that statement means. If a strategy is dubbed "cost-effective" and the term is used as its creators intended, it means that the new strategy is a good value. Note that being cost-effective does not mean that the strategy saves money, and just because a strategy saves money doesn't mean that it is cost-effective. Also note that the very notion of cost-effective requires a value judgment—what you think is a good price for an additional outcome, someone else may not.

It's also worthwhile to recognize that CEA is only relevant to certain decisions. The various way a new strategy might compare with an existing approach. Note that a CEA is relevant only if a new strategy is *both* more effective and more costly.

TRANSACTION COSTS

Transaction costs are commissions and processing charges incurred as part of a business transaction. In some cases, this transaction cost is a percentage of the total sale. In other cases, it may be a flat fee. In general, the money spent on the transaction costs is often referred to as a *spread*.

Understanding transaction costs is very important for anyone who is looking to buy or sell any financial product, whether it is stocks, bonds, currency or valuable metals. It does not matter whether you are buying or selling assets, transaction costs can be incurred in a number of different situations. It is important to read all policies and agreements of the company executing the transaction in order to have full awareness of which transaction costs you may incur.

One of the most common types of transaction costs is the buy/sell spread. While they can go by several different names, spreads are the costs that an investment manager charges to execute a transaction. To provide a real-world example, let's assume the currency exchange rate is $2 US Dollar for every 1 Euro. Though someone may expect to get 5 Euros if they pay $10 USD, it is likely that he will receive somewhat less than that.

Why is it that a trader may get less than the published rate? Because of the buy/sell spread. The person or agency executing the trade takes out a cut in order to provide the service. The amount charged for that service will likely be different, depending on the person or firm.

Some firms will actually use their transaction costs as an incentive to attract customers. If an investment firm has a competitive rate in their transaction costs, this can lead to a substantial cost savings for an investor, especially if that investor executes a large number of trades as a general practice.

Though it is not as prevalent as it once was, several trading firms specializing in online trades advertise their transaction costs regularly.

TOTAL COST

In economics, and cost accounting, total cost describes the total economic cost of production and is made up of variable costs, which vary just as to the quantity of a good produced and include inputs such as labour and raw materials, plus fixed costs, which are independent of the quantity of a good produced and include inputs that cannot be varied in the short term, such as buildings and machinery. Total cost in economics includes the total opportunity cost of each factor of production in addition to fixed and variable costs.

The rate at which total cost changes as the amount produced changes is called marginal cost. This is also known as the marginal unit variable cost.

If one assumes that the unit variable cost is constant, as in cost-volume-profit analysis developed and used in cost accounting by the accountants, then total cost is linear in volume, and given by: total cost = fixed costs + unit variable cost amount.

ABSORPTION COSTING

Absorption costing is a method for appraising or valuing a firm's total inventory by including all the manufacturing costs incurred to produce those goods.

Product Costs

- *Direct Materials*: These are the raw materials such as wood, metal, bricks, etc that are used in order to create a finished usable good which will be demanded by the market.
- *Direct Labour*: Direct Labour is the manwork and total factory hours put behind assembling the raw materials, creating the finished good, etc.
- *Fixed Manufacturing Overhead*: This includes expenses such as rent of factory where the raw materials are

turned into finished goods, amortization of factory building, utilities, etc.

- *Variable Manufacturing Overhead*: These are the general and administrative expenses in the manufacturing process.

Absorption costing is different from the other costing methods because it takes into account fixed manufacturing overhead. It is hard to factor in the fixed manufacturing overhead expenses into calculating the per unit price of goods, therefore other methods such as Variable Costing do not take it into account.

One drawback of absorption costing is that managers can increase production levels without taking into account total sales. With higher production levels, this year's expenses can be deferred to next year, thus lowering this year's costs. What does this mean? The managers get a fat bonus and pay raises thanks to more "profits."

Inventory Production and Absorption Costing

When beginning inventory and ending inventory levels are different, profit calculations using the Absorption costing can be difficult.

Here are the effects of fluctuating inventory levels:

- If Beginning Inventory = Ending Inventory, then Absorption Costing = Variable Costing
- If Inventory Levels = Low, then Variable Costing Profit > Absorption Costing Profit
- If Inventory Levels = High, then Absorption Costing Profit >Variable Costing Profit

SUNK COSTS

Sunk costs are sums that have already been spent and can not be recovered. The concept is important because sunk costs are irrelevant to financial decisions. Many people tend to feel instinctively that because an investment has been made it is necessary to get a return on it.

This can lead to people rejecting one course of action in favour of another that actually generates smaller cash flows.

This can happen to business, portfolio investment and personal decisions.

Suppose a hotel has calculated that their cost for providing a room is £100 per night, of which £50 covers their rental of the building and £20 covers their other fixed costs and £30 covers the costs that result from having an extra guest.

Now suppose the market rate for hotel rooms goes down and they are only able to charge £50 per night. The hotel is committed to remaining open. It appears that the hotel will make a £50 loss on each night per guest so they should not accept bookings until prices rise. Of course this is wrong as the rent and other fixed costs are already committed to and have to be paid anyway. The hotel should accept bookings at any price it can get above £30, as these make a positive contribution.

A common mistake made by investors is reluctance to sell securities at a loss. It does not matter what you paid for shares, if the market price has fallen you have already made that loss. It is a sunk cost and should be forgotten about. What matters is whether the shares are worth holding or not at the current market price. A key question is whether the shares would still be worth buying at current prices. If not, they are probably not worth holding.

SEMI-VARIABLE COSTS

Semi-variable costs are those that have both fixed cost and variable cost elements. For example, a manufacturer's electricity bill may include elements that are fixed and elements that are variable.

SEARCH COST

Search costs are one facet of transaction costs or switching costs. Rational consumers will continue to search for a better product or service until the marginal cost of searching exceeds the marginal benefit. Search theory is a branch of microeconomics that studies decisions of this type.

The costs of searching are divided into external and internal costs. External costs include the monetary costs of acquiring the information, and the opportunity cost of the time taken up in searching. External costs are not under the consumer's control. All they can do is choose whether or not to incur them. Internal costs include the mental effort given over to undertaking the search, sorting the incoming information, and integrating it with what the consumer already knows. Internal costs are determined by the consumer's ability to undertake the search, and this in turn depends on intelligence, prior knowledge, education and training. These internal costs are the background to the study of bounded rationality.

The Internet was expected to eliminate search costs. For example, electronic commerce was predicted to cause disintermediation as search costs become low enough for end-consumers to incur them directly instead of employing retailers to do this for them. This would in turn lead to lower prices and less variation between prices quoted by different sellers.

REPUGNANCY COSTS

Repugnancy costs are costs borne by an individual or entity as a result of a stimulus that goes against that individual or entity's cultural mores. The cost could be emotional, physical, mental or figurative. The stimulus could be anything from food to people to an idea.

These costs are perspective-dependent and individual. These costs may be different for different groups of people; countries, states, ethnicities, etc. The term allows for a clear and understandable way of representing the concept of contextual stigma in a literal and applicable sense.

QUALITY COST

Quality cost is the sum of all costs a company invests into the release of a quality product.

When developing a software product, there are four types of quality costs: prevention costs, appraisal costs, internal failure costs, and external failure costs:

1. *Prevention costs:* Represent everything a company

spends to prevent software errors, documentation errors, and other product-related errors. These include requirements and usability analysis, for example. Dollars spent on prevention costs are the most effective quality dollars, because preventing errors from getting into the product is much cheaper than fixing errors later. If there is an error in a requirement or the intended usability, and money is spent on developing the software to the erroneous requirement, the costs of identifying the error, determining how to fix it, and then developing new code to correct it will arise later.

2. *Appraisal costs:* Include the money spent on the actual testing activity. Any and all activities associated with searching for errors in the software and associated product materials falls into this category. This includes all testing: by the developers themselves, by an internal test team, and by an outsourced software test organization. This also includes all associated hardware, software, labour, and other costs. Once a product is in the coding phases, the goal is to do the most effective appraisal job, so that internal failure work is streamlined and well-managed and prevents skyrocketing external failure costs.
3. *Internal failure costs*: Are the costs of coping with errors discovered during development and testing. These are bugs found before the product is released. The further in the development process the errors are discovered, the more costly they are to fix. So the later the errors are discovered, the higher their associated internal failure costs will be.
4. *External failure costs*: Are the costs of coping with errors discovered after the product is released. These are typically errors found by your customers. These costs can be much higher than internal failure costs, because the stakes are much higher. These costs include post-release customer and technical support. Errors at this stage can also be costly in terms of your

company's reputation and may lead to lost customers.

The following table in shows examples of costs that fall into each of the four categories of quality costs.

Prevention	Appraisal
Staff training Requirements analysis Early prototyping Fault tolerant design Defensive programming Usability analysis Clear specification Accurate internal documentation Pre-purchase evaluation of the reliability of development tools	Design reviews Code inspection Glass box testing Black box testing Beta testing Test automation Usability testing Pre-release out-of-box testing by customer service staff
Internal Failure	**External Failure**
Bug fixes Regression testing Wasted in-house user time Wasted tester time Wasted writer time Wasted marketer time Wasted advertisements Direct cost of late shipment Opportunity cost of late shipment	Technical support calls Answer books Investigating complaints Refunds and recalls Interim bug fix releases Shipping product updates Warranty, liability costs PR to soften bad reviews Lost sales Lost customer goodwill Supporting multiple versions in the field Reseller discounts to keep them selling the product

The Four Categories of Quality Costs

All the costs can be effectively reduced through smarter

test efforts that include a high degree of test automation. Test automation when done *right* leads to greater test coverage, resulting in higher-quality products.

Higher-quality products require less technical support, fewer patches, and lead to greater customer satisfaction. Smarter automated testing also speeds up the release process and incrementally reduces the manual test costs. But most of all, more test coverage gives you and your customers more confidence in your product.

You will feel more comfortable knowing that there are not bugs lurking in your software that have not been exposed yet because of insufficient test coverage. You will also not have to scramble at the last minute to deal with a problem and fix it to your customer's satisfaction in a rush.

The solution to quality cost problems is to get a better understanding of your investment in product quality and manage your costs better. The first place most organizations look for a better understanding is in the highest cost area: the software test effort or lack thereof.

For example, if you do not test at all, your testing or appraisal cost is low. You will ship on time but your external failure costs will skyrocket. Your prevention and appraisal costs will result in finding errors that can be corrected while they are still internal failures, where they are cheaper to deal with than when they are external failures.

The goal of understanding quality costs is to analyse where you spend your time and money to *get the most bang for the buck*. It is well known that it is faster and cheaper to find and fix a bug during unit testing done by developers early in the development cycle. Should we then spend most of our time/budget on unit testing? No. There are many limitations to unit testing.

Unit testing is not capable of finding many varieties of bugs, including graphical user interface (GUI) bugs, usability problems, end-to-end bugs, and configuration bugs. For most organizations, getting a better unit test effort will help you release a better product sooner. It is not a replacement for the test effort done by skilled software testers, but it may reduce the time that test effort takes. Understanding quality costs will hopefully help you shift some of your test effort to the most cost-effective places.

In the following, the total quality cost is shown in the upper bathtub-shaped curve. On the bottom axis is the quality of performance, ranging from totally defective to zero defects. On the left axis is the cost per good unit of product. You can see that with highly defective software, your prevention and appraisal costs are very low, but your failure costs are very high, yielding a high total quality cost.

With zero defect software, likewise, your failure costs are very low, but your prevention and appraisal costs are very high. To optimize your total quality costs, you want to be between these extremes, at the bottom of the bathtub curve.

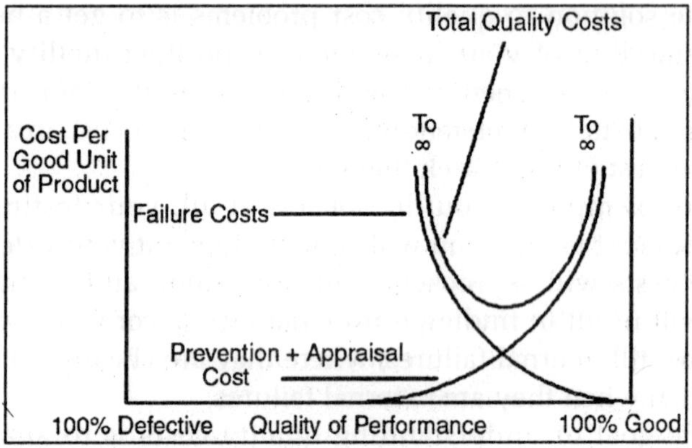

Theoretical Model of Optimum Quality Cost

This offers two challenges: First, a sufficiently sophisticated accounting system allowing a typical mid-sized company to track the total cost of quality has yet to be developed.

To optimize total quality cost, you need to have the appropriate categories in your accounting system and keep track of the related costs. Second, you need to be able to track your external quality costs. You may not even have enough information from customers on why the software is not working for them. How are you going to know what to book into your accounting system for external failure costs? The point here is that while capturing this data is difficult and expensive, you know that the benefit is reducing your overall cost of quality.

You need to determine if the benefits of tracking your total quality cost will give you enough of a return on investment to make setting up the appropriate accounting system and paying for the implementation of the programme worthwhile.

ECONOMIC COST

The economic cost of a decision depends on both the cost of the alternative chosen and the benefit that the best alternative would have provided if chosen. Economic cost differs from accounting cost because it includes opportunity cost. As an example, consider the economic cost of attending college. The accounting cost of attending college includes tuition, room and board, books, food, and other incidental expenditures while there.

The opportunity cost of college also includes the salary or wage that otherwise could be earning during the period. So for the two to four years an individual spends in school, the opportunity cost includes the money that one could have been making at the best possible job. The economic cost of college is the accounting cost plus the opportunity cost.

Thus, if attending college has a direct cost of $20,000 dollars a year for four years, and the lost wages from not working during that period equals $25,000 dollars a year, then the total economic cost of going to college would be $180,000 dollars ($20,000 × 4 years + $25,000 × 4 years).

EXPLICIT COST

An explicit cost is an easily accounted cost, such as wage, rent and materials. It can be transacted in the form of money payment and is lost directly, as opposed to monetary implicit costs.

Explicit cost are those which the entrepreneur has to pay from his own pocket.\ Explicit costs require an outlay of money by the firm.

Implicit Costs, Explicit Costs, and Total Costs

Implicit cost + explicit cost = total cost. Implicit cost is not equal to total cost, but a component of it. A simple example: Sean builds a cabinet. He spends 2 hours building the cabinet. He could have been working instead and normally makes $25/hour at his job. Since he was building a cabinet he wasn't paid for this time.

The materials to make the cabinet cost him $20:

- *His Explicit Costs are*: $20 in materials
- *His Implicit Costs are*: $25/hr x 2 hrs= $50 of foregone pay
- *His Total Costs are*: $20 in materials + $50 of foregone pay = $70 Total Costs

INDIRECT COSTS

Indirect costs are costs that are not directly accountable to a cost object. Indirect costs may be either fixed or variable. Indirect costs include taxes, administration, personnel and security costs, and are also known as overhead.

Indirect vs. Direct Costs

Direct costs are those for activities or services that benefit specific projects, e.g., salaries for project staff and materials required for a particular project. Because these activities are easily traced to projects, their costs are usually charged to projects on an item-by-item basis.

Indirect costs are those for activities or services that benefit more than one project. Their precise benefits to a specific project are often difficult or impossible to trace. For example, it may be difficult to determine precisely how the activities of the director of an organization benefit a specific project.

It is possible to justify the handling of almost any kind of cost as either direct or indirect. Labour costs, for example, can be indirect, as in the case of maintenance personnel and executive officers; or they can be direct, as in the case of project staff members.

Similarly, materials such as miscellaneous supplies purchased in bulk—pencils, pens, paper—are typically handled as indirect costs, while materials required for specific projects are charged as direct costs.

ISOCOST

In economics an isocost line represents a combination of inputs which all cost the same amount. Although similar to the budget constraint in consumer theory, the use of the isocost pertains to cost-minimization in production, as opposed to utility-maximization. The typical isocost line represents the ratio of costs of labour and capital, so the formula is often written as:

$$rK+wL=c$$

Where w represents the wage of labour, and r represents the rental rate of capital.

The slope is:

$$-w/r$$

or the negative ratio of wages divided by rental fees.

The isocost line is combined with the isoquant line to determine the optimal production point.

The Cost Function for a Firm with Two Variable Inputs

Consider a firm that uses two inputs and has the production function F. This firm minimizes its cost of producing any given output y if it chooses the pair (z1, z2) of inputs to solve the problem

Min z1,z2w1s conditional input demand functions.

The firm's minimal cost of producing the output y is w1z1*(y,w1, w2) + w2z2*(y,w1, w2) (the value of its total cost for the values of z1 and z2 that minimize that cost). The function TC defined by

$$Tc(y, w1, w2) = w1z1 * (y, w1, w2) + w2z2 * (y, w1, w2)$$

which is called the firm's (total) cost function. (Note that the hard part of the problem is finding the conditional input demands; once you have found these, then finding the cost function is simply a matter of adding the conditional input ogether with the weights w1 and w2.)

An Isocost line shows all the combinations of capital and labour that can be bought for a given total cost"

LOCK-IN (DECISION-MAKING)

Lock-in can be seen as the escalating commitment of decision-makers to an ineffective course of action.

It concerns institutional lock-in as compared to technical lock-in of which the QWERTY keyboard is a famous example.

The decision-making process is characterised by various informal and formal decision-making moments and decision-makers can become committed to the project before the formal decision to build was taken.

The formation of commitment is not necessarily bad, but when commitment turns into lock-in, it has by definition a negative influence on the project performance.

Lock-in can occur at the decision-making level or at the project level. There are possibilities to avoid lock-in when decision-makers can be made aware of this phenomenon. However, lock-in can also be used intentionally, in which case, it is much more difficult to prevent and hence manage cost overruns.

Decision Making I rocess

The decision-making process of large infrastructure projects is marked by the formal decision to build the project. However, there are several possible moments in the decision-making process before the formal decision is taken at which decision-makers are committed to the project.

The extent of which decision-makers are committed to the project is of importance here. Early commitment, commitment to the project before the formal decision to build has been taken, is in itself not necessarily negative. It could be advantageous to the decision-making process as it could enforce a decision.

This eventually could limit delay and contribute to the projects' performance.

Early commitment can result in negative outcomes once

the commitment turns into escalating commitment and lock-in. As lock-in is based on escalating commitment, it has, by definition, a negative influence on project performance. Lock-in has the potential to explain the large cost overruns in large scale transportation infrastructure projects.

Formation

Lock-in with respect to decision-making is created when sub-optimal policies are used as a consequence of e.g. path dependency, even though a better alternative is present. The term refers to the escalating commitment of decision-makers to an ineffective course of action.

Escalating commitment itself refers to the style of psychological coping associated with the inability to withdraw from obligations.

The process of escalating commitment is also known as "entrapment", the "sunk-cost effect", the "knee-deep in the big muddy" effect, and the "too-much-invested-to-quit" effect.

Occurrence

Lock-in can occur both at the decision-making level and can influence the extent of overruns in two ways:

1. The first involves the "methodology" of calculating cost overruns just as to the "formal decision to build". Due to lock-in, however, the "real decision to build" is made much earlier in the decision-making process and the costs estimated at that stage are often much lower than those that are estimated at a later stage in the decision-making process, thus increasing cost overruns.
2. The second way that lock-in can affect cost overruns is through "practice". Although decisions about the project need to be made, lock-in can lead to inefficient decisions that involve higher costs. Sunk costs in terms of both time and money, the need for justification, escalating commitment, and inflexibility and the closure of alternatives are indicators of lock-in.

Prevention

There are different types of lock-in; conscious/unconscious and intentional/unintentional lock-in. Some of these types of lock-in can be avoided. Decision-makers can be made conscious about their behaviour, for example by confronting them with the lack of sufficient alternatives. When these decision-makers are willing to change their behaviour and consider other alternatives, they are less likely to become committed to one project alternative and hence, the chance for lock-in can be partly avoided.

However, other types of lock-in are more difficult to control, especially intentional lock-in. Intentional lock-in is the result of specific behaviour of parties that performance deliberately in the interest of their project.

Cost overruns may thus be partly unnecessary or avoidable if such deliberate creation of lock-in had not taken place, and be partly unavoidable due to the incapacity of decision-makers to make optimal decisions.

MARGINAL COST OF CAPITAL SCHEDULE

Marginal Cost of Capital (MCC) Schedule is a graph that relates the firm's weighted average cost of each dollar of capital to the total amount of new capital raised.

The WACC is the minimum rate of return allowable, and still meeting financial obligationts such as debt, interest payments, dividends etc... Therefore, the WACC averages the required returns from all long-term financing sources.

the WACC is based on cash flows, which are after-tax. By the same notion then, the WACC should be calculated on an after-tax basis.

MARGINAL COST

In economics and finance, marginal cost is the change in total cost that arises when the quantity produced changes by one unit. That is, it is the cost of producing one more unit of a good. Mathematically, the marginal cost (MC) function is expressed as the first derivative of the total cost (TC) function with respect to quantity (Q). Note that the marginal cost may change with volume, and so at each level of production, the marginal cost is the cost of the next unit produced.

$$MC = \frac{dTC}{dQ}$$

In general terms, marginal cost at each level of production includes any additional costs required to produce the next unit. If producing additional vehicles requires, for example, building a new factory, the marginal cost of those extra vehicles includes the cost of the new factory. In practice, the analysis is segregated into short and long-run cases, and over the longest run, all costs are marginal. At each level of production and time period being considered, marginal costs include all costs which vary with the level of production, and other costs are considered fixed costs.

A number of other factors can affect marginal cost and its applicability to real world problems. Some of these may be considered market failures. These may include information asymmetries, the presence of negative or positive externalities, transaction costs, price discrimination and others.

Cost Functions and Relationship to Average Cost

In the simplest case, the total cost function and its derivative are expressed as follows, where Q represents the production quantity, VC represents variable costs, FC represents fixed costs and TC represents total costs.

$$MC = \frac{dTC}{dQ} = \frac{d(FC + VC)}{dQ} = \frac{dVC}{dQ}$$

Since fixed costs do not vary with production quantity, it drops out of the equation when it is differentiated. The important cease is that marginal cost is not related to fixed costs. This can be compared with average total cost or ATC, which is the total cost divided by the number of units produced and does include fixed costs.

$$ATC = \frac{FC + VC}{Q}$$

For discrete calculation without calculus, marginal cost

equals the change in total cost that comes with each additional unit produced. For instance, suppose the total cost of making 1 shoe is $30 and the total cost of making 2 shoes is $40. The marginal cost of producing the second shoe is $40 – $30 = $10.

Economies of Scale

Production may be subject to economies of scale. Increasing returns to scale are said to exist if additional units can be produced for less than the per unit, that is, average cost is falling. This can only occur if average cost at any given level of production is higher than the marginal cost. Conversely, there may be levels of production where marginal cost is higher than average cost, and average cost will rise for each unit of production after that point. This type of production function is generally known as diminishing marginal productivity: at low levels of production, productivity gains are easy and marginal costs falling, but productivity gains become smaller as production increases; eventually, marginal costs rise because increasing output becomes more expensive. For this generic case, minimum average cost occurs at the point where average cost and marginal cost are equal; this point will not be at the minimum for marginal cost if fixed costs are greater than zero.

Externalities

Externalities are costs that are not borne by the parties to the economic transaction. A producer may, for example, pollute the environment, and others may bear those costs. A consumer may consume a good which produces benefits for society, such as education; because the individual does not receive all of the benefits, he may consume less than efficiency would suggest. Alternatively, an individual may be a smoker or alcoholic and impose costs on others. In these cases, production or consumption of the good in question may differ from the optimum level.

Negative Externalities of Production

Much of the time, private and social costs do not diverge

from one another, but at times social costs may be either greater or less than private costs. When marginal social costs of production are greater than that of the private cost function, we see the occurrence of a negative externality of production.

Such externalities are a result of firms externalising their costs onto a third party in order to reduce their own total cost. As a result of externalising such costs we see that members of society will be negatively affected by such behaviour of the firm. In this case, we see that an increased cost of production on society creates a social cost curve that depicts a greater cost than the private cost curve.

In an equilibrium state we see that markets creating negative externalities of production will overproduce that good. As a result, the socially optimal production level would be lower than that observed.

Positive Externalities of Production

When marginal social costs of production are less than that of the private cost function, we see the occurrence of a positive externality of production. An example of such a public good, which creates a divergence in social and private costs, includes the production of education. It is often seen that education is a positive for any whole society, as well as a positive for those directly involved in the market.

Examining the relevant diagram we see that such production creates a social cost curve that is less than that of the private curve. In an equilibrium state we see that markets creating positive externalities of production will under produce that good. As a result, the socially optimal production level would be greater than that observed.

Social Costs

Of great importance in the theory of marginal cost is the distinction between the marginal private and social costs. The marginal private cost shows the cost associated to the firm in question. It is the marginal private cost that is used by business decision makers in their profit maximization goals, and by individuals in their purchasing and consumption choices.

Marginal social cost is similar to private cost in that it includes the cost functions of private enterprise but also that of society as a whole, including parties that have no direct association with the private costs of production. It incorporates all negative and positive externalities, of both production and consumption.

Hence, when deciding whether or how much to buy, buyers take account of the cost to society of their actions if private and social marginal cost coincide. The equality of price with social marginal cost, by aligning the interest of the buyer with the interest of the community as a whole is a necessary condition for economically efficient resource allocation.

4

Financial Analysis

FINANCIAL ANALYSIS

Financial analysis refers to an assessment of the viability, stability and profitability of a business, sub-business or project.

It is performed by professionals who prepare reports using ratios that make use of information taken from financial statements and other reports. These reports are usually presented to top management as one of their bases in making business decisions.

Based on these reports, management may:

- Continue or discontinue its main operation or part of its business;
- Make or purchase certain materials in the manufacture of its product;
- Acquire or rent/lease certain machineries and equipment in the production of its goods;
- Issue stocks or negotiate for a bank loan to increase its working capital;
- Make decisions regarding investing or lending capital;
- Other decisions that allow management to make an informed selection on various alternatives in the conduct of its business.

GOALS

Financial analysts often assess the firm's:

1. *Profitability*: Its ability to earn income and sustain growth in both short-term and long-term. A

company's degree of profitability is usually based on the income statement, which reports on the company's results of operations;

2. *Solvency*: Its ability to pay its obligation to creditors and other third parties in the long-term;
3. *Liquidity*: Its ability to maintain positive cash flow, while satisfying immediate obligations; Both 2 and 3 are based on the company's balance sheet, which indicates the financial condition of a business as of a given point in time.
4. *Stability*: The firm's ability to remain in business in the long run, without having to sustain significant losses in the conduct of its business. Assessing a company's stability requires the use of both the income statement and the balance sheet, as well as other financial and non-financial indicators.

METHODS

Financial analysts often compare financial ratios:

- *Past Performance*: Across historical time periods for the same firm,
- *Future Performance*: Using historical figures and certain mathematical and statistical techniques, including present and future values, This extrapolation method is the main source of errors in financial analysis as past statistics can be poor predictors of future prospects.
- *Comparative Performance*: Comparison between similar firms.

These ratios are calculated by dividing a account balances, taken from the balance sheet and/or the income statement, by another, for example:

n/equity = return on equity

Net income/total assets = return on assets

Stock price/earnings per share = P/E-ratio

Comparing financial ratios is merely one way of conducting financial analysis.

Financial ratios face several theoretical challenges:

- They say little about the firm's prospects in an absolute sense. Their insights about relative performance require a reference point from other time periods or similar firms.
- One ratio holds little meaning. As indicators, ratios can be logically interpreted in at least two ways. One can partially overcome this problem by combining several related ratios to paint a more comprehensive picture of the firm's performance.
- Seasonal factors may prevent year-end values from being representative. A ratio's values may be distorted as account balances change from the beginning to the end of an accounting period. Use average values for such accounts whenever possible.
- Financial ratios are no more objective than the accounting methods employed. Changes in accounting policies or choices can yield drastically different ratio values.
- They fail to account for exogenous factors like investor behaviour that are not based upon economic fundamentals of the firm or the general economy.

Financial analysts can also use percentage analysis which involves reducing a series of figures as a percentage of some base amount.

For example, a group of items can be expressed as a percentage of net income. When proportionate changes in the same figure over a given time period expressed as a percentage is know as horizontal analysis.

Vertical or common-size analysis, reduces all items on a statement to a "common size" as a percentage of some base value which assists in comparability with other companies of different sizes.

Another method is comparative analysis. This provides a better way to determine trends. Comparative analysis presents the same information for two or more time periods and is presented side-by-side to allow for easy analysis.

FINANCIAL ANALYSIS TOOLS

ANALYSIS OF THE COMPOSITION OF THE BALANCE SHEET

The balance sheet can be broken down into groups of accounts. A comparative analysis of the percentage relationships of the different groups of accounts that make up assets, liabilities, and equity can serve to detect, control, and manage trends or shifts in the composition of your net business resources.

The asset side of the balance sheet can be broken down into:

- Cash and cash equivalents, such as deposits and liquid marketable securities,
- Realizable assets, including short-term investments, trade accounts receivable from customers or clients, and other receivables,
- Inventories, and
- Fixed assets.

The liabilities and equity side can be separated into:

- Short-term liabilities,
- Long-term debt, and
- Owner's equity.

VERTICAL ANALYSIS

A vertical analysis can then be done by calculating the percentage that each group of assets represents in terms of total assets, and that each group of liabilities and equity represents in terms of total liabilities and equity. A graph of these relationships may be useful for visualizing the relationships.

This vertical analysis will provide you with an idea of where your resources are invested. If your business requires a significant portion of your resources to be liquid, for example, your analysis will probably show a strong percentage in cash and cash equivalents. If it does not, you may need to evaluate ways of freeing up more resources. If the level of inventory you carry is a significant aspect of your business, you will probably want to closely monitor how much of your resources are invested in inventory.

On the liability side, if you have a relatively rapid turnover of working capital, current liabilities will probably be significant. If your business is more capital intensive, with a significant investment in fixed assets, your long-term debt may be a more significant portion of total liabilities.

And while the amount of owner's equity will vary depending on how your business is financed, how profitable your business has been, and how you distribute earnings, owner's equity should be maintained at a level that is appropriate for the financial health and solvency of your business.

STATIC AND DYNAMIC ANALYSIS

A static analysis of these percentages at any given point in time can be useful. But a dynamic analysis, comparing the evolution of these percentages from period to period can be even more useful in seeing overall trends, and thereby knowing how resources are being allocated, what type of debt is being incurred, and how owner's equity is being affected by operations.

This type of dynamic analysis can be performed by choosing a certain period or year as a baseline (N), and then comparing the percentages for period N with the percentages for the following period (N+1), or with the percentages from as many other periods (N+2, N+3, N–1, N–2, etc.) as you wish, in order to see the trends over the periods in which you are interested.

PARAMETRES

Based on your experience with your business and its operations, you may be able to set some parametres or guidelines to use in analyzing the percentages and determining where actions need to be taken to make changes or modifications.

The following are some examples:

- Current assets should be greater than, and if possible double the amount of short-term liabilities.
- Realizable assets plus cash and cash equivalents

should be approximately equal to short-term liabilities.
- Owner's equity should amount to 40% or 50% of total liabilities and owner's equity.

You may also use benchmarking to compare the status of your business, in terms of relative proportions of different groups of assets and liabilities, with industry standards, or other comparable operations.

DEBT CHARACTERISTICS

The total amount of debt your business is carrying is important, but it is also important to know what type of debt you are carrying. In this regard, it can be useful to prepare an analysis, or table of debt characteristics.

Some of the data you may want to include in this type of analysis include:

- Type of debt
- Amount of each type of debt
- Interest rate
- Due dates
- Annual debt servicing cost
- Annual installments
- Collateral provided

Having a clear picture of the structure of your debt will allow you to make decisions regarding potential alternative sources of financing, if necessary.

INCOME STATEMENT ANALYSIS

The income statement can also be broken down into its component parts and analysed on a percentage basis.

PERCENTAGE BREAKDOWN

Some of the principle items in an income statement, that could be expressed as a percentage of sales, for example, include:

- Sales
- Cost of Sales
- Gross Margin
- Fixed Costs or Overhead

- Net Income Before Interest and Taxes
- Interest Expense and Financing Costs
- Net Income Before Income Tax
- Income Tax
- Net After-Tax Income

By doing a comparative analysis based on percentages over different periods, you can see how the different components of the income statement are evolving. Here again, graphs would be a useful visual tool.

BASELINE

You can also analyse income statement accounts by using a baseline period. The baseline period could be your budget, a break-even point, your first year of operations, any period of actual results against which you want to compare other periods; or the baseline could be industry benchmark data or the results of a similar business, such as a competitor.

The results of any period you are comparing to the baseline period would be expressed in terms of a percentage of the corresponding amount from the baseline period. By doing this type of analysis over more than one period, you can see the absolute variances in the amounts of each element of the income statement as compared to the baseline, as well as relative variances from one period to another. For example, if your baseline indicates gross profit as 40% of sales, you will be able to track, period by period, how your actual gross profit compares.

MARKET SHARE AND PARTICIPATION BY PRODUCT

If you have access to data on your particular market, you can determine your share of the market as:

- Market Share = Your Company's Sales/Total Sales in Your Market Sector

This ratio could be calculated in terms of volume of units sold, dollar value of sales, or both. If your business involves more than one type of product, you can determine the relative importance of each product, in terms of your total sales, as:

- Participation of Product A in Total Sales = Sales of Product A/Total Sales

To obtain an indication of how well you are renewing your product line, you can use the following ratio:

- Level of Renewal of Product Line = Sales of New Products/Total Sales

The more information you have regarding the sales and costs of each of your own products, and the associated figures relating to your market sector, the more types of analyses you can perform. By breaking down your actual sales by individual product, or line of products, and comparing these figures with the corresponding market figures, you can determine:

- The growth of your sales of each product, period by period, and how your growth compares to the market.
- Changes in your market share, by product by period.
- Changes in the make-up of your sales – how much of your sales was for each product, and how is this evolving over time.

INCOME STATEMENTS BY PRODUCT

If you have the capability to generate income statements by product, or by product lines, you will have good insight as to where resources and efforts can be allocated more efficiently and profitably. If this information is not readily available from your accounting system, you may be able to prepare pro forma income statements by product.

Certain costs may be more readily assignable to specific products than others.

Costs that may be allocable by product include:

- Materials and supplies
- Direct labour
- Manufacturing cost
- Sales commissions
- Advertising and publicity

By breaking down sales by product, and then allocating these direct costs, you can determine a gross margin by product. This will be helpful in showing which products are contributing the most to your bottom line.

RATIOS

If you use a baseline period expressed in terms of 1.00, the percentage increase or decrease in sales, gross margin, net income, or any other income statement line item will be evident from the comparative analysis. Other ratios that may be useful could be based on other types of data.

For example, in a labour-intensive environment where the output of each individual employee is a key factor in sales and profitability, useful ratios could include:

- Sales by Employee = Total Sales/Number of Employees
- Added Value by Employee = Total Added Value (Gross or Net Profit)/Number of Employees

In a capital-intensive environment, ratios related to the investment in equipment, or maintenance costs may be more relevant:

EXPENSE ANALYSIS RATIOS

One type of ratios that can be used to track expenses is by comparing different categories of expenses to sales:

- Fixed Expenses or Overhead/Sales
- Variable Expenses/Sales
- Personnel-related Expenses/Sales

This type of ratios will be useful to the extent there are parametres established, comparison is made using benchmark data, or the evolution of expenses is compared from one period to another. Another way to analyse expenses is by comparison to an associated criteria, such as number of employees, customers, or products.

These ratios give a type of unit cost which, when compared to a parametre, or when followed over time, can provide indications of where variances are occurring:

- Customer Service Expenses/Number of Customers
- Advertising Expenses/Number of Products
- Production Expenses/Number of Units Produced

- Personnel-related Expenses/Average Number of Employees

PRODUCTIVITY RATIOS

Productivity rations are intended to show the results obtained with the expenses incurred or the resources employed.

Some overall ratios include:

- Net Income/Expenses
- Sales/Expenses
- Production/Expenses
- Trade Accounts Receivable/Expenses

More specific ratios can be calculated using virtually any type of criteria. Ratios that are meaningful will depend on the nature of the business; that is, what factors affect productivity and can be tracked and controlled.

Another productivity ratio, that is probably more oriented toward a manufacturing or production environment, is:

- Utilization of Productive Capacity = Production Obtained/Production Capacity

RATIOS OF EFFECTIVENESS

Effectiveness has to do with comparing actual results with budgeted, forecast, or expected results. These ratios can be calculated on any item for which actual and expected results are available, and which are of interest in managing the business.

Some examples include:

- Forecast Profit/Actual Profit
- Forecast Sales/Actual Sales
- Forecast Production/Actual Production
- Forecast Trade Receivables/Actual Trade Receivables

It should be noted that calculating the ratios as indicated above will yield a ratio greater than 1.0 if actual results are lower than forecast results. If you want to see a ratio of less than 1.0 if actual results are lower you would have to invert the ratios.

To see how efficiently you controlled expenses, you could

calculate efficiency ratios of any individual expense item, or any grouping or total expenses:

- Efficiency = Forecast Expenses/Actual Expenses
- In addition to effectiveness and efficiency, quality control is another concern that can be expressed through ratio analysis:
- Number of Customer Complaints/Number of Customers
- Number of Late Deliveries/Total Orders Delivered
- Quality Evaluation and Assurance Costs/Sales
- Costs of Damages and Defects/Sales
- Cost of Service After the Sale/Sales

FINANCIAL RATIO ANALYSIS

The Balance Sheet and the Statement of Income are essential, but they are only the starting point for successful financial management. Apply Ratio Analysis to Financial Statements to analyse the success, failure, and progress of your business.

Ratio Analysis enables the business owner/manager to spot trends in a business and to compare its performance and condition with the average performance of similar businesses in the same industry. To do this compare your ratios with the average of businesses similar to yours and compare your own ratios for several successive years, watching especially for any unfavourable trends that may be starting. Ratio analysis may provide the all-important early warning indications that allow you to solve your business problems before your business is destroyed by them.

BALANCE SHEET RATIO ANALYSIS

Important Balance Sheet Ratios measure liquidity and solvency and leverage. They include the following ratios:

Liquidity Ratios

These ratios indicate the ease of turning assets into cash. They include the Current Ratio, Quick Ratio, and Working Capital.

Current Ratios. The Current Ratio is one of the best known measures of financial strength. It is figured as shown:

$$\text{Current Ratio} = \frac{\text{Total Current Assest}}{\text{Total Current Liabilities}}$$

The main question this ratio addresses is: "Does your business have enough current assets to meet the payment schedule of its current debts with a margin of safety for possible losses in current assets, such as inventory shrinkage or collectable accounts?" A generally acceptable current ratio is 2 to 1. But whether or not a specific ratio is satisfactory depends on the nature of the business and the characteristics of its current assets and liabilities. The minimum acceptable current ratio is obviously 1:1, but that relationship is usually playing it too close for comfort.

If you decide your business's current ratio is too low, you may be able to raise it by:

- Paying some debts.
- Increasing your current assets from loans or other borrowings with a maturity of more than one year.
- Converting non-current assets into current assets.
- Increasing your current assets from new equity contributions.
- Putting profits back into the business.

Quick Ratios. The Quick Ratio is sometimes called the "acid-test" ratio and is one of the best measures of liquidity. It is figured as shown:

$$\text{Quick Ratio} = \frac{\text{Cash} + \text{Government Securities} + \text{Receivables}}{\text{Total Current Liabilities}}$$

The Quick Ratio is a much more exacting measure than he Current Ratio. By excluding inventories, it concentrates on the really liquid assets, with value that is fairly certain. It helps answer the question: "If all sales revenues should disappear, could business meet its current obligations with the readily convertible `quick' funds on hand?"

An acid-test of 1:1 is considered satisfactory unless the majority of your "quick assets" are in accounts receivable, and the pattern of accounts receivable collection lags behind the schedule for paying current liabilities.

Working Capital. Working Capital is more a measure of cash flow than a ratio. The result of this calculation must be a positive number. It is calculated as shown: Working Capital = Total Current Assets - Total Current Liabilities.

Bankers look at Net Working Capital over time to determine a company's ability to weather financial crises. Loans are often tied to minimum working capital requirements. A general observation about these three Liquidity Ratios is that the higher they are the better, especially if you are relying to any significant extent on creditor money to finance assets.

Leverage Ratio

This Debt/Worth or Leverage Ratio indicates the extent to which the business is reliant on debt financing:

$$\text{Debt/Worth Ratio} = \frac{\text{Total Liabilities}}{\text{Net Worth}}$$

Generally, the higher this ratio, the more risky a creditor will perceive its exposure in your business, making it correspondingly harder to obtain credit.

INCOME STATEMENT RATIO ANALYSIS

The following important State of Income Ratios measure profitability:

Gross Margin Ratio

This ratio is the percentage of sales dollars left after subtracting the cost of goods sold from net sales. It measures the percentage of sales dollars remaining available to pay the overhead expenses of the company. Comparison of your business ratios to those of similar businesses will reveal the relative strengths or weaknesses in your business.

The Gross Margin Ratio is calculated as follows:

$$\text{Gross Margin Ratio} = \frac{\text{Gross Profit}}{\text{Net Sales}}$$

(Gross Profit = Net Sales - Cost of Goods Sold)

Net Profit Margin Ratio

This ratio is the percentage of sales dollars left after subtracting the Cost of Goods sold and all expenses, except income taxes. It provides a good opportunity to compare your company's "return on sales" with the performance of other companies in your industry. It is calculated before income tax because tax rates and tax liabilities vary from company to company for a wide variety of reasons, making comparisons after taxes much more difficult.

The Net Profit Margin Ratio is calculated as follows:

$$\text{Net Profit Margin Ratio} = \frac{\text{Net Profit Before Tax}}{\text{Net Sales}}$$

Management Ratios

Other important ratios, often referred to as Management Ratios, are also derived from Balance Sheet and Statement of Income information.

Inventory Turnover Ratio

This ratio reveals how well inventory is being managed. It is important because the more times inventory can be turned in a given operating cycle, the greater the profit.

The Inventory Turnover Ratio is calculated as follows:

$$\text{Inventory Turnover Ratio} = \frac{\text{Net Sales}}{\text{Average Inventory at Cost}}$$

Accounts Receivable Turnover Ratio

This ratio indicates how well accounts receivable are being collected. If receivables are not collected reasonably in accordance with their terms, management should rethink its collection policy. If receivables are excessively slow in being converted to cash, liquidity could be severely impaired.

The Accounts Receivable Turnover Ratio is calculated as follows:

$$\frac{\text{Net Credit Sales/Year}}{\text{365 Days/Year}} = \text{Daily Credit Sales}$$

$$\text{Accounts Receivable Turnover (in days)} = \frac{\text{Accounts Receivable}}{\text{Daily Credit Sales}}$$

Return on Assets Ratio

This measures how efficiently profits are being generated from the assets employed in the business when compared with the ratios of firms in a similar business. A low ratio in comparison with industry averages indicates an inefficient use of business assets.

The Return on Assets Ratio is calculated as follows:

$$\text{Return on Assets} = \frac{\text{Net Profit Before Tax}}{\text{Total Assets}}$$

Return on Investment (ROI) Ratio

The ROI is perhaps the most important ratio of all. It is the percentage of return on funds invested in the business by its owners. In short, this ratio tells the owner whether or not all the effort put into the business has been worthwhile. If the ROI is less than the rate of return on an alternative, risk-free investment such as a bank savings account, the owner may be wiser to sell the company, put the money in such a savings instrument, and avoid the daily struggles of small business management.

The ROI is calculated as follows:

$$\text{Return on Assets} = \frac{\text{Net Profit Before Tax}}{\text{Net Worth}}$$

These Liquidity, Leverage, Profitability, and Management Ratios allow the business owner to identify trends in a business and to compare its progress with the performance of others through data published by various sources. The owner may thus determine the business's relative strengths and weaknesses.

ADVANTAGES AND USES OF RATIO ANALYSIS

There are various groups of people who are interested in

analysis of financial position of a company. They use the ratio analysis to workout a particular financial characteristic of the company in which they are interested.

Ratio analysis helps the various groups in the following manner:

- *To workout the profitability*: Accounting ratio help to measure the profitability of the business by calculating the various profitability ratios. It helps the management to know about the earning capacity of the business concern. In this way profitability ratios show the actual performance of the business.
- *To workout the solvency*: With the help of solvency ratios, solvency of the company can be measured. These ratios show the relationship between the liabilities and assets. In case external liabilities are more than that of the assets of the company, it shows the unsound position of the business. In this case the business has to make it possible to repay its loans.
- *Helpful in analysis of financial statement*: Ratio analysis help the outsiders just like creditors, shareholders, debenture-holders, bankers to know about the profitability and ability of the company to pay them interest and dividend etc.
- *Helpful in comparative analysis of the performance*: With the help of ratio analysis a company may have comparative study of its performance to the previous years. In this way company comes to know about its weak point and be able to improve them.
- *To simplify the accounting information*: Accounting ratios are very useful as they briefly summarise the result of detailed and complicated computations.
- *To workout the operating efficiency*: Ratio analysis helps to workout the operating efficiency of the company with the help of various turnover ratios. All turnover ratios are worked out to evaluate the performance of the business in utilising the resources.
- *To workout short-term financial position*: Ratio analysis helps to workout the short-term financial position of

the company with the help of liquidity ratios. In case short-term financial position is not healthy efforts are made to improve it.

- *Helpful for forecasting purposes*: Accounting ratios indicate the trend of the business. The trend is useful for estimating future. With the help of previous years' ratios, estimates for future can be made. In this way these ratios provide the basis for preparing budgets and also determine future line of action.

LIMITATIONS OF RATIO ANALYSIS

In spite of many advantages, there are certain limitations of the ratio analysis techniques and they should be kept in mind while using them in interpreting financial statements.

The following are the main limitations of accounting ratios:

- *Limited Comparability*: Different firms apply different accounting policies. Therefore the ratio of one firm can not always be compared with the ratio of other firm. Some firms may value the closing stock on LIFO basis while some other firms may value on FIFO basis. Similarly there may be difference in providing depreciation of fixed assets or certain of provision for doubtful debts etc.
- *False Results*: Accounting ratios are based on data drawn from accounting records. In case that data is correct, then only the ratios will be correct. For example, valuation of stock is based on very high price, the profits of the concern will be inflated and it will indicate a wrong financial position. The data therefore must be absolutely correct.
- *Effect of Price Level Changes*: Price level changes often make the comparison of figures difficult over a period of time. Changes in price affects the cost of production, sales and also the value of assets. Therefore, it is necessary to make proper adjustment for price-level changes before any comparison.
- *Qualitative factors are ignored*: Ratio analysis is a

technique of quantitative analysis and thus, ignores qualitative factors, which may be important in decision making. For example, average collection period may be equal to standard credit period, but some debtors may be in the list of doubtful debts, which is not disclosed by ratio analysis.

- *Effect of window-dressing*: In order to cover up their bad financial position some companies resort to window dressing. They may record the accounting data just as to the convenience to show the financial position of the company in a better way.
- *Costly Technique*: Ratio analysis is a costly technique and can be used by big business houses. Small business units are not able to afford it.
- *Misleading Results*: In the absence of absolute data, the result may be misleading. For example, the gross profit of two firms is 25%. Whereas the profit earned by one is just Rs. 5,000 and sales are Rs. 20,000 and profit earned by the other one is Rs. 10,00,000 and sales are Rs. 40,00,000. Even the profitability of the two firms is same but the magnitude of their business is quite different.
- *Absence of standard university accepted terminology*: There are no standard ratios, which are universally accepted for comparison purposes. As such, the significance of ratio analysis technique is reduced.

COMMON SIZE FINANCIAL STATEMENTS

Common size ratios are used to compare financial statements of different-size companies, or of the same company over different periods.

By expressing the items in proportion to some size-related measure, standardized financial statements can be created, revealing trends and providing insight into how the different companies compare.

The common size ratio for each line on the financial statement is calculated as follows:

$$\text{Common Size Ratio} = \frac{\text{Item of Interest}}{\text{Reference Item}}$$

For example, if the item of interest is inventory and it is referenced to total assets, the common size ratio would be:

$$\text{Common Size Ratio for Inventory} = \frac{\text{Inventory}}{\text{Total Assest}}$$

The ratios often are expressed as percentages of the reference amount.

Common size statements usually are prepared for the income statement and balance sheet, expressing information as follows:

- *Income statement items*: Expressed as a percentage of total revenue
- *Balance sheet items*: Expressed as a percentage of total assets

The following example income statement shows both the dollar amounts and the common size ratios:

Table. Common Size Income Statement

	Income Statement	**Common-Size Income Statement**
Revenue	70,134	100%
Cost of Goods Sold	44,221	63.1%
Gross Profit	25,913	36.9%
SG&A Expense	13,531	19.3%
Operating Income	12,382	17.7%
Interest Expense	2,862	4.1%
Provision for Taxes	3,766	5.4%
Net Income	5,754	8.2%

For the balance sheet, the common size percentages are referenced to the total assets. The following sample balance sheet shows both the dollar amounts and the common size ratios:

Table. Common Size Balance Sheet

	Balance Sheet	Common-Size Balance Sheet
Assets		
Cash & Marketable Securities	6,029	15.1%
Accounts Receivable	14,378	36.0%
Inventory	17,136	42.9%
Total Current Assets	37,543	93.9%
Property, Plant, & Equipment	2,442	6.1%
Total Assets	39,985	100%
Liabilities And Shareholders' Equity		
Current Liabilities	14,251	35.6%
Long-Term Debt	12,624	31.6%
Total Liabilities	26,875	67.2%
Shareholders' Equity	13,110	32.8%
Total Liabilities & Equity	39,985	100%

The common size statements are prepared in a vertical analysis, referencing each line on the financial statement to a total value on the statement in a given period.

The ratios in common size statements tend to have less variation than the absolute values themselves, and trends in the ratios can reveal important changes in the business. Historical comparisons can be made in a time-series analysis to identify such trends. Common size statements also can be used to compare the firm to other firms.

COMPARISONS BETWEEN COMPANIES

Common size financial statements can be used to compare multiple companies at the same point in time. A common-size analysis is especially useful when comparing companies of different sizes. It often is insightful to compare a firm to the best performing firm in its industry.

A firm also can be compared to its industry as a whole. To compare to the industry, the ratios are calculated for each firm in the industry and an average for the industry is calculated. Comparative statements then may be constructed with the company of interest in one column and the industry averages in another. The result is a quick overview of where the firm stands in the industry with respect to key items on the financial statements.

LIMITATIONS

As with financial statements in general, the interpretation of common size statements is subject to many of the limitations in the accounting data used to construct them.

For example:

- Different accounting policies may be used by different firms or within the same firm at different points in time. Adjustments should be made for such differences.
- Different firms may use different accounting calendars, so the accounting periods may not be directly comparable.

TREND ANALYSIS

Trend analysis is a form of comparative analysis that is often employed to identify current and future movements of an investment or group of investments. The process may involve comparing past and current financial ratios as they related to various institutions in order to project how long the current trend will continue. This type of information is extremely helpful to investors who wish to make the most from their investments.

The process of a trend analysis begins with identifying the category of the investments that are under consideration. For example, if the investor wishes to get an idea on the potential for making a profit with pork bellies, the focus will be on the performance of pork bellies in a commodities market. The trend analysis will include more than one supplier for the commodity, in order to get a more accurate picture of the current status of pork bellies on the market.

Once the focus is established, the investor takes a long at the general performance for the category over the last couple of years. This helps to identify key factors that led to the current trend of performance for the investment under consideration. By understanding how a given investment reached the current level of performance, it is then possible to determine if all or most of those factors are still exerting an influence.

After identifying past and present factors that are maintaining a current trend in performance, the investor can analyse each factor and project which factors are likely to continue exerting influence on the direction of the investment. Assuming that all or most of the factors will continue to exert an influence for the foreseeable future, the investor can make an informed decision on whether to buy or sell a given asset.

A trend analysis may be used to identify and project upswings in the performance of a stock or commodity, or to identify the potential for an upcoming downturn in value. By comparing the financial ratio of the past with the present and identifying key factors that helped the investment to arrive at the current point, it is possible to use the process of trend analysis to project future worth and adjust the components of the financial portfolio accordingly.

FUNDS FLOW STATEMENT

The estimated amount of tuition and living expenses for 1 year is US $ 23,422 which is approximately equal to Rs. 11.48 lakhs per year.

Year	Semester	Funds required	Sources of funds	Funds arranged
First	Sem 1 Aug 2002	Rs. 5.74 lakhs	33% of current bank balance	Rs. 5.8 lakhs
	Sem 2 Jan 2003	Rs. 5.74 lakhs	33% of current bank balance	Rs. 5.8 lakhs
Second	Sem 3 Aug 2003	Rs. 5.74 lakhs	25% of current bank Balance 30% of Post Office Savings Deposit	Rs. 4.4 lakhs Rs. 1.5 lakhs ------------- Rs. 5.9 lakhs
	Sem 4 Jan 2004	Rs. 5.74 lakhs	60% of Post Office Savings Deposit 50% of fixed deposits and recurring deposit with UBI 40% of General Provident Fund	Rs. 3.0 lakhs Rs. 1.6 lakhs Rs. 1.2 lakhs ------------- Rs. 5.8 lakhs
Total		Rs. 22.96 lakhs		Rs. 23.3 lakhs

Balance Assets after meeting with all the expenses:

Movable Assets:	Rs. 12.68 lakhs
Immovable Assets:	Rs. 73.52 lakhs
Total balance Assets:	Rs. 86.20 lakhs

Besides this, parents have a steady annual income of about Rs. 8.03 lakhs per year.

(Name of Applicant)

CASH FLOW STATEMENT

In financial accounting, a cash flow statement, also known as *statement of cash flows* or *funds flow statement,* is a financial statement that shows how changes in balance sheet accounts and income affect cash and cash equivalents, and breaks the analysis down to operating, investing, and financing activities. Essentially, the cash flow statement is concerned with the flow of cash in and cash out of the business.

The statement captures both the current operating results and the accompanying changes in the balance sheet. As an analytical tool, the statement of cash flows is useful in determining the short-term viability of a company, particularly its ability to pay bills.

International Accounting Standard 7 is the International Accounting Standard that deals with cash flow statements.

People and groups interested in cash flow statements include:

- Accounting personnel, who need to know whether the organization will be able to cover payroll and other immediate expenses
- Potential lenders or creditors, who want a clear picture of a company's ability to repay
- Potential investors, who need to judge whether the company is financially sound
- Potential employees or contractors, who need to know whether the company will be able to afford compensation
- Shareholders of the business.

PURPOSE

The cash flow statement as the flow of funds statement. The cash flow statement reflects a firm's liquidity. The balance sheet is a snapshot of a firm's financial resources and obligations at a single point in time, and the income statement summarizes a firm's financial transactions over an interval of time. These two financial statements reflect the accrual basis accounting used by firms to match revenues with the expenses associated with generating those revenues.

The cash flow statement includes only inflows and outflows of cash and cash equivalents; it excludes transactions that do not directly affect cash receipts and payments. These noncash transactions include depreciation or write-offs on bad debts or credit losses to name a few. The cash flow statement is a cash basis report on three types of financial activities: operating activities, investing activities, and financing activities. Noncash activities are usually reported in footnotes.

The cash flow statement is intended to:

- Provide information on a firm's liquidity and solvency and its ability to change cash flows in future circumstances
- Provide additional information for evaluating changes in assets, liabilities and equity
- Improve the comparability of different firms' operating performance by eliminating the effects of different accounting methods
- Indicate the amount, timing and probability of future cash flows

The cash flow statement has been adopted as a standard financial statement because it eliminates allocations, which might be derived from different accounting methods, such as various timeframes for depreciating fixed assets.

HISTORY AND VARIATIONS

Cash basis financial statements were common before accrual basis financial statements. The "flow of funds" statements of the past were cash flow statements. In 1863, the Dowlais Iron Company had recovered from a business slump, but had no cash to invest for a new blast furnace, despite having made a profit. To explain why there were no funds to invest, the manager made a new financial statement that was called a *comparison balance sheet*, which showed that the company was holding too much inventory. This new financial statement was the genesis of Cash Flow Statement that is used today.

In the United States in 1971, the Financial Accounting Standards Board defined rules that made it mandatory under Generally Accepted Accounting Principles to report sources and uses of funds, but the definition of "funds" was not clear."Net working capital" might be cash or might be the difference between current assets and current liabilities. From the late 1970 to the mid-1980s, the FASB discussed the usefulness of predicting future cash flows.

In 1987, FASB Statement No. 95 mandated that firms provide cash flow statements. In 1992, the International Accounting Standards Board issued International Accounting Standard 7, *Cash Flow Statements,* which became effective in 1994, mandating that firms provide cash flow statements.

US GAAP and IAS 7 rules for cash flow statements are similar.

Differences include:

- IAS 7 requires that the cash flow statement include changes in both cash and cash equivalents. US GAAP permits using cash alone or cash and cash equivalents.
- IAS 7 permits bank borrowings in certain countries to be included in cash equivalents rather than being considered a part of financing activities.
- IAS 7 allows interest paid to be included in operating activities or financing activities. US GAAP requires that interest paid be included in operating activities.
- US GAAP requires that when the direct method is used to present the operating activities of the cash flow statement, a supplemental schedule must also present a cash flow statement using the indirect method. The IASC strongly recommends the direct

method but allows either method. The IASC considers the indirect method less clear to users of financial statements. Cash flow statements are most commonly prepared using the indirect method, which is not especially useful in projecting future cash flows.

CASH FLOW ACTIVITIES

The cash flow statement is partitioned into three segments, namely: cash flow resulting from operating activities, cash flow resulting from investing activities, and cash flow resulting from financing activities. The money coming into the business is called cash inflow, and money going out from the business is called cash outflow.

Operating Activities

Operating activities include the production, sales and delivery of the company's product as well as collecting payment from its customers. This could include purchasing raw materials, building inventory, advertising, and shipping the product.

Under IAS 7, operating cash flows include:

1. Receipts from the sale of goods or services
2. Receipts for the sale of loans, debt or equity instruments in a trading portfolio
3. Interest received on loans
4. Dividends received on equity securities
5. Payments to suppliers for goods and services
6. Payments to employees or on behalf of employees
7. Interest payments

Items which are added back to the net income figure to arrive at cash flows from operations generally include:

- Depreciation
- Deferred tax
- Amortization
- Any gains or losses associated with the sale of a non-current asset, because associated cash flows do not belong in the operating section.

Investing Activities

Examples of Investing activities are:

- Purchase or Sale of an asset
- Loans made to suppliers or received from customers
- Payments related to mergers and acquisitions

Financing Activities

Financing activities include the inflow of cash from investors such as banks and shareholders, as well as the outflow of cash to shareholders as dividends as the company generates income. Other activities which impact the long-term liabilities and equity of the company are also listed in the financing activities section of the cash flow statement.

Under IAS 7,:

- Proceeds from issuing short-term or long-term debt
- Payments of dividends
- Payments for repurchase of company shares
- Repayment of debt principal, including capital leases
- For non-profit organizations, receipts of donor-restricted cash that is limited to long-term purposes

Items under the financing activities include:

- Dividends paid
- Sale or repurchase of the company's stock
- Net borrowings
- Payment of dividend tax

DISCLOSURE OF NONCASH ACTIVITIES

Under IAS 7, noncash investing and financing activities are disclosed in footnotes to the financial statements. Under US General Accepted Accounting Principles, noncash activities may be disclosed in a footnote or within the cash flow statement itself.

Noncash financing activities may include:

- Leasing to purchase an asset
- Converting debt to equity
- Exchanging noncash assets or liabilities for other noncash assets or liabilities
- Issuing shares in exchange for assets

PREPARATION METHODS

The direct method of preparing a cash flow statement results is a more easily understood report. The indirect method is almost universally used, because FAS 95 requires a supplementary report similar to the indirect method if a company chooses to use the direct method.

Direct Method

The direct method for creating a cash flow statement reports major classes of gross cash receipts and payments. Under IAS 7, dividends received may be reported under operating activities or under investing activities.

If taxes paid are directly linked to operating activities, they are reported under operating activities; if the taxes are directly linked to investing activities or financing activities, they are reported under investing or financing activities.

Sample cash flow statement using the direct method:

Cash flows from operating activities		
Cash receipts from customers	27,500	
Cash paid to suppliers and employees	(20,000)	
Cash generated from operations (sum)	7,500	
Interest paid	(2,000)	
Income taxes paid	(4,000)	
Net cash flows from operating activities		1,500
Cash flows from (used in) investing activities		
Proceeds from the sale of equipment	7,500	
Dividends received	3,000	
Net cash flows from investing activities		10,500
Cash flows from (used in) financing activities		
Dividends paid	(2,500)	
Net cash flows used in financing activities		(2,500)
Net increase in cash and cash equivalents		9,500
Cash and cash equivalents, beginning of year		1,000
Cash and cash equivalents, end of year		$10,500

Indirect Method

The indirect method uses net-income as a starting point,

makes adjustments for all transactions for non-cash items, then adjusts for all cash-based transactions. An increase in an asset account is subtracted from net income, and an increase in a liability account is added back to net income. This method converts accrual-basis net income into cash flow by using a series of additions and deductions.

Rules

The following rules are used to make adjustments for changes in current assets and liabilities, operating items not providing or using cash and nonoperating items:

Table. Example: Cash flow of Citigroup

Citigroup Cash Flow Statement (all numbers in millions of US$):			
Period ending	12/31/2007	12/31/2006	12/31/2005
Net income	21,538	24,589	17,046
Operating activities, cash flows provided by or used in:			
Depreciation and amortization	2,790	2,592	2,747
Adjustments to net income	4,617	621	2,910
Decrease (increase) in accounts receivable	12,503	17,236	--
Increase (decrease) in liabilities (A/P, taxes payable)	131,622	19,822	37,856
Decrease (increase) in inventories	--	--	--
Increase (decrease) in other operating activities	(173,057)	(33,061)	(62,963)
Net cash flow from operating activities	13	31,799	(2,404)
Investing activities, cash flows provided by or used in:			
Capital expenditures	(4,035)	(3,724)	(3,011)
Investments	(201,777)	(71,710)	(75,649)
Other cash flows from investing activities	1,606	17,009	(571)
Net cash flows from investing activities	(204,206)	(58,425)	(79,231)
Financing activities, cash flows provided by or used in:			
Dividends paid	(9,826)	(9,188)	(8,375)
Sale (repurchase) of stock	(5,327)	(12,090)	133
Increase (decrease) in debt	101,122	26,651	21,204
Other cash flows from financing activities	120,461	27,910	70,349
Net cash flows from financing activities	206,430	33,283	83,311
Effect of exchange rate changes	645	(1,840)	731
Net increase (decrease) in cash and cash equivalents	2,882	4,817	2,407

- Decrease in non-cash current assets are added to net income
- Increase in non-cash current asset are subtracted from net income
- Increase in current liabilities are added to net income

- Decrease in current liabilities are subtracted from net income
- Expenses with no cash outflows are added back to net income
- Revenues with no cash inflows are subtracted from net income
- Non operating losses are added back to net income
- Non operating gains are subtracted from net income

5

Emerging Dimensions in Accounting

PRICE LEVEL ACCOUNTING

Price level accounting method of measuring the impact of changes in general purchasing power of the dollar. Inflation is measured and reported in the financial statements. Balance sheet and income statement accounts are restated to average current year dollars using the Consumer Price Index. *Purchasing power gains and losses* on monetary item are reflected in the price-level income statement.

PRICING POLICY AND STRATEGY

Managers should start setting prices during the development stage as part of strategic pricing to avoid launching products or services that cannot sustain profitable prices in the market.

This approach to pricing enables companies to either fit costs to prices or scrap products or services that cannot be generated cost-effectively. Through systematic pricing policies and strategies, companies can reap greater profits and increase or defend their market shares.

Setting prices is one of the principal tasks of marketing and finance managers in that the price of a product or service often plays a significant role in that product's or service's success, not to mention in a company's profitability.

Generally, pricing policy refers how a company sets the prices of its products and services based on costs, value, demand, and competition. Pricing strategy, on the other hand, refers to how a company uses pricing to achieve its strategic goals, such as offering lower prices to increase sales volume or higher prices to decrease backlog. Despite some degree of difference, pricing policy and strategy tend to overlap, and the different policies and strategies are not necessarily mutually exclusive.

After establishing the bases for their prices, managers can begin developing pricing strategies by determining company pricing goals, such as increasing short-term and long-term profits, stabilizing prices, increasing cash flow, and warding off competition. Managers also must take into account current market conditions when developing pricing strategies to ensure that the prices they choose fit market conditions. In addition, effective pricing strategy involves considering customers, costs, competition, and different market segments.

Pricing strategy entails more than reacting to market conditions, such as reducing pricing because competitors have reduced their prices. Instead, it encompasses more thorough planning and consideration of customers, competitors, and company goals. Furthermore, pricing strategies tend to vary depending on whether a company is a new entrant into a market or an established firm. New entrants sometimes offer products at low cost to attract market share, while incumbents' reactions vary.

Incumbents that fear the new entrant will challenge the incumbents' customer base may match prices or go even lower than the new entrant to protect its market share. If incumbents do not view the new entrant as a serious threat, incumbents may simply resort to increased advertising aimed at enhancing customer loyalty, but have no change in price in efforts to keep the new entrant from stealing away customers.

Various ways companies develop pricing policy and strategy. First, cost-based pricing is considered. This is followed by the second topic of value-based pricing. Third, demand-based pricing is addressed followed by competition-based pricing. After this, several strategies for new and established pricing strategies are explained.

COST-BASED PRICING

The traditional pricing policy can be summarized by the formula:

Cost + Fixed profit percentage = Selling price.

Cost-based pricing involves the determination of all fixed and variable costs associated with a product or service. After the total costs attributable to the product or service have been determined, managers add a desired profit margin to each unit such as a 5 or 10 per cent markup. The goal of the cost-oriented approach is to cover all costs incurred in producing or delivering products or services and to achieve a targeted level of profit.

By itself, this method is simple and straightforward, requiring only that managers study financial and accounting records to determine prices. This pricing approach does not involve examining the market or considering the competition and other factors that might have an impact on pricing. Cost-oriented pricing also is popular because it is an age-old practice that uses internal information that managers can obtain easily. In addition, a company can defend its prices based on costs, and demonstrate that its prices cover costs plus a markup for profit.

However, critics contend that the cost-oriented strategy fails to provide a company with an effective pricing policy. One problem with the cost-plus strategy is that determining a unit's cost before its price is difficult in many industries because unit costs may vary depending on volume. As a result, many business analysts have criticized this method, arguing that it is no longer appropriate for modern market conditions. Cost-based pricing generally leads to high prices in weak markets and low prices in strong markets, thereby impeding profitability because these prices are the exact opposites of what strategic prices would be if market conditions were taken into consideration.

While managers must consider costs when developing a pricing policy and strategy, costs alone should not determine prices. Many managers of industrial goods and service companies sell their products and services at incremental cost, and make their substantial profits from their best customers and from short-notice deliveries. When considering costs, managers should ask what costs they can afford to pay, taking into account the prices the market allows, and still allow for a profit on the sale.

In addition, managers must consider production costs in order to determine what goods to produce and in what amounts. Nevertheless, pricing generally involves determining what prices customers can afford before determining what amount of products to produce. By bearing in mind the prices they can charge and the costs they can afford to pay, managers can determine whether their costs enable them to compete in the low-cost market, where customers are concerned primarily with price, or whether they must compete in the premium-price market, in which customers are primarily concerned with quality and features.

VALUE-BASED PRICING

Value pricers adhere to the thinking that the optimal selling price is a reflection of a product or service's perceived value by customers, not just the company's costs to produce or provide a product or service. The value of a product or service is derived from customer needs, preferences, expectations, and financial resources as well as from competitors' offerings.

Consequently, this approach calls for managers to query customers and research the market to determine how much they value a product or service. In addition, managers must compare their products or services with those of their competitors to identify their value advantages and disadvantages.

Yet, value-based pricing is not just creating customer satisfaction or making sales because customer satisfaction may be achieved through discounting alone, a pricing strategy that could also lead to greater sales. However, discounting may not necessarily lead to profitability. Value pricing involves setting prices to increase profitability by tapping into more of a product or service's value attributes. This approach to pricing also depends heavily on strong advertising, especially for new products or services, in order to communicate the value of products or services to customers and to motivate customers to pay more if necessary for the value provided by these products or services.

DEMAND-BASED PRICING

Managers adopting demand-based pricing policies are, like value pricers, not fully concerned with costs. Instead, they concentrate on the behaviour and characteristics of customers and the quality and characteristics of their products or services. Demand-oriented pricing focuses on the level of demand for a product or service, not on the cost of materials, labour, and so forth.

This pricing policy, managers try to determine the amount of products or services they can sell at different prices. Managers need demand schedules in order to determine prices based on demand. Using demand schedules, managers can figure out which production and sales levels would be the most profitable.

To determine the most profitable production and sales levels, managers examine production and marketing costs estimates at different sales levels. The prices are determined by considering the cost estimates at different sales levels and expected revenues from sales volumes associated with projected prices.

The success of this strategy depends on the reliability of demand estimates. Hence, the crucial obstacle managers face with this approach is accurately gauging demand, which requires extensive knowledge of the manifold market factors that may have an impact on the number of products sold. Two common options managers have for obtaining accurate estimates are enlisting the help from either sales representatives or market experts.

Managers frequently ask sales representatives to estimate increases or decreases in demand stemming from specific increases or decreases in a product or service's price, since sales representatives generally are attuned to market trends and customer demands. Alternatively, managers can seek the assistance of experts such as market researchers or consultants to provide estimates of sales levels at various unit prices.

COMPETITION-BASED PRICING

With a competition-based pricing policy, a company sets its prices by determining what other companies competing in the market charge. A company begins developing competition-based prices by identifying its present competitors.

Next, a company assesses its own product or service. After this step, a company sets it prices higher than, lower than, or on par with the competitors based on the advantages and disadvantages of a company's product or service as well as on the expected response by competitors to the set price. This last consideration-the response of competitors-is an important part of competition-based pricing, especially in markets with only a few competitors. In such a market, if one competitor lowers its price, the others will most likely lower theirs as well.

This pricing policy allows companies to set prices quickly with relatively little effort, since it does not require as accurate market data as the demand pricing. Competitive pricing also makes distributors more receptive to a company's products because they are priced within the range the distributor already handles. Furthermore, this pricing policy enables companies to select from a variety of different pricing strategies to achieve their strategic goals. In other words, companies can choose to mark their prices above, below, or on par with their competitors' prices and thereby influence customer perceptions of their products.

For example, if a Company A sets its prices above those of its competitors, the higher price could suggest that Company A's products or services are superior in quality. Harley Davidson used this with great success. Although Harley-Davidson uses many of the same parts suppliers as Honda, Kawasaki, Yamaha, and Honda, they price well above the competitive price of these competitors. Harley's high prices combined with its customer loyalty and mystique help overcome buyer resistance to higher prices. Production efficiencies over the last two decades, however, have made quality among motorcycle producers about equal, but pricing above the market signals quality to buyers, whether or not they get the quality premium they pay for.

STRATEGIES FOR NEW AND ESTABLISHED PRODUCTS

Product pricing strategies frequently depend on the stage a product or service is in its life cycle; that is, new products often require different pricing strategies than established products or mature products.

New Product Pricing Strategy

Entrants often rely on pricing strategies that allow them to capture market share quickly. When there are several competitors in a market, entrants usually use lower pricing to change consumer spending habits and acquire market share. To appeal to customers effectively, entrants generally implement a simple or transparent pricing structure, which enables customers to compare prices easily and understand that the entrants have lower prices than established incumbent companies.

Complex pricing arrangements, however, prevent lower pricing from being a successful strategy in that customers cannot readily compare prices with hidden and contingent costs.

The long-distance telephone marketemphasizes this point; large corporations have lengthy telephone bills that include numerous contingent costs, which depend on location, use, and service features. Consequently, competitors in the corporate long-distance telephone service market do not use lower pricing as the primary pricing strategy, as they do in the consumer and small-business markets, where telephone billing is much simpler.

Another example is the computer industry. Dell, Fujitsu, HP, and many others personal computer makers offer bundles of products that make it more difficult for consumers to sort out the true differences among these competitors. For example, consumers purchasing an HP computer from the retailer, Best

Buy, will have not only the computer itself, but also six months of "free" Internet access bundled into the price. Comparing the absolute value of each personal computer become more difficult as an increasing number of other products such as Quicken, Adobe's Photoshop Elements, and other software are sold together with the purchase.

For Macintosh users or for those who might consider switching from a personal computer to a Macintosh, Apple announced in 2005 that it would begin selling the Mac Mini, a Macintosh that, as with PC makers, bundles its iLife software into the mix.

By extending its brand to non-premium price tiers, Apple will compete head-to-head with established firms. And although the Mac Mini is at a low price point, starting at $499, it will be difficult for consumers to directly compare the bundled products of PCs directly with the bundled products of Apple's Mac Mini. The complexity of these comparisons is what can make such new product pricing successful.

Established Product Pricing Strategy

Sometimes established companies need not adjust their prices at all in response to entrants and their lower prices, because customers frequently are willing to pay more for the products or services of an established company to avoid perceived risks associated with switching products or services.

However, when established companies do not have this advantage, they must implement other pricing strategies to preserve their market share and profits. When entrants are involved, established companies sometimes attempt to hide their actual prices by embedding them in complex prices. This tactic makes it difficult for customers to compare prices, which is advantageous to established companies competing with entrants that have lower prices.

In addition, established companies also may use a more complex pricing plan, such as a two-part pricing tactic. This tactic especially benefits companies with significant market power. Local telephone companies, for example, use this strategy, charging both fixed and per-minute charges.

MARKET SEGMENTATION

Because all customers do not have the same needs, expectations, and financial resources, managers can improve their pricing strategies by segmenting markets. Successful segmentation comes about when managers determine what motivates particular markets and what differences exist in the market when taken as a whole. For example, some customers may be motivated largely by price, while others are motivated by functionality and utility.

The idea behind segmentation is to divide a large group into a set of smaller groups that share significant characteristics such as age, income, geographic location, lifestyle, and so on. By dividing a market into two or more segments, a company can devise a pricing plan that will appeal to the motivations of each of the different market segments or it can decide to target only particular segments of the market that best correspond to its products or services and their prices.

Managers can use market segmentation strategically to price products or services in order to attain company objectives. Companies can set prices differently for different segments based on factors such as location, time of sale, quantity of sale, product design, and a number of others, depending on the way companies divide up the market. By doing so, companies can increase their profits, market share, cash flow, and so forth.

HUMAN RESOURCE ACCOUNTING

The past few decades have witnessed a global transition from manufacturing to service based economies. The fundamental difference between the two lies in the very nature of their assets. In the former, the physical assets like plant, machinery, material etc. are of utmost importance. In contrast, in the latter, knowledge and attitudes of the employees assume greater significance. For instance, in the case of an IT firm, the value of its physical assets is negligible when compared with the value of the knowledge and skills of its personnel. Similarly, in hospitals, academic institutions, consulting firms etc., the total worth of the organisation depends mainly on the skills of its employees and the services they render. Hence, the success of these organizations is contingent on the quality of their Human Resource- its knowledge, skills, competence, motivation and understanding of the organisational culture. In knowledge –driven economies therefore, it is imperative that the humans be recognised as an integral part of the total worth of an organisation. However, in order to estimate and project the worth of the human capital, it is necessary that some method of quantifying the worth of the knowledge, motivation, skills, and contribution of the human element as well as that of the organisational processes, like recruitment, selection, training etc., which are used to build and support these human aspects, is developed. Human resource accounting denotes just this process of quantification/ measurement of the Human Resource.

WHAT IS HRA

The American Accounting Association's Committee on Human Resource Accounting has defined Human Resource Accounting as "the process of identifying and measuring data about human resources and communicating this information to interested parties". HRA, thus, not only involves measurement of all the costs/investments associated with the recruitment, placement, training and development of employees, but also the quantification of the economic value of the people in an organisation. Flamholtz too has offered a similar definition for HRA.

They define HRA as "the measurement and reporting of the cost and value of people in organizational resources". As far as the statutory requirements go, the Companies Act, 1956 does not demand furnishing of HRA related information in the financial statements of the companies. The Institute of Chartered Accountants of India too, has not been able to bring any definitive standard or measurement in the reporting of human resources costs. While qualitative pronouncements regarding the importance of Human Resources is often made by the chairmen, in the AGM, quantitative information about their contribution is rarely recorded or communicated. There are a few organizations, however, that do recognize the value of their human resources, and furnish the related information in their annual reports. In India, some of these companies are: Infosys, Bharat Heavy Electricals Ltd; the Steel Authority of India Ltd., the Minerals and Metals Trading Corporation of India Ltd., the Southern Petrochemicals Industries Corporation of India, the Associated Cement Companies Ltd, Madras Refineries Ltd., the Hindustan Zinc Ltd., Engineers India Ltd, the Oil and Natural Gas Commission, Oil India Ltd., the Cement Corporation of India Ltd. Etc.

WHY HRA

Likert, HRA serves the following purposes in an organisation:

- It furnishes cost/value information for making management decisions about acquiring, allocating, developing, and maintaining human resources in order to attain cost-effectiveness;
- It allows management personnel to monitor effectively the use of human resources;
- It provides a sound and effective basis of human asset control, that is, whether the asset is appreciated, depleted or conserved;
- It helps in the development of management principles by classifying the financial consequences of various practices

Basically, HRA is a management tool which is designed to assist senior management in understanding the long term cost and benefit implications of their HR decisions so that better business decisions can be taken.

If such accounting is not done, then the management runs the risk of taking decisions that may improve profits in the short run but may also have severe repercussions in future. For example, very often organisations hire young people from outside on very high salaries because of an immediate business requirement.

Later on, however, they find that the de-motivating impact of this move on the existing experienced staff has caused immense long term harm by reducing their productivity and by creating salary distortions across the organisational structure. HRA also provides the HR professionals and management with information for managing the human resources efficiently and effectively.

Such information is essential for performing the critical HR functions of acquiring, developing, allocating, conserving, utilizing, evaluating and rewarding in a proper way.

These functions are the key transformational processes that convert human resources from'raw' inputs to outputs in the form of goods and services. HRA indicates whether these processes are adding value or enhancing unnecessary costs.

In addition to facilitating internal decision making processes, HRA also enables critical external decision makers, especially the investors in making realistic investment decisions. Investors make investment decisions based on the total worth of the organisation. HRA provides the investors with a more complete and accurate account of the organisations' total worth, and therefore, enables better investment decisions.

For example, conventional financial statements treat HR investments as"expenditures. Consequently, their income statement projects expenditures to acquire, place and train human resources as expenses during the current year rather than capitalizing and amoritizing them over their expected service life.

The balance sheet, thus, becomes distorted as it inaccurately presents the"total Assets" as well as the"net income" and, thereby, the"rate of return" which is the ratio of net income to the total assets. HRA helps in removing this distortion.

Furthermore, in a business environment where corporate social responsibility is rapidly gaining ground, HRA reflects the extent to which organisation contributes to society's human capital by investing in its development. Finally, in an era where performance is closely linked to rewards and, therefore, the performance of all groups/departments/functions needs to be quantified to the extent possible, HRA helps in measuring the performance of the HR function as such.

HISTORICAL DEVELOPMENT OF HRA

The traces of a rudimentary HRA can be found in the Medieval European practice of calculating the cost of keeping a prisoner versus the expected future earnings from him. The prisoners in those days were seen to be the general property of the capturing side.

Consequently, after the victory a quick decision regarding whether to capture a prisoner or to kill him had to be taken based on the costs involved in keeping him and the benefits accruing from killing him. However, these represented very rough measurements with limited use. The development of HRA as a systematic and detailed academic activity, Eric G Falmholtz began in sixties. He divides the development into five stages.

These are:

- *First stage*: This marks the beginning of academic interest in the area of HRA. However, the focus was primarily on deriving HRA concepts from other studies like the economic theory of capital, psychological theories of leadership- effectiveness, the emerging concepts of human resource as different from personnel or human relations; as well as the measurement of corporate goodwill.
- *Second stage*: The focus here was more on developing and validating different models for HRA. These models covered both costs and the monetary and non-monetary value of HR. The aim was to develop some tools that would help the organisations in assessing and managing their human resource/asset in a more realistic manner. One of the earliest studies here was that of Roger Hermanson, who as part of his Ph.D. studied the problem of measuring the value of human assets as an element of goodwill. Inspired by his work, a number of research projects were undertaken by the researchers to develop the concepts and methods of accounting for human resource
- *Third Stage*: This period was marked by a widespread

interest in the field of HRA leading to a rapid growth of research in the area. The focus in most cases was on the issues of application of HRA in business organisations. R.G. Barry experiments contributed substantially during this stage.

- *Fourth Stage*: This was a period of decline in the area of HRA primarily because the complex issues that needed to be explored required much deeper empirical research than was needed for the earlier simple models. The organisations, however, were not prepared to sponsor such research. They found the idea of HRA interesting but did not find much use in pumping in large sums or investing lot of time and energy in supporting the research.
- *Stage Five:* There was a sudden renewal of interest in the field of HRA partly because most of the developed economies had shifted from manufacturing to service economies and realised the criticality of human asset for their organisations. Since the survival, growth and profits of the organisations were perceived to be dependent more on the intellectual assets of the companies than on the physical assets, the need was felt to have more accurate measures for HR costs, investments and value.

An important outcome of this renewed interest was that unlike the previous decades, when the interests were mainly academic with some practical applications, from mid 90s the focus has been on greater application of HRA to business management. Different types of models to suit the specific requirements of the organisations have been developed incorporating both the tangible and the intangible aspects. Also, larger number of organisations actually began to use HRA as part of their managerial and financial accounting practice.

Today, human and intellectual capital are perceived to be the strategic resources and therefore, clear estimation of their value has gained significant importance. The increased pressures for corporate governance and the corporate code of conduct demanding transparency in accounting have further supported the need for developing methods of measuring human value.

In India, human resource valuation has not yet been institutionalized though many public as well as private have adopted HRA.

INFORMATION MANAGEMENT IN HRA

Like any accounting exercise, the HRA too depends heavily on the availability of relevant and accurate information. HRA is essentially a tool to facilitate better planning and decision making based on the information regarding actual HR costs and organisational returns. The kind of data that needs to be managed systematically depends upon the purpose for which the HRA is being used by an organisation.

For example, if the purpose is to control the personnel costs, a system of standard costs for personnel recruitment, selection and training has to be developed.

It helps in analyzing projected and actual costs of manpower and thereby, in taking remedial action, wherever necessary.

Information on turnover costs generates awareness regarding the actual cost of turnover and highlights the need for efforts by the management towards retention of manpower. Accountability in the management process is often enhanced when information involving an evaluation of managerial effectiveness is generated Finally, information on the intangibles like intellectual capital/human capital becomes necessary to measure the true worth of the organisation. This information, though unaudited, needs to be communicated to the board and the stockholders.

MEASUREMENTS IN HRA

The biggest challenge in HRA is that of assigning monetary values to different dimensions of HR costs, investments and the worth of employees.

The two main approaches usually employed for this are:

1. The cost approach which involves methods based on the costs incurred by the company, with regard to an employee.
2. The economic value approach which includes methods based on the economic value of the human resources and their contribution to the company's gains. This approach looks at human resources as assets and tries to identify the stream of benefits flowing from the asset.

COST APPROACH

Cost is a sacrifice incurred to obtain some anticipated benefit or service. All costs have two portions, viz., the expense and the asset portions.

The expense portion is that which provides benefits during the current accounting period whereas the asset portion is that which is expected to give rise to benefits in the future. Arriving at a clear distinction between the two, however, remains an accounting problem even today.

Two types of costs are of special importance in HRA. These are original or historical cost, and replacement cost. The historical cost of human resources is the sacrifice that was made to acquire and develop the resource. These include the costs of recruiting, selection, hiring, placement, orientation, and on the job training.

While some of the costs like salaries, for instance, are direct costs, other costs like the time spent by the supervisors during induction and training, are indirect costs. Sometimes, opportunity cost method, that is, a calculation of what would have been the returns if the money spent on HR was spent on something else, is also used.

However, this method is seen to be not as objective as desired. Hence its use is restricted to internal reporting and not external reporting.

The replacement cost of human resources is the cost that would have to be incurred if present employees are to be replaced. For instance, if an employee were to leave today, several costs of recruiting, selection, hiring, placement, orientation, and on the job training would have to be incurred in order to replace him. Such costs have two dimensions-positional replacement costs or the costs incurred to replace the services rendered by an employee only to a particular position; and personal replacement cost or the cost incurred to replace all the services expected to be rendered by the employee at the various positions that he might have occupied during his work life in the organisation.

Though replacement cost method can be adapted for determining the cost of replacement of groups, this method is used essentially to determine the replacement cost of individuals. Other cost based methods that may be used are the standard cost method and the competitive bidding method. In the standard cost method, the standard costs associated with the recruitment, hiring, training and developing per grade of employees are determined annually. The total costs for all the personnel signify the worth of the human resources.

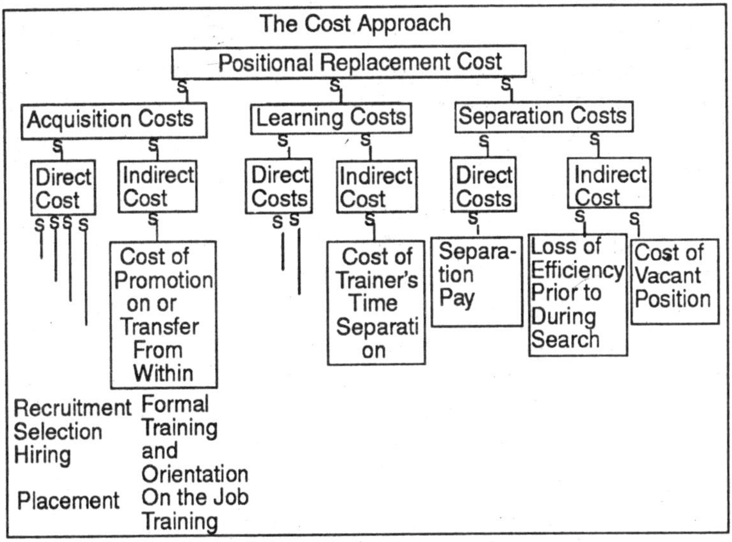

ECONOMIC VALUE APPROACH

The value of an object, in economic terms, is the present value of the services that it is expected to render in future.

Similarly, the economic value of human resources is the present worth of the services that they are likely to render in future. This may be the value of individuals, groups or the total human organisation. The methods for calculating the economic value of individuals may be classified into monetary and non-monetary methods.

Monetary Measures for Assessing Individual Value

Flamholtz's Model of Determinants of Individual Value to Formal Organisations

Flamholtz, the value of an individual is the present worth of the services that he is likely to render to the organisation in future. As an individual moves from one position to another, at the same level or at different levels, the profile of the services provided by him is likely to change. The present cumulative value of all the possible services that may be rendered by him during his/her association with the organisation, is the value of the individual.

Typically, this value is uncertain and has two dimensions. The first is the expected conditional value of the individual. This is the amount that the organisation could potentially realise from the services of an individual during his/her productive service life in the organization.

It is composed of three factors:

1. Productivity or performance;
2. Transferability;
3. Promotability.

These three factors depend, to a great extent, on individual determinants like activation level of the individual and organizational determinants like opportunity to use these skills or roles and the reward system.

The second dimension of an individual value is the expected realizable value, which is a function of the expected conditional value, and the probability that the individual will remain in the organisation for the duration of his/her productive service life. Since individuals are not owned by the organisation and are free to leave, ascertaining the probability of their turnover becomes important. The interaction between the individual and organizational determinants leads to job satisfaction.

The higher is the level of job satisfaction, the lower is the probability of employee turnover. Therefore, higher is the expected realizable value.

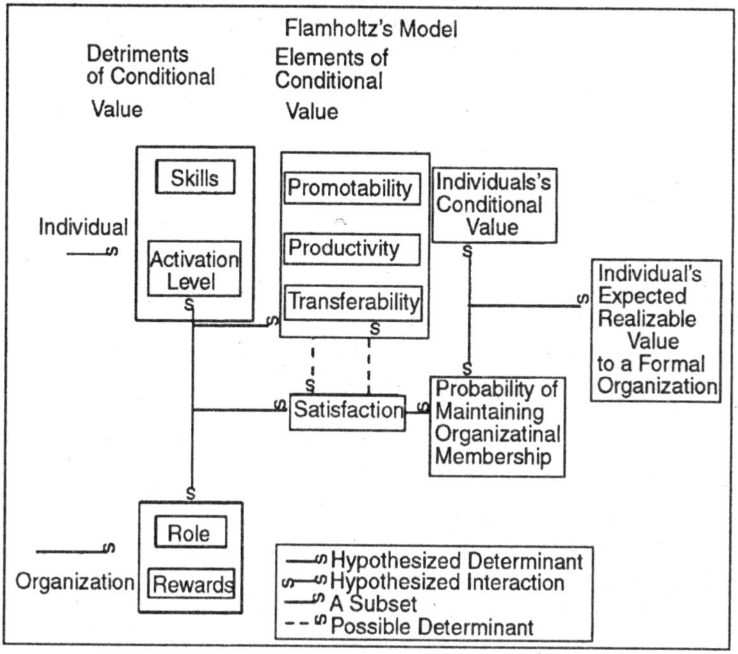

Flamholtz's Stochastic Rewards Valuation Model

The movement or progress of people through organizational 'states' or roles is called a stochastic process. The Stochastic Rewards Model is a direct way of measuring a person's expected conditional value and expected realizable value.

It is based on the assumption that an individual generates value as he occupies and moves along organizational roles, and renders service to the organisation. It presupposes that a person will move from one state in the organisation, to another, during a specified period of time. In this model, exit is also considered to be a state.

Use of this model necessitates the following information:

- The set of mutually exclusive states that an individual may occupy in the system during his/her career;
- The value of each state, to the organisation;
- Estimates of a person's expected tenure in the organisation
- The probability that in future, the person will occupy each state for the specified time.
- The discount rate to be applied to the future cash flows.

A person's expected conditional value and expected realizable value will be equal, if the person is certain to remain in the organisation, in the predetermined set of states, throughout his expected service life. The main drawback of this model, however, is the extent of information required to make the necessary estimates of the values of the service states, the expected tenure, and the probability that the individual will occupy the state for the specified period of time. However, if this information can be made available, this model emerges as one of the most sophisticated models for determining the value of individuals.

The Lev and Schwartz Model

The Lev and Schwartz model is the basic model employed by Indian organisations. The value of human capital embodied in a person who is 'y' years old, is the present value of his/her future earnings from employment and can be calculated by using the following formula

$$E(Vy) = \sum_{T=Y} Py(t+1) \sum_{T} I(T)/(I+R)^{t-y}$$

where

E (Vy) = expected value of a 'y' year old person's human capital

T = the person's retirement age

Py (t) = probability of the person leaving the organisation

I(t) = expected earnings of the person in period I

r = discount rate

The basic theme of Lev, Schwartz model is to compute the present value of the future direct and indirect payments to their employees as a measure of their human resource value. While doing so, the common assumptions set by the Indian companies are the pattern of employee compensation, normal career growth, and weightage for efficiency.

Moreover, companies adapt this model to their practical requirements by making necessary alterations. For instance, different organisations use different discount rates for ascertaining the present value of future cash flows.

This method of accounting is basically oriented towards measuring changes in the employees' value rather than employers' gains from the employees.

Unless the employees' payments are directly linked to employee productivity or the company performance, the changes in the value of employees will not reflect the changes in the employees' contribution.

As pointed out by Prabhakara Rao under the Lev, Schwartz model, the value of human resources will be more or less increasing, even if the organisations continuously incur losses/decrease in profitability.

The attitude and morale of the employees, the contribution of the employees to the organisation, and such other factors are out of the purview of the Lev, Schwartz model.

Table. Lev and Schwartz Model

	Sail		Bhel		MMTC	
Year	**Number**	**Value**	**Number**	**Value**	**Number**	**Value**
1984-85	74464	1216	206414	9581	3638	95
1985-86	75915	1358	206198	9589	3760	121
1986-87	74918	1588	203292	10828	3830	140
1987-88	74813	1827	197296	12013	3862	158
1988-89	75116	2183	194872	12725	3825	174
1989-90	74436	2673	193223	15790	3825	196

Table. NTPC's Human Resource Value, (Discount factor of 0.12)

Category employees	No. of (Rs. lakhs)	Per capita (Rs Crores)	Total value
Executives	6841	17.76	1215
Supervisors	3010	15.11	455
Workmen	12445	13.71	1705
Total	22296	15.14	3375

Hekimian and Jones Competitive Bidding Model

In this method, an internal market for labour is developed and the value of the employees is determined by the managers. Managers bid against each other for human resources already available within the organisation. The highest bidder 'wins' the resource.

There is no criteria on which the bids are based. Rather, the managers rely only on their judgement.

NON-MONETARY METHODS FOR DETERMINING VALUE

The non-monetary methods for assessing the economic value of human resources also measure the Human Resource but not in dollar or money terms. Rather they rely on various indices or ratings and rankings. These methods may be used as surrogates of monetary methods and also have a predictive value.

The non-monetary methods may refer to a simple inventory of skills and capabilities of people within an organization or to the application of some behavioural measurement technique to assess the benefits gained from the Human resource of an organisation.

- The skills or capability inventory is a simple listing of the education, knowledge, experience and skills of the firm's human resources.
- Performance evaluation measures used in HRA include ratings, and rankings. Ratings reflect a

person's performance in relation to a set of scales. They are scores assigned to characteristics possessed by the individual. These characteristics include skills, judgment, knowledge, interpersonal skills, intelligence etc. Ranking is an ordinal form of rating in which the superiors rank their subordinates on one or more dimensions.

- Assessment of potential determines a person's capacity for promotion and development. It usually employs a trait approach in which the traits essential for a position are identified. The extent to which the person possesses these traits is then assessed.
- Attitude measurements are used to assess employees' attitudes towards their job, pay, working conditions, etc., in order to determine their job satisfaction and dissatisfaction.

MEASUREMENTS OF GROUP VALUE

The Likert and Bowers Model

Causal, intervening and end-result variables. Likert and Bowers propose causal, intervening, and end-result variables, which determine the group's value to an organization. Causal variables are those which can be controlled by the organization.

These variables include managerial behaviour and organisational structure. Intervening variables reflect organizational capabilities and involve group processes, peer leadership, organization climate, and the subordinates' satisfaction. Both, the causal and the intervening variables determine the end result variables of the organization. Figureemphasizes the elements used to measure human organisational causal and intervening variables.

The end-result, dependent variables reflect the achievements of the organization or the total productive efficiency in terms of sales, costs, earnings, market performance, etc. They are dependent on the causal and the intervening variables.

Table. Elements used to Measure Human Resource Organisational Causal and Intervening Variables

	Managerial and Peer Leadership
Support :	Friendly; pays attention to what you are saying;
Team Building:	Listens to subordinates' problems; encourages subordinates to work as a team' encourages exchange of opinions and ideas
Goal Emphasis:	Encourages best efforts; maintains high standards.
Help with work:	Shows ways to do a better job; helps subordinates plan,organize and schedule; offers new ideas, and solutions
	Organisational Climate
Communication	Communication flow is amicable
Decision making practices	Subordinates know what is going on; superiors are receptive.
Concern for persons	Subordinates are involved in setting goals; decisions are made at levels of accurate information; persons affected by decisions are asked for their ideas; know-how of people of all levels is used.
Influence on department	The organization is interested in individual's welfare; tries to improve working conditions; organizes work activities sensibly.
Technological adequacy	From lower level supervisors, employees who have no subordinates.
Motivation	Improved methods are quickly adopted; equipment and resources are well managed. Differences and disagreements are accepted and worked through; people in organization work hard for money, promotions, job satisfaction and to meet high money, promotion, job satisfaction and to meet high expectations from others and are encouraged to do so by policies, working conditions, and people.

Group process
l Planning together, coordinating efforts. l Making good decision's solving problems l Knowing jobs and how to do them well l Sharing information l Wanting to meet objectives l Having confidence and trust in other members l Ability to meet unusual work demands.
Satisfaction
With fellow workers; superiors; jobs; this organization compared with others; pay; progress in the organization upto now; chances for getting ahead in the future.

Brummet, Flamholtz, and Pyle's Economic Value Model

The Brummet, Flamholtz, and Pyle model follows the principle that a resource's value is equal to the present worth of the future services it can be expected to provide, and therefore it can provide a basis of measuring the value of a group of people. Groups of human resources should be valued by estimating their contribution to the total economic value of the firm. Thus a firm's forecasted future earnings are discounted to determine the firm's present value, and a portion of these earnings is allocated to human resources just as to their contribution.

Hermanson's Unpurchased Goodwill Model

Hermanson, the unpurchased goodwill notion is based on the premise that 'the best available evidence of the present existence of un-owned resources is the fact that a given firm earned a higher than normal rate of income for the most recent year. Here Hermanson is proposing that supernormal earning are an indication of resources not shown on the balance sheet, such as human assets. Even though his method of valuing human resources is explicitly intended for use in a company's published financial statements rather than for internal consumption, this would necessarily involve forecasting future earnings and allocating any excess above normal expected earnings to human resources of the organization.

However, the assumptions would be subject to the uncertainties involved in any forecast of future events. This method suffers from several limitations: Firstly, since the methods limits recognition of human resources to the amount of earnings in excess of normal, the human resource base that is required to carry out normal operations is totally ignored. As a result, the value of human assets will be an underestimation. Secondly, the method only uses the actual earnings of the most recent year as the basis for calculating human assets, thereby, ignoring the forecasts of future earnings that are equally relevant for managerial decision making.

Human Organizational Dimensions Method

Based on the Likert-Bowers model of group's value to an organization, discussed earlier, this method is based on the relationship among causal, intervening and end-result variables. The causal variables influence the intervening variables, which, in turn, determine the organization's end result variables. Hence changes in the key dimensions of organisation can be used as dependable indicators for forecasting future changes in productivity and financial performance. Monetary estimations of changes in human value of organisations.

For computing a monetary estimate of the expected change in the value of human organization, the following steps are suggested:

- Measure the key dimensions of human organization, using a Likert scale at specified time periods. These are in non-monetary measurements.
- The scaled responses to questionnaire items called'scores' are then standardized by statistical methods to take into account the degree of variability of the set of responses. This is done for responses in each time period.
- The difference between two standardized scores from one period to the next is then calculated. This

difference represents the change in an index of specified dimensions of the human organization.

- From present changes in dimensions of the human organization, the expected future change in end result variables is estimated. Specifically, for a given variable the delta is multiplied by coefficient or correlation between that variable and the end result variable. This provides an estimate in standard scores of the anticipated change in the end result variable attributable to a change in the human organisational dimension believed to cause that change.
- Lastly, the standard scores are converted into the measuring monetary units for the end result variables.

Likert points out that changes in the productive capability of a firm's human organization cannot be assessed correctly unless periodic measurements of causal and intervening dimensions of that organization are taken regularly. Current profit and loss reports often encourage us to believe that changes are occurring. When profits increase, it is often assumed that the human organization has become more productive, but steps taken to maintain earnings or prevent losses may actually result in a decrease in the productive capability of the human organization. There is some controversy about the validity and reliability of this method. Flamholtz, future research on this method is necessary because its validity and feasibility have not yet been established. Likert, however, maintains that the method is feasible where reliable and valid measurements of the coefficients are available.

Methods for Valuation of Expense Centre Groups

Flamholtz proposes three methods for valuation of expense centre groups. In all these measures, the surrogate value is used for estimation.

The three methods are:

1. Capitalization of Compensation
2. Replacement Cost Valuation, and
3. Original Cost Valuation

Capitalization

The capitalisation method involves capitalizing a person's salary and using it as a surrogate measure of human value. This value may be ascertained for groups as well as individuals.

The value of the group is essentially the aggregate value of the individuals compromising the group. Capitalization of compensation method is not considered an ideal method of group valuation because it ignores the possible effects of synergy. However, this method may be used to arrive at an approximation of a group's value to the firm.

Replacement Cost Valuation

The replacement cost of a group is defined as the sacrifice that would have to be incurred today to recruit, select, hire, train and develop a substitute group capable of providing a set of services equivalent to that of a group presently employed. This method involves considerable subjective estimates, which reduce its validity and replicability.

Original Cost Valuation

The original cost valuation method involves estimation of the original cost of recruiting, selecting, hiring, training, and developing a firm's existing human organization. The need for using original costs to value groups arises out of the necessity of estimating the cost of developing an effectively functioning team.

Teamwork is essential for effective communication, decision-making, coordination and several other critical organisational processes. Yet, when the original costs are used to make an estimation of the value of the expense centre, the costs of generating this teamwork are largely ignored.

SOCIAL ACCOUNTING

Social accounting is a type of accounting that a business performs to place a value on the influence its operations have on society. It requires that enterprises look closely at all that it does and what kind of impact its activities have on people, places, and the environment. Social accounting doesn't deal with the type of assets that financial accounting does; rather, it focuses on business behaviours and what kind of impact that behaviour has. Any business can undergo this type of evaluation, regardless of its size.

This process was an accounting phenomenon of the latter portion of the 20th century. Its growth as an accounting discipline stems from the pressures the environmental movement placed on large corporations. Also, it stems from the demand from governments and the public that businesses be more transparent concerning activities and the implications of those activities.

The performance of social accounting attempts to put a figure on the costs and benefits of an enterprise's operations in relation to society and the environment. An enterprise may measure the impact of its smokestack emissions on a surrounding region.

A business may measure the impact of its community involvement and charitable contributions in the city or town in which it operates. It could measure the effectiveness of its hiring programme and whether the programme influences a region's unemployment rate.

Social accounting, unlike financial accounting, looks to understand the contributions, or lack thereof, that businesses make to society. It concerns itself with business behaviour that contributes to the well-being of people and the planet. Consequently, social accounting often goes by the name social and environmental accounting, corporate social reporting, or corporate social responsibility reporting.

Because of its focus away from the financial reporting aspects of a business, social accounting also goes by the names non-financial reporting and sustainability accounting. The term sustainability applies to the entire operations of a business. A business can analyse whether it is sustainable as an entity from a social, environmental, cultural, and financial perspective. A business can also analyse its ability to embark on and then sustain its commitment to conducting its activities in a way that benefits society.

Social accounting is a process that any kind of entity can perform, not just businesses that are focused on growth and profitability. This includes governmental agencies, not-for-profit businesses, and charitable organizations. In essence, social accounting deals with accountability - it demands that organizations put in place practices that contribute to the planet's sustainability and to the overall well being of humanity.

PURPOSE

Social accounting challenges conventional accounting, in particular financial accounting, for giving a narrow image of the interaction between society and organizations, and thus artificially constraining the subject of accounting.

Social accounting, a largely normative concept, seeks to broaden the scope of accounting in the sense that it should:

- Concern itself with more than only economic events;
- Not be exclusively expressed in financial terms;
- Be accountable to a broader group of stakeholders;
- Broaden its purpose beyond reporting financial success.

It points to the fact that companies influence their external environment through their actions and should therefore account for these effects as part of their standard accounting practices. Social accounting is in this sense closely related to the economic concept of externality.

Social accounting offers an alternative account of significant economic entities. It has the "potential to expose the tension between pursuing economic profit and the pursuit of social and environmental objectives". The purpose of social accounting can be approached from two different angles, namely for management control purposes or accountability purposes.

Accountability

Social accounting for accountability purposes is designed to support and facilitate the pursuit of society's objectives. These objectives can be manifold but can typically be described in terms of social and environmental desirability and sustainability. In order to make informed choices on these objectives, the flow of information in society in general, and in accounting in particular, needs to cater for democratic decision-making. In democratic systems, Gray argues, there must then be flows of information in which those controlling the resources provide accounts to society of their use of those resources: a system of corporate accountability.

Society is seen to profit from implementing a social and environmental approach to accounting in a number of ways, e.g.:

- Honouring stakeholders' rights of information;
- Balancing corporate power with corporate responsibility;
- Increasing transparency of corporate activity;
- Identifying social and environmental costs of economic success.

Management Control

Social accounting for the purpose of management control is designed to support and facilitate the achievement of an organization's own objectives. Because social accounting is concerned with substantial self-reporting on a systemic level, individual reports are often referred to as social audits.

Organizations are seen to benefit from implementing social accounting practices in a number of ways, e.g.:

- Increased information for decision-making;
- More accurate product or service costing;
- Enhanced image management and Public Relations;
- Identification of social responsibilities;
- Identification of market development opportunities;
- Maintaining legitimacy.

BITC the "process of reporting on responsible businesses performance to stakeholders" helps integrate such practices into business practices, as well as identifying future risks and opportunities.

The management control view thus focuses on the individual organization.Critics of this approach point out that the benign nature of companies is assumed. Here, responsibility, and accountability, is largely left in the hands of the organization concerned.

SCOPE

Formal Accountability

In social accounting the focus tends to be on larger organisations such as multinational corporations and their visible, external accounts rather than informally produced accounts or accounts for internal use. The need for formality in making MNCs accountability is given by the spatial, financial and cultural distance of these organisations to those who are affecting and affected by it.

Social accounting also questions the reduction of all meaningful information to financial form. Financial data is seen as only one element of the accounting language.

Self-reporting and Third Party Audits

In most countries, existing legislation only regulates a fraction of accounting for socially relevant corporate activity. In consequence, most available social, environmental and sustainability reports are produced voluntarily by organisations and in that sense often resemble financial statements. While companies' efforts in this regard are usually commended, there seems to be a tension between voluntary reporting and accountability, for companies are likely to produce reports favouring their interests.

The rearrangement of social and environmental data companies already produce as part of their normal reporting practice into an independent social audit is called a silent or shadow account.

An alternative phenomenon is the creation of external social audits by groups or individuals independent of the accountable organisation and typically without its encouragement. External social audits thus also attempt to blur the boundaries between organisations and society and to establish social accounting as a fluid two-way communication process. Companies are sought to be held accountable regardless of their approval. It is in this sense that external audits part with attempts to establish social accounting as an intrinsic feature of organisational behaviour. The reports of Social Audit Ltd in the 1970s on e.g. Tube Investments, Avon Rubber and Coalite and Chemical, laid the foundations for much of the later work on social audits.

Reporting Areas

Unlike in financial accounting, the matter of interest is by definition less clear-cut in social accounting; this is due to an aspired all-encompassing approach to corporate activity. It is generally agreed that social accounting will cover an organisations relationship with the natural environment, its employees, and ethical issues concentrating upon consumers and products, as well as local and international communities. Other issues include corporate action on questions of ethnicity and gender.

Audience

Social accounting supersedes the traditional audit audience, which is mainly composed of a company's shareholders and the financial community, by providing information to all of the organisation's stakeholders. A stakeholder of an organisation is anyone who can influence or is influenced by the organisation. This often includes, but is not limited to, suppliers of inputs, employees and trade unions, consumers, members of local communities, society at large and governments. Different stakeholders have different rights of information. These rights can be stipulated by law, but also by non-legal codes, corporate values, mission statements and moral rights. The rights of information are thus determined by "society, the organisation and its stakeholders".

ENVIRONMENTAL ACCOUNTING

Environmental accounting, is a subset of social accounting, focuses on the cost structure and environmental performance of a company. It principally describes the preparation, presentation, and communication of information related to an organisation's interaction with the natural environment. Although environmental accounting is most commonly undertaken as voluntary self-reporting by companies, third-party reports by government agencies, NGOs and other bodies posit to pressure for environmental accountability.

Accounting for impacts on the environment may occur within a company's financial statements, relating to liabilities, commitments and contingencies for the remediation of contaminated lands or other financial concerns arising from pollution. Such reporting essentially expresses financial issues arising from environmental legislation. More typically, environmental accounting describes the reporting of quantitative and detailed environmental data within the non-financial parts of the annual report or in separate environmental reports. Such reports may account for pollution emissions, resources used, or wildlife habitat damaged or re-established.

In their reports, large companies commonly place primary emphasis on eco-efficiency, referring to the reduction of resource and energy use and waste production per unit of product or service. A complete picture which accounts for all inputs, outputs and wastes of the organisation, must not necessarily emerge. Whilst companies can often demonstrate great success in eco-efficiency, their ecological footprint, that is an estimate of total environmental impact, may move independently following changes in output.

Legislation for compulsory environmental reporting exists in some form e.g. in Denmark, Netherlands, Australia and Korea. The United Nations has been highly involved in the adoption of environmental accounting practices, most notably in the United Nations Division for Sustainable Development publication Environmental Management Accounting Procedures and Principles.

APPLICATIONS

Social accounting is a widespread practice in a number of large organisations in the United Kingdom. Royal Dutch

Shell, BP, British Telecom, The Co-operative Bank, The Body Shop, and United Utilities all publish independently audited social and sustainability accounts. In many instances the reports are produced in compliance with the sustainability reporting guidelines set by the Global Reporting Initiative.

Traidcraft plc, the fair trade organisation, claims to be the first public limited company to publish audited social accounts in the UK, starting in 1993. The website of the Centre for Social and Environmental Accounting Research contains a collection of exemplary reporting practices and social audits.

Format

Companies and other organisations may publish annual corporate responsibility reports, in print or online. The reporting format can also include summary or overview documents for certain stakeholders, a corporate responsibility or sustainability part on its corporate website, or integrate social accounting into its annual report and accounts.

Companies may seek to adopt a social accounting format that is audience specific and appropriate. For example, HandM, asks stakeholders how they would like to receive reports on its website; Vodafone publishes separate reports for 11 of its operating companies as well as publishing an internal report in 2005; Weyerhaeuser produced a tabloid-size, four-page mini-report in addition to its full sustainability report.

6

Cost Accounting

INTRODUCTION

Cost accounting is an approach to evaluating the overall costs that are associated with conducting business. Generally based on standard accounting practices, cost accounting is one of the tools that managers utilize to determine what type and how much expenses is involved with maintaining the current business model. At the same time, the principles of cost accounting can also be utilized to project changes to these costs in the event that specific changes are implemented.

When it comes to measuring how wisely company resources are being utilized, cost accounting helps to provide the data relevant to the current situation. By identifying production costs and further defining the cost of production by three or more successive business cycles, it is possible to note any trends that indicate a rise in production costs without any appreciable changes or increase in production of goods and services. By using this approach, it is possible to identify the reason for the change, and take steps to contain the situation before bottom line profits are impacted to a greater degree.

Product development and marketing strategies are also informed by the utilization of cost accounting. In terms of product development, it is possible to determine if a new product can be produced at a reasonable price, considering the cost of raw materials and the labour and equipment necessary to product a finished product. At the same time, marketing protocols can make use of cost accounting to project if the product will sell enough units to make production a viable option.

Cost accounting is helpful in making a number of business decisions. By weighing the actual costs versus the anticipated benefit, cost accounting can help a company to avoid launching a product with no real market, prevent the purchase of unnecessary goods and services, or alter the current operational model in a manner that will decrease efficiency. Whether utilized to evaluate the status of a department within the company or as a tool to project the feasibility of opening new locations or closing older ones, cost accounting can provide important data that may impact the final decision.

ORIGINS

Cost accounting has long been used to help managers understand the costs of running a business. Modern cost accounting originated during the industrial revolution, when the complexities of running a large scale business led to the development of systems for recording and tracking costs to help business owners and managers make decisions.

In the early industrial age, most of the costs incurred by a business were what modern accountants call "variable costs" because they varied directly with the amount of production. Money was spent on labour, raw materials, power to run a factory, etc. in direct proportion to production. Managers could simply total the variable costs for a product and use this as a rough guide for decision-making processes.

Some costs tend to remain the same even during busy periods, unlike variable costs, which rise and fall with volume of work. Over time, the importance of these "fixed costs" has become more important to managers. Examples of fixed costs include the depreciation of plant and equipment, and the cost of departments such as maintenance, tooling, production control, purchasing, quality control, storage and handling, plant supervision and engineering. In the early twentieth century, these costs were of little importance to most businesses. However, in the twenty-first century, these costs are often more important than the variable cost of a product, and allocating them to a broad range of products can lead to bad decision making. Managers must understand fixed costs in order to make decisions about products and pricing.

For example: A company produced railway coaches and had only one product. To make each coach, the company needed to purchase $60 of raw materials and components, and pay 6 laborers $40 each. Therefore, total variable cost for each coach was $300. Knowing that making a coach required spending $300, managers knew they couldn't sell below that price without losing money on each coach. Any price above $300 became a contribution to the fixed costs of the company. If the fixed costs were, $1000 per month for rent, insurance and owner's salary, the company could therefore sell 5 coaches per month for a total of $3000 or 10 coaches for a total of $4500 and make a profit of $500 in both cases.

ELEMENTS OF COST

- Material
  - Direct material
  - Indirect material
- Labour
  - Direct labour
  - Indirect labour
- Overhead
  - Indirect material
  - Indirect labour

They are grouped further based on their functions as:

- Production or works overheads
- Administration overheads
- Selling overheads
- Distribution overheads

Standard Cost Accounting

In modern cost accounting, the concept of recording historical costs was taken further, by allocating the company's fixed costs over a given period of time to the items produced during that period, and recording the result as the total cost of production. This allowed the full cost of products that were not sold in the period they were produced to be recorded in inventory using a variety of complex accounting methods, which was consistent with the principles of GAAP. It also essentially enabled managers to ignore the fixed costs, and look at the results of each period in relation to the"standard cost" for any given product.

For example: if the railway coach company normally produced 40 coaches per month, and the fixed costs were still $1000/month, then each coach could be said to incur an overhead of $25. Adding this to the variable costs of $300 per coach produced a full cost of $325 per coach.

This method tended to slightly distort the resulting unit cost, but in mass-production industries that made one product line, and where the fixed costs were relatively low, the distortion was very minor. For example: if the railway coach company made 100 coaches one month, then the unit cost would become $310 per coach ($300 + ($1000/100)). If the next month the company made 50 coaches, then the unit cost = $320 per coach ($300 + ($1000/50)), a relatively minor difference.

An important part of standard cost accounting is a variance analysis, which breaks down the variation between actual cost and standard costs into various components (volume variation, material cost variation, labour cost variation, etc.) so managers can understand why costs were different from what was planned and take appropriate action to correct the situation.

Development of Throughput Accounting

As business became more complex and began producing a greater variety of products, the use of cost accounting to make decisions to maximize profitability came under question. Management circles became increasingly aware of the Theory of Constraints in the 1980s, and began to understand that"every production process has a limiting factor" somewhere in the chain of production. As business management learned to identify the constraints, they increasingly adopted throughput accounting to manage them and"maximize the throughput dollars" (or other currency) from each unit of constrained resource.

For example: The railway coach company was offered a contract to make 15 open-topped streetcars each month, using a design that included ornate brass foundry work, but very little of the metalwork needed to produce a covered rail coach. The buyer offered to pay $280 per streetcar. The company had a firm order for 40 rail coaches each month for $350 per unit.

The company accountant determined that the cost of operating the foundry vs. the metalwork shop each month was as follows:

Overhead Cost by Department	Total Cost	Hours Available per month	Cost per hour
Foundry	$ 7,300.00	160	$45.63
Metal shop	$ 3,300.00	160	$20.63
Total	$10,600.00	320	$33.13

The company was at full capacity making 40 rail coaches each month. And since the foundry was expensive to operate, and purchasing brass as a raw material for the streetcars was expensive, the accountant determined that the company would lose money on any streetcars it built. He showed an analysis of the estimated product costs based on standard cost accounting and recommended that the company decline to build any streetcars.

Standard Cost Accounting Analysis	Streetcars	Rail coach
Monthly Demand	15	40
Price	$280	$350
Foundry Time (hrs)	3.0	2.0
Metalwork Time (hrs)	1.5	4.0
Total Time	4.5	6.0
Foundry Cost	$136.88	$ 91.25
Metalwork Cost	$ 30.94	$ 82.50
Raw Material Cost	$120.00	$ 60.00
Total Cost	$287.81	$233.75
Profit per Unit	$ (7.81)	$116.25

However, the company's operations manager knew that recent investment in automated foundry equipment had created idle time for workers in that department. The constraint on production of the railcoaches was the metalwork shop.

She made an analysis of profit and loss if the company took the contract using throughput accounting to determine the profitability of products by calculating "throughput" (revenue less variable cost) in the metal shop.

Throughput Cost Accounting Analysis	Decline Contract	Take Contract
Coaches Produced	40	34
Streetcars Produced	0	15
Foundry Hours	80	113
Metal shop Hours	160	159
Coach Revenue	$14,000	$11,900
Streetcar Revenue	$ 0	$ 4,200
Coach Raw Material Cost	$(2,400)	$(2,040)
Streetcar Raw Material Cost	$ 0	$(1,800)
Throughput Value	$11,600	$12,260
Overhead Expense	$(10,600)	$(10,600)
Profit	$1,000	$1,660

After the presentations from the company accountant and the operations manager, the president understood that the metal shop capacity was limiting the company's profitability. The company could make only 40 rail coaches per month. But by taking the contract for the streetcars, the company could make nearly all the railway coaches ordered, and also meet all the demand for streetcars. The result would increase throughput in the metal shop from $6.25 to $10.38 per hour of available time, and increase profitability by 66 per cent.

ACTIVITY-BASED COSTING

Activity-based costing (ABC) is a system for assigning costs to products based on the activities they require. In this case, activities are those regular actions performed inside a company."Talking with customer regarding invoice questions" is an example of an activity inside most companies.

Accountants assign 100% of each employee's time to the different activities performed inside a company (many will use surveys to have the workers themselves assign their time to the different activities).

The accountant then can determine the total cost spent on each activity by summing up the percentage of each worker's salary spent on that activity.

A company can use the resulting activity cost data to determine where to focus their operational improvements. For example, a job-based manufacturer may find that a high percentage of its workers are spending their time trying to figure out a hastily written customer order.

Via ABC, the accountants now have a currency amount pegged to the activity of"Researching Customer Work Order Specifications". Senior management can now decide how much focus or money to budget for resolving this process deficiency. Activity-based management includes (but is not restricted to) the use of activity-based costing to manage a business.

While ABC may be able to pinpoint the cost of each activity and resources into the ultimate product, the process could be tedious, costly and subject to errors.

As it is a tool for a more accurate way of allocating fixed costs into product, these fixed costs do not vary just as to each month's production volume. For example, an elimination of one product would not eliminate the overhead or even direct labour cost assigned to it. ABC better identifies product costing in the long run, but may not be too helpful in day-to-day decision-making.

LEAN ACCOUNTING

Lean accounting has developed in recent years to provide the accounting, control, and measurement methods supporting lean manufacturing and other applications of lean thinking such as healthcare, construction, insurance, banking, education, government, and other industries.

There are two main thrusts for Lean Accounting. The first is the application of lean methods to the company's accounting, control, and measurement processes. This is not different from applying lean methods to any other processes. The objective is to eliminate waste, free up capacity, speed up the process, eliminate errors and defects, and make the process clear and understandable.

The second (and more important) thrust of Lean Accounting is to fundamentally change the accounting, control, and measurement processes so they motivate lean change and improvement, provide information that is suitable for control and decision-making, provide an understanding of customer value, correctly assess the financial impact of lean improvement, and are themselves simple, visual, and low-waste.

Lean Accounting does not require the traditional management accounting methods like standard costing, activity-based costing, variance reporting, cost-plus pricing, complex transactional control systems, and untimely and confusing financial reports.

These are replaced by:

- Lean-focused performance measurements
- Simple summary direct costing of the value streams
- Decision-making and reporting using a box score
- Financial reports that are timely and presented in"plain English" that everyone can understand
- Radical simplification and elimination of transactional control systems by eliminating the need for them
- Driving lean changes from a deep understanding of the value created for the customers
- Eliminating traditional budgeting through monthly sales, operations, and financial planning processes (SOFP)
- Value-based pricing
- Correct understanding of the financial impact of lean change

As an organization becomes more mature with lean thinking and methods, they recognize that the combined methods of lean accounting in fact creates a lean management system (LMS) designed to provide the planning, the operational and financial reporting, and the motivation for change required to prosper the company's on-going lean transformation.

MARGINAL COSTING

This method is used particularly for short-term decision-making.

Its principal tenets are:

- Revenue (per product) – variable costs (per product) = contribution (per product)
- Total contribution – total fixed costs = (total profit or total loss)

Thus, it does not attempt to allocate fixed costs in an arbitrary manner to different products. The short-term objective is to maximize contribution per unit. If constraints exist on resources, then Managerial Accounting dictates that marginal cost analysis be employed to maximize contribution per unit of the constrained resource.

SCOPE OF COST ACCOUNTING

The terms 'costing' and 'cost accounting' are many times used interchangeably. However, the scope of cost accounting is broader than that of costing.

Following functional activities are included in the scope of cost accounting:

- *Cost book-keeping:* It involves maintaining complete record of all costs incurred from their incurrence to their charge to departments, products and services. Such recording is preferably done on the basis of double entry system.
- *Cost system:* Systems and procedures are devised for proper accounting for costs.
- *Cost ascertainment:* Ascertaining cost of products,

processes, jobs, services, etc., is the important function of cost accounting. Cost ascertainment becomes the basis of managerial decision making such as pricing, planning and control.

- *Cost Analysis:* It involves the process of finding out the causal factors of actual costs varying from the budgeted costs and fixation of responsibility for cost increases.
- *Cost comparisons:* Cost accounting also includes comparisons between cost from alternative courses of action such as use of technology for production, cost of making different products and activities, and cost of same product/service over a period of time.
- *Cost Control:* Cost accounting is the utilisation of cost information for exercising control. It involves a detailed examination of each cost in the light of benefit derived from the incurrence of the cost. Thus, we can state that cost is analysed to know whether the current level of costs is satisfactory in the light of standards set in advance.
- *Cost Reports:* Presentation of cost is the ultimate function of cost accounting. These reports are primarily for use by the management at different levels. Cost Reports form the basis for planning and control, performance appraisal and managerial decision making.

CLASSIFICATION OF COSTS

Classification of cost means, the grouping of costs just as to their common characteristics.

The important ways of classification of costs are:

- *By nature or element*: Materials, labour, expenses
- *By functions*: Production, selling, distribution, administration, R&D, development,
- As direct and indirect
- *By variability*: Fixed, variable, semi-variable

- *By controllability*: Controllable, uncontrollable
- *By normality*: Normal, abnormal

ABSORPTION COSTING

Absorption costing means that all of the manufacturing costs are *absorbed* by the units produced. In other words, the cost of a finished unit in inventory will include direct materials, direct labour, and both variable and *fixed manufacturing overhead*.

As a result, absorption costing is also referred to as full costing or the full absorption method.

Absorption costing is often contrasted with variable costing or direct costing.

Under variable or direct costing, the fixed manufacturing overhead costs are not allocated or assigned to the products manufactured. Variable costing is often useful for management's decision-making. However, absorption costing is required for external financial reporting and for income tax reporting.

BREAK-EVEN ANALYSIS

Break-even analysis is a technique widely used by production management and management accountants. It is based on categorising production costs between those which are "variable" and those that are "fixed".

Total variable and fixed costs are compared with sales revenue in order to determine the level of sales volume, sales value or production at which the business makes neither a profit nor a loss.

THE BREAK-EVEN CHART

In its simplest form, the break-even chart is a graphical representation of costs at various levels of activity shown on the same chart as the variation of income with the same variation in activity.

The point at which neither profit nor loss is made is known as the "break-even point" and is represented on the chart by the intersection of the two lines:

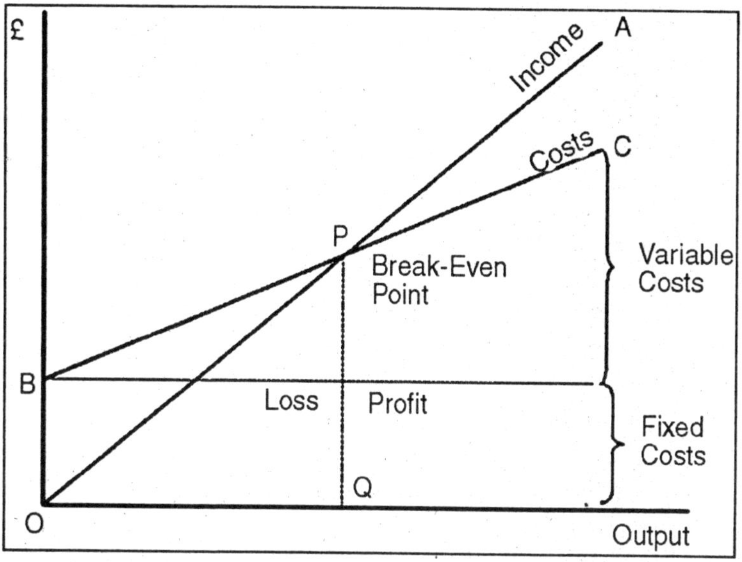

The line OA represents the variation of income at varying levels of production activity. OB represents the total fixed costs in the business. As output increases, variable costs are incurred, meaning that total costs also increase. At low levels of output, Costs are greater than Income. At the point of intersection, P, costs are exactly equal to income, and hence neither profit nor loss is made.

FIXED COSTS

Fixed costs are those business costs that are not directly related to the level of production or output. In other words, even if the business has a zero output or high output, the level of fixed costs will remain broadly the same. In the long term fixed costs can alter - perhaps as a result of investment in production capacity or through the growth in overheads required to support a larger, more complex business.

Examples of fixed costs:

- Rent and rates
- Depreciation
- Research and development
- Marketing costs
- Administration costs

VARIABLE COSTS

Variable costs are those costs which vary directly with the level of output. They represent payment output-related inputs such as raw materials, direct labour, fuel and revenue-related costs such as commission.

A distinction is often made between "Direct" variable costs and "Indirect" variable costs.

Direct variable costs are those which can be directly attributable to the production of a particular product or service and allocated to a particular cost centre. Raw materials and the wages those working on the production line are good examples.

Indirect variable costs cannot be directly attributable to production but they do vary with output. These include depreciation, maintenance and certain labour costs.

SEMI-VARIABLE COSTS

Whilst the distinction between fixed and variable costs is a convenient way of categorising business costs, in reality there are some costs which are fixed in nature but which increase when output reaches certain levels. These are largely related to the overall "scale" and/or complexity of the business. For example, when a business has relatively low levels of output or sales, it may not require costs associated with functions such as human resource management or a fully-resourced finance department. However, as the scale of the business grows then more resources are required. If production rises suddenly then some short-term increase in warehousing and/or transport may be required. In these circumstances.

7

Cost Control Techniques

INTRODUCTION

The cost control definition suggests that a company should investigate good procedures for finding out the reason why the costs of the company are not as per the pre-decided or budgeted costs. Thus, cost control can help a company determine, if it is really spending more than it should actually spend.

Though it is not essential to be a finance expert to understand the definition of cost control, planning and actually implementing the cost control techniques can be quite a big challenge.

It is essential for the senior level managers to have a good understanding of the cost control software which is a part of effective cost control techniques. The next few paragraphs will give you more information about the cost control management and the cost control techniques.

TECHNIQUES AND WAYS FOR CONTROLLING COSTS

The first step in the cost control management is to find out the cost centres and arrive at a cease in how much percentage they differ or vary from the standards of the industry.

It is also important to study how the close competitors of your company manage to control their costs and in turn, maximize their profits. Before discussing about the cost control methods or the cost control techniques, it is very important to carry out a very proper cost analysis. The costs incurred by all the departments of the company should be considered so that, you can chalk out some smart cost control strategies to overcome these financial problems. It is very important to find out the exact and relevant reasons for why the costs of the company are more than the standards adhered to by the industry.

The most important of all the cost control techniques is to appoint a small team of highly qualified and experienced people well versed in the financial management team to manage the daily finances of the company in a very professional and systematic manner.

The finance team should take correct decisions in favour of the company and opt for less expensive materials and resources for the company without compromising on their quality.

You should be very clear about the number of employees you require for a particular project. There are many companies who find it difficult to earn decent profits as their employee count is way beyond the necessity. You can also consider the idea of recruiting employees on contract basis to cut down your costs.

While deciding how much salary to pay to a particular employee, you need to be very careful. You should decide the salary strictly on the basis of overall performance. Instead of giving awards to the employees in the form of frequent salary hikes, you should give out bonuses to eligible employees. Following practices recommended in cost method of accounting may benefit your company.

The cost control software can be helpful in doing the work in comparatively less time and with more accuracy. In the times of recession, many firms resort to cost control techniques such as reducing the extra facilities to the employees such as the recreational facilities.

The cost control techniques might also include cutting down the expenditure incurred on traveling by air and luxury hotel accommodations in order to harness the cash flow. As a part of the cost cutting measure, few firms may postpone or cancel their plans of acquiring new companies, investing in new businesses and buying new machinery or systems. The cost control techniques should be utilized to save cash and bring back the financial strength of the company.

The cost control techniques used by different organizations are different and are largely dependent on their business model and strength of their balance sheet. The better the implementation of these techniques, the better would be the future of the concerned organizations.

BUDGET

A budget is generally a list of all planned expenses and revenues. It is a plan for saving and spending. A budget is an important concept in microeconomics, which uses a budget line toemphasize the trade-offs between two or more goods. In other terms, a budget is an organizational plan stated in monetary terms.

In summary, the purpose of budgeting is to:

- Provide a forecast of revenues and expenditures i.e. construct a model of how our business might perform financially speaking if certain strategies, events and plans are carried out.
- Enable the actual financial operation of the business to be measured against the forecast.

BUSINESS START-UP BUDGET

The process of calculating the costs of starting a small business begins with a list of all necessary purchases including tangible assets and services, working capital, sources and collateral. The budget should contain a narrative explaining how you decided on the amount of this reserve and a description of the expected financial results of business activities. The assets should be valued with each and every cost. All other expenses are like labour factory overhead all freshmen expenses are also included into business budgeting

CORPORATE BUDGET

The budget of a company is often compiled annually, but

may not be. A finished budget, usually requiring considerable effort, is a plan for the short-term future, typically one year. While traditionally the Finance department compiles the company's budget, modern software allows hundreds or even thousands of people in various departments to list their expected revenues and expenses in the final budget.

If the actual figures delivered through the budget period come close to the budget, this suggests that the managers understand their business and have been successfully driving it in the intended direction. On the other hand, if the figures diverge wildly from the budget, this sends an 'out of control' signal, and the share price could suffer as a result.

EVENT MANAGEMENT BUDGET

A budget is a fundamental tool for an event director to predict with reasonable accuracy whether the event will result in a profit, a loss or will break-even. A budget can also be used as a pricing tool.

BUDGET TYPES

- *Sales budget*: The sales budget is an estimate of future sales, often broken down into both units and dollars. It is used to create company sales goals.
- *Production budget*: Product oriented companies create a production budget which estimates the number of units that must be manufactured to meet the sales goals. The production budget also estimates the various costs involved with manufacturing those units, including labour and material.
- *Cash Flow/Cash budget*: The cash flow budget is a prediction of future cash receipts and expenditures for a particular time period. It usually covers a period in the short term future. The cash flow budget helps the business determine when income will be sufficient to cover expenses and when the company will need to seek outside financing.
- *Marketing budget*: The marketing budget is an estimate of the funds needed for promotion,

advertising, and public relations in order to market the product or service.

- *Project budget*: The project budget is a prediction of the costs associated with a particular company project. These costs include labour, materials, and other related expenses. The project budget is often broken down into specific tasks, with task budgets assigned to each.
- *Revenue budget*: The Revenue Budget consists of revenue receipts of government and the expenditure met from these revenues. Tax revenues are made up of taxes and other duties that the government levies.
- *Expenditure budget*: A budget type which include of spending data items.

BUDGET PREPARATION

A critical aspect of intervention planning is preparing a budget of income and expenses. The budget must include funding for materials and supplies for the intervention activities, but also for staff, facilities, and promotion. Keep in mind that each intervention requires different resources, and organizations have unique capacities to conduct interventions with existing resources. The following are typical budget categories.

CATEGORIES FOR AN INTERVENTION BUDGET

- *Personnel and benefits expense:* Personnel includes all individuals who will have responsibilities in the intervention. Others who may be hired to help with the project, such as consultants or contractors, are not budgeted in Personnel, rather are included in the Purchased, Consultant or Contractual Services. Fringe benefits are typically budgeted at a per cent of the personnel salary, and are dependent upon the benefits paid by the employer.
- *Things to consider:* Do you have enough people to implement the intervention? Will you need to hire

additional part-time or full-time staff to help you? What benefits will be paid and to whom? Will your staffing needs change over the duration of your intervention from year to year?

Examples: Principal investigator, project director, project staff, paid interns – full and part-time

- *General Office Expenses:* Includes office supplies needed to support the intervention.
- *Things to consider:* What basic materials or supplies are needed to support the intervention? You should be able to budget more for office supplies the first year of the project and less in subsequent years.

  Examples: Computers, software, office supplies/ materials, telephones, copy machines, office furniture, postage, etc.
- *Intervention Supplies and Materials*: Intervention materials are the actual materials you will need to implement your intervention.
- *Things to consider*: How many participants you are anticipating? Can you prepare the materials yourself or do you need to hire someone to prepare them for you? Do you need to conduct research or a needs assessment before designing your materials?

  Examples: Educational materials or curriculum, incentive or promotional materials, copies of pre/post surveys, brochures, posters, equipment for a physical activity intervention.
- *Meeting and Activity Expenses*: Space outside your organization's office may be needed for meetings or intervention activities. Some places may charge a rental fee as well as for use of audio visual equipment, such as projectors or TVs. Food and drinks provided at the meeting may be included in this category or in Intervention Supplies, depending on the organization's preference.
- *Things to consider*: Does your current office space accommodate everything you will need for the

intervention? Do you have room to conduct meetings with other partners or internal staff? Do you have appropriate space to conduct your intervention activities or will you need to use other spaces? Will any of your partners donate space for meetings or intervention activities? Will you need to rent facilities to conduct your intervention? Will you need to travel to your intervention's participants or partners, if so where will you meet with them?

Examples: Meeting rooms, church basements, school gymnasiums, community centres, multi-purpose rooms, park pavilions, etc.

- *Transportation/Travel Expenses*: Transportation can involve providing a means for participants to travel to your intervention activities in order to increase participation or providing transportation for you and your staff to travel to other locations to conduct intervention activities. This may also include fees or stipends to attend professional meetings or perform interviews and surveys out-of-town.
- *Things to consider*: Do your participants have access to public or personal transportation or will you need to provide it? Do your staff members need to travel to participants' homes or communities to conduct intervention activities? Will your staff need to travel to conferences or to make presentations outside of your city?

  Examples: Bus tokens or cab fare for programme participants, rental vans to pick up participants, mileage reimbursement for staff members conducting intervention activities, travel stipends, air fare and per diem for out-of-town travel
- *Purchased, Consultant or Contractual Service Expenses*: These expenses are payments to individuals or companies for a specific service, usually occurring temporarily during the project, that are not completed by the regular project staff.
- *Things to consider*: What specific expertise and services

will you need in planning, implementing and evaluating your intervention?

Examples: Development and placement of media ads;consultant for identifying interventions for priority populations; contractor to conduct an evaluation of the intervention.

- *Indirect Costs*: Indirect costs are the expenses incurred by the organization to keep the organization operating. Indirect cost are typically calculated by multiplying an agreed upon percentage by the total direct costs, or by the total of personnel and benefit costs. These costs are sometimes also referred to as administrative costs.
- *Things to consider:* Will your organization obtain sufficient indirect costs from your intervention income? Are there partners who are willing to cover some indirect costs?

  Examples: Rent, utilities, telecommunications, property insurance, legal expenses, or building maintenance costs.

An "in-kind" donation is a contribution of time, service or goods made by a donor to help support the operations or services provided by your organization. It isn't cash. Therefore the donor does retain a degree of control over the donation that doesn't occur when the donor gives you a cash donation. Because of this "relationship" your organization should keep the donor well informed on how their donation is being used.

Some examples of in-kind donations include:

- Bookkeeping service
- Copying
- Office equipment
- Office/meeting space
- Printing
- Professional services
- Refreshments
- Volunteer time

As you prepare your budget it is critical you account for anticipated in-kind donations. If you don't track these donations, you aren't truly acknowledging the total capacity of your organization. Also tracking these donations will help you better acknowledge the donors for their contribution.

BUDGET PREPARATION WORKSHEET

When creating your intervention budget, take into consideration that your budget and allocation of funds may vary from year to year.

For example, in Year 1, many of your funds may go into buying supplies or investing money in materials for start-up. In Year 2 and beyond, you may be spending most of your budget disseminating your intervention materials or on evaluation efforts. It is important to create your yearly intervention budget to reflect these changes.

Personnel

Personnel refers to all staff members who will be involved in the various intervention activities. Others helping with the intervention, such as consultants or technical assistance, are not considered Personnel, but are rather included in the Purchased Services Total. Remember: When creating Year 2 and beyond budgets, it is important to adjust for Personnel salaries based on increases in cost of living. When calculating Personnel salaries for Year 2 and beyond, multiply personnel by the expected increase of cost of living for each year.

Calculating Personnel:

- *Base Salary*: For each personnel position, state the base salary for the position.
  - Example: Principal Investigator -$75,000
- *% of Time*: For each personnel position, determine the per cent of that person's total time that will be used to work on the intervention project.
  - *Example*: A Principal Investigator may only contribute 25% of his/her time to oversee the project, while interns or research assistants may be using 100% of their time on intervention activities.
- *Project Salary*: For each personnel position, determine

the project salary by multiplying base salary by% of time.

  - *Example*: Principal Investigator [$75,000 X 25% (% of time) =$ 18,750 (Project Salary)]

- *Fringe Benefit%*: Fringe benefits include all taxes, as well as health insurance, paid time off, retirement, and other benefits provided. Fringe benefits may or may not be offered to all employees. Fringe benefit%s are at the discretion of the organization based on amount of funding and what it offers its employees in terms of benefits. Fringe benefit for a graduate research assistant may be a little as 3% perhaps providing worker's compensation only, as opposed to 20- 40% for senior full time employee of the project receiving full benefits.
  - *Example*: Full time employees may receive a fringe benefit rate of 30%
- *Fringe Amount*: To determine fringe amount, multiple the fringe benefit percentage rate by the project salary amount. (Remember: {Base Salary} X {% of Time} = {Project Salary})
  - *Example*: Principal Investigator [$18,750 (Project Salary) x 30% (Fringe Benefit%) = $5,625(Fringe Amount)]
- *Total*: To determine the total cost of each personnel position, add the project salary + the fringe amount.
  - *Example*: Principal Investigator [$18,750 (Project Salary) + $5,625 (Fringe Amount) = $24,375 (Total Salary Cost)]

Principal Investigator

Includes project time associated with such positions as project direct, principal investigator, or any co-principal investigators that provide the main leadership to the project.

Project Staff

Includes salary costs of the project staff such as project manager, project coordinator, or senior staff, who directly work on the project. Project staff can also include nurses, statisticians, researchers, graduate assistants, epidemiologist or any other staff with roles directly related to aspects of the project.

Administrative Staff

Includes any staff providing administrative support, such as secretaries, administrative assistant, bookkeeper, data entry staff or any staff used for this type of work.

Other Staff

Any other staff not included in the other personnel categories, such as a stipend or salary for interns or fellows.

Example:

Your budget calculation for Principal Investigator would look like this:						**Total**
Position	Base Salary	% of Effort	Project Salary	Fringe %	Fringe Amount	(Project Salary + Fringe Amount)
Principal Investigator	$75,000	25%	$18,750	30%	$5,625	$24,375

Other Direct Costs

These are direct non-personnel cost of any materials and resources that are necessary for completing the research or intervention.

General Office Supplies and Materials

Includes any of the fixed costs of having your organization remain in operation. Office operations and equipment are included in this category.

These categories encompass computers, software, office supplies/materials, telephones, copy machines, office furniture, postage, etc.

You may spend more on office supplies and materials in your first year of the intervention than in subsequent years.

Example:

Your budget calculation for office equipment would look like this:	**Total**
Office Computers (4 @$700)	2,800
Statistical Software	200
Laser printer	1,000
Office Furniture	1,500
Office Telephones	200
Total office equipment:	$5,700

Intervention Materials

Intervention materials are those that are needed to implement your programme that are not already included general office supplies and materials.

Intervention materials include any money spent on incentives or promotions for intervention participants. This can also include the costs for materials such as pre/post surveys and copies, other intervention materials such as brochures, posters, or any other materials created to promote the intervention, including distribution costs of intervention materials. Intervention material costs may vary from year to year.

Example:

Your budget calculation to distribute a three-page pre-intervention survey to 100 participants by mail would look like this:	**Total**
3 page survey X 100 copies = 300 pages 300 pages @ $.05 per page	15
100 envelopes	8
100 survey recipients X $.37 postage each	37
Total intervention survey cost:	$60

Meeting and Intervention Activity Space

Includes cost for the use of meeting or intervention activity space. If these types of activities occur outside the office, you may need to rent a meeting room. Some places may also charge a fee for use of audio visual equipment, such as projectors or

TVs. Food and drinks provided at the meeting should also be included in this category.

Example:

Your budget calculation for one 4-hour workshop with 20 of your partners and community members, would look like this:	Total
Meeting Space Rental for 4 hours:	75
AV Equipment Rental	10
Food/Drink	80
Total meeting cost:	$165

Transportation/Travel

Refers to travel and transportation costs for project staff or consultants to perform intervention duties. This may include fees or stipends to attend professional meetings or perform interviews or surveys out-of-town. Transportation/Travel costs can also include those incurred by providing a means for participants to get to your intervention activities in order to increase participation.

Example:

Your budget calculation for your principal investigator to attend a 3 day conference in Washington, D.C., would look like this:	Total
Air Fare	350
Conference Registration Fee	75
Per diem for 3 days @ $150.00/day	450
Local Transportation	25
Total personnel travel cost:	$900

Other

Refers to any other costs not covered in the other direct costs. This might include workshop fees, data purchases, and subscriptions to journals or any other miscellaneous programme costs.

Purchased Services

This refers to fees paid to individuals or companies for a specific service, usually occurring temporarily during the intervention that is not completed by the regular project staff. Purchased services may vary from project year to project year.

Consultants

Includes individuals providing expert or professional advice for an agreed per diem rate. Consultants could provide services such as proposal review, speaking engagements, or services for an advisory board/committee. Consultants are usually hired on an hourly or daily rate. When calculating consultant fees, include the hourly rate and how many hours you expect them to be needed for that project year.

Example:

If you and your partnership need help with data analysis from your needs assessment, you may want to hire an epidemiologist as a consultant for your intervention, for a brief period of time.	**Total**
Epidemiology consultant for 2 days @ $300/per day	300
Total consultant cost:	$600

Contracts

Includes agreements entered into with individuals or companies, to provide a specific service to the project. Contracts could include hiring a company to survey participants by phone or to design intervention materials. Contracts are usually negotiated for a set amount for the provided service.

Example:

If you would like to hire a graphic design company to design an intervention logo and materials, your contract for development may look like this:	**Total**
Contract with Graphic Design Company to design intervention materials	800
Total contract cost:	$800

Technical Assistance

Includes any fees for professional technical services, such as; setting up or maintaining computer systems, providing training on software programmes, or providing repairs for office technology.

Technical assistance can vary from company to company and by service, some may charge an hourly rate or charge a set amount for maintenance.

Example:

If your intervention requires special software or computer programming, you may want to figure into your budget the cost for computer technical support.	**Total**
Computer technical support for 15 hours @ $50/hour	750
Total technical assistance cost:	$750

Indirect Costs

This is a percentage that includes costs incurred by the organization as a result of the intervention, but that is not easily identifiable with any specific component of the intervention. Indirect costs are sometimes also referred to as facilities and administrative costs.

Indirect costs include building maintenance costs, utilities, property insurance, accounting, or legal expenses. If your intervention is being housed in university space, your indirect cost may be upwards of 30-60%, however if your space is in a community organization's building, it may be much lower, for instance, 10-15%. Remember: Indirect Cost is a percentage that is multiplied by the total direct cost to determine your total project cost

Example:

If your organization has calculated a 10% indirect cost needed to cover the cost of building maintenance costs, utilities, property insurance, accounting, or legal expenses.	**Total**
Total Direct Costs (Personnel + Other Direct Costs)*	165,652
Indirect Cost %	10%
Total indirect cost (10% X $165,652.00):	$16,565

Grand Total

Project budget total (Personnel Total + Other Direct Cost Total + Indirect Cost Total) for Year 1.

Total	
Total Direct Costs (Personnel + Other Direct Costs)	165,652
Total Indirect Cost:	16,565
Grand Total Year 1:	$182,217

Remember that you are calculating your project budget by year or cycle, and that your expenses may fluctuate from year to year. You will need to take into consideration how your budget will change from year to year and what categories may need more or less money during the course of the intervention. It is also important to remember increases in cost of living for personnel salaries.

BUDGET CONTROL SYSTEM

The State University of New York Fiscal and Accounting Procedures for Mandatory Student Activity Fee Programmes require the custodial and disbursing agent to establish and maintain budgetary accounts. The basic structure for recording and monitoring revenues and expenditures is the Annual Operating Budget. As part of its accounting system, Sub-Board provides a Budgetary Control System modeled after those commonly used by governments and other not-for-profit entities which satisfies the fiscal guidelines, policies and procedures of the Board of Trustees and the State University of New York. All student governments and clients for whom Sub-Board acts as Fiscal Agent must use the Budgetary Control System.

WHAT IS A BUDGET?

A budget is your management's plan or blueprint, in structured form, which projects or anticipates the desired outcome of financial activity for a specific set of resources, for a fixed period, usually one year.

For our purposes, the Annual Operating Budget is divided into two separate components:

1. *Estimated Revenues*: What are the anticipated sources of revenue and how much can management realistically expect to receive?

2. *Estimated Expenditures*: How much does management expect to spend, and for what purposes are resources to be spent?

WHY IS A BUDGET IMPORTANT?

A budget acts as the formal process that establishes the authority on how funds are to be collected and spent. Management's objective is to provide a logical, detailed and realistic spending plan.

Once a plan has been decided upon and is formally adopted by the student government/client governing body, the budget acts as an effective management tool by providing a means of identifying and allocating limited resources and monitoring their use.

The budget also is used to help prevent the student government/client from overspending. Budget reports provide management with information on operations, allowing the organization to monitor and control spending and revenue collection while they are in progress. Hence, budgets alone are meaningless unless they are used to motivate responsible action and to direct operations toward accomplishing objectives that have been established by management as desirable.

The budget is the single most important source of financial information. Almost all financial transactions are recorded in the budget. The budget is used to track all cash receipts, encumbrances and cash disbursements, and provides a means of tracking these transactions back to original source documents.

HOW IS THE BUDGET STRUCTURED?

In determining the basic elements of Estimated Revenues and Estimated Expenditures, a logical structure must be developed to codify and arrange the elements into parts that reflect the nature and structure of the operations themselves. The basic structural tool is the budgetary account. A budgetary account identifies a specific source of revenue or a particular type of expenditure by using a budgetary account number.

Sub-Board's Budgetary Control System uses the following budgetary account number format:

- *Fund*: The first three digits of the account number identify the student government/client and the overall purpose of the funds accounted for in a particular budget, e.g. operating funds, capital funds, etc.
- *Department*: The next four digits of the account number identify the department, division, activity centre, etc. within the internal operations of the student government/client.
- *Line Item*: The next four digits of the account number identify the specific source of revenue or the type of expenditure for a particular department, e.g. Advertising Revenue, or Telephone Expense.
- *Project*: In certain situations, the account number may be extended by an additional four digits to further identify a particular project.

Therefore, the account number format is:

XXX. XXXX. XXXX. XXXX

Fund. Department. Line Item. Project

Sub-Board assigns budgetary account numbers for all student governments/clients just as to a Chart of Accounts.

HOW DOES THE BUDGETARY PROCESS BEGIN?

The first step in the budgetary process is for the student government/client to review its operations. What is working well and what needs to be changed? What are the goals and objectives for the coming budget year? What projects does the student government/client wish to support? Which recognized clubs and organizations has management agreed to fund? What are the primary sources of revenue? Clubs, organizations, project managers and department heads may be required to submit budget requests to whoever is responsible for preparing the initial or "proposed" budget. These requests can then be reviewed and modified before being incorporated into the proposed budget. It may also be helpful for whoever is preparing the proposed budget to review past budgets – historical information can be very helpful in determining how the student government/client has operated in the past and can help identify areas that management would like to continue, eliminate or change.

All student governments/clients must prepare their budgets just as to the fiscal year. The fiscal year begins on August 1 and ends on July 31 of the following year.

Once the proposed budget has been prepared, it must be formally approved or adopted in accordance with the student government/client constitution, by-laws or governing rules. During this process, the budget may be discussed, modified, or challenged before being formally adopted.

For student governments/clients that maintain more that one fund in addition to the operating budget, a separate budget for each Fund must be adopted.

AFTER THE BUDGET IS ADOPTED, WHAT IS THE NEXT STEP?

For all student governments/clients subject to administrative review and certification, approved budgets must be submitted using the Required Budget Format to the Administrative Designee no later than June 1 prior to the start of the fiscal year. A copy of the approved budget must also be submitted to the SBI Accounting Office by the same date, June 1. For independent clients whose budgets are not subject to administrative review and certification, approved budgets must be submitted to the SBI Accounting Office no later than June 1 prior to the start of the Fiscal Year. Budgets must be accompanied by a completed Certification of Budget Form signed by at least two officers or authorized representatives of the student government/client, attesting that adoption and approval procedures were correctly followed. For student governments/clients that maintain more than one budget, a separate Certification of Budget Form must be submitted with each budget. In order to continue operating without an interruption in accounting services, budgets must be submitted by the due date of June 1.

WHAT HAPPENS AFTER THE BUDGET IS SUBMITTED AND CERTIFIED?

Upon receiving the adopted budget, Sub-Board will review the budget for accuracy and conformity to fiscal guidelines. Budgets must be balanced; i.e.

Total Estimated Revenue must equal or exceed Total Estimated Expenditures. Unbalanced budgets will be returned to the student government/client unprocessed. Estimated Revenues and Estimated Expenditures must be based on realistic projections.

Assuming that budgets have been submitted by the required deadline, in the required format, and with the proper officer certification, and the administrative designee, where applicable, has approved the budgets, Sub- Board will enter the adopted budgets into the accounting system. On August 1, the adopted budgets will go into effect. All student governments/clients will receive initial budget reports as of August 1, before any activity begins, as verification that Sub-Board has accurately entered the budgets. The student government/client should closely review these initial budget reports and report any problems or errors immediately to the SBI Accounting Office for correction.

WILL ANY ACTIVITY FROM THE PRIOR YEAR BUDGET HAVE AN EFFECT ON THE CURRENT BUDGET?

Since there may be financial activity in process between the end of one fiscal year and the beginning of the next, the budget will be affected in several ways.

First, on the revenue side, the Fund's cash balance as of July 31 will be added to Estimated Revenues and Annual Revenue Receipts in the new budget on the first day of the new fiscal year, August 1. This cash balance, if sufficient, can be used as a reserve to accommodate outstanding encumbrances and accrued payroll expenses. Any remaining cash balance not reserved for other purposes may be re-appropriated in the new budget. This adjustment will take place as soon as all cash activity has been recorded and reconciled for July, usually sometime in early August. Second, on the expenditure side, any encumbrances outstanding at the end of the fiscal year will be added to budgeted expenditures in the next fiscal year's budget. The date that this adjustment actually takes place depends on the final accounting of year-end activity, preparation of year-end financial statements, the progress of the annual independent audit, etc., and usually takes place sometime after October 15. Until this final accounting for outstanding encumbrances is completed and the prior year budget is "closed", the accounting system will automatically account for encumbrances from the prior fiscal year that are paid in the new fiscal year. This is done so that budgetary expenditures for the new fiscal year are not depleted by payments for which encumbrances existed in the prior fiscal year's budget.

Third, accrued payroll expenses, if any, as of July 31 will be added to Estimated Expenditures in the next fiscal year when the new budget goes into effect on August 1. You must provide a sufficient reserve in your budget to accommodate this additional appropriation and to maintain a balanced budget. This adjustment to the budget will take place after all payroll activity has been received and recorded, usually sometime in September.

WHAT IF THE BUDGET NEEDS TO BE MODIFIED OR ADJUSTED DURING THE COURSE OF THE FISCAL YEAR?

It is not realistic to prepare a budget at the beginning of the fiscal year and then leave it as a rigid plan of action. Important unforeseen changes in internal or external conditions may require budget revisions during the fiscal year. It is essential that management receive timely information on its actual results in comparison with the plan. A comparison of actual operating results with the original budget plan would show management what the organization did in comparison with what it initially planned to do. It may not reveal, however, how well the organization did with regard to how it should have performed under the conditions which actually existed.

Therefore, Sub-Board will provide periodic budget reports to assess performance of actual results with the original plan and the adjusted budget plan.

Whenever an adjustment or revision to the original budget is necessary, the student government/client must notify Sub-Board of the adjustment(s) to be made by entering a Budget Adjustment into the on-line KVS Accounting System. Budget Adjustments require the approval of two officers. In addition, student governments and independent clients who are subject to administrative review must have all budget adjustments or changes to the budget reviewed and certified by the administrative designee. All approvals can be done on-line. Sub-Board will update the budget adjustments only after all approvals have been obtained.

ZERO-BASED BUDGETING

Zero-based budgeting is a technique of planning and decision-making which reverses the working process of traditional budgeting. In traditional incremental budgeting, departmental managers justify only increases over the previous year budget and what has been already spent is automatically sanctioned. No reference is made to the previous level of expenditure. By contrast, in zero-based budgeting, every department function is reviewed comprehensively and all expenditures must be approved, rather than only increases. Zero-based budgeting requires the budget request be justified in complete detail by each division manager starting from the zero-base. The zero-base is indifferent to whether the total budget is increasing or decreasing.

The term"zero-based budgeting" is sometimes used in personal finance to describe the practice of budgeting every dollar of income received, and then adjusting some part of the budget downward for every other part that needs to be adjusted upward. It is more technically correct to refer to this practice as"zero-sum budgeting".

Zero based budgeting also refers to the identification of a task or tasks and then funding resources to complete the task independent of current resourcing.

ADVANTAGES OF ZERO-BASED BUDGETING

- Efficient allocation of resources, as it is based on needs and benefits.
- Drives managers to find cost effective ways to improve operations.
- Detects inflated budgets.
- Useful for service departments where the output is difficult to identify.
- Increases staff motivation by providing greater initiative and responsibility in decision-making.
- Increases communication and coordination within the organization.
- Identifies and eliminates wasteful and obsolete operations.
- Identifies opportunities for outsourcing.
- Forces cost centres to identify their mission and their relationship to overall goals.

DISADVANTAGES OF ZERO-BASED BUDGETING

- Difficult to define decision units and decision packages, as it is time-consuming and exhaustive.
- Forced to justify every detail related to expenditure. The R&D department is threatened whereas the production department benefits.
- Necessary to train managers. Zero-based budgeting must be clearly understood by managers at various levels to be successfully implemented. Difficult to administer and communicate the budgeting because more managers are involved in the process.
- In a large organization, the volume of forms may be so large that no one person could read it all. Compressing the information down to a usable size might remove critically important details.
- Honesty of the managers must be reliable and uniform. Any manager that exaggerates skews the results.

INCREMENTAL BUDGETING

Incremental Budgeting uses a budget prepared using a previous period's budget or actual performance as a base, with incremental amounts added for the new budget period. The allocation of resources is based upon allocations from the previous period. This approach is not recommended as it fails to take into account changing circumstances. Moreover, it encourages "spending up to the budget" to ensure a reasonable allocation in the next period. It leads to a "spend it or lose it" mentality.

Advantages of incremental budgeting:

- The budget is stable and change is gradual.
- Managers can operate their departments on a consistent basis.
- The system is relatively simple to operate and easy to understand.
- Conflicts are avoided when departments appear to be treated similarly.
- Co-ordination between budgets is easier to achieve.
- The impact of change can be seen quickly.

Disadvantages of incremental budgeting:

- Assumes activities and methods of working will continue in the same way.
- No incentive for developing new ideas.
- No incentive to reduce costs.
- Encourages spending up to the budget so that the budget is maintained next year.
- The budget may become out-of-date and no longer relate to the level of activity or type of work being carried out.
- The priority for resources may have changed since the budgets were originally set.
- There may be budgetary slack built into the budget, which is never reviewed. Managers might have overestimated their requirements in the past in order to obtain a budget which is easier to work within, and which will allow them to achieve favourable results.

STANDARD COSTING

Standard costing is an important subtopic of cost accounting. Standard costs are usually associated with a manufacturing company's costs of direct material, direct labour, and manufacturing overhead.

Rather than assigning the actual costs of direct material, direct labour, and manufacturing overhead to a product, many manufacturers assign the expected or standard cost. This means that a manufacturer's inventories and cost of goods sold will begin with amounts reflecting the standard costs, not the actual costs, of a product. Manufacturers, of course, still have to pay the actual costs. As a result there are almost always differences between the actual costs and the standard costs, and those differences are known as variances.

Standard costing and the related variances is a valuable management tool.

If a variance arises, management becomes aware that manufacturing costs have differed from the standard costs:

- If actual costs are greater than standard costs the variance is unfavourable. An unfavourable variance tells management that if everything else stays constant the company's actual profit will be less than planned.
- If actual costs are less than standard costs the variance is favourable. A favourable variance tells management that if everything else stays constant the actual profit will likely exceed the planned profit.

The sooner that the accounting system reports a variance, the sooner that management can direct its attention to the difference from the planned amounts.

If we assume that a company uses the perpetual inventory system and that it carries all of its inventory accounts at standard cost then the standard cost of a finished product is the sum of the standard costs of the inputs:

- Direct material
- Direct labour
- Manufacturing overhead
  - Variable manufacturing overhead
  - Fixed manufacturing overhead

Usually there will be two variances computed for each input:

Input for Product	Variance #1	Variance #2
Direct material	Price (or cost)	Usage (or quantity)
Direct labor	Rate (or cost)	Efficiency (or quantity)
Manufacturing overhead-variable	Spending	Efficiency
Manufacturing overhead-fixed	Budget	Volume

VARIANCE ANALYSIS

Variance analysis is usually associated with explaining the difference (or variance) between actual costs and the standard costs allowed for the good output. For example, the difference in materials costs can be divided into a materials price variance and a materials usage variance.

The difference between the actual direct labour costs and the standard direct labour costs can be divided into a rate variance and an efficiency variance. The difference in manufacturing overhead can be divided into spending, efficiency, and volume variances. Mix and yield variances can also be calculated. Variance analysis helps management to understand the present costs and then to control future costs.

Variance analysis is also used to explain the difference between the actual sales dollars and the budgeted sales dollars. Examples include sales price variance, sales quantity variance, and sales mix variance. A difference in the relative proportion of sales can account for some of the difference in a company's profits.

TYPES OF VARIANCES

RESPONSIBILITY ACCOUNTING

Responsibility accounting is an underlying concept of accounting performance measurement systems. The basic idea is that large diversified organizations are difficult, if not impossible to manage as a single segment, thus they must be decentralized or separated into manageable parts.

These parts, or segments are referred to as responsibility centres that include:

- Revenue centres,
- Cost centres,
- Profit centres and
- Investment centres.

This approach allows responsibility to be assigned to the segment managers that have the greatest amount of influence over the key elements to be managed. These elements include revenue for a revenue centre costs for a cost centre a measure of profitability for a profit centre and return on investment for an investment centre.

CONTROLLABILITY CONCEPT

An underlying concept of responsibility accounting is referred to as controllability. Conceptually, a manager should only be held responsible for those aspects of performance that he or she can control. This concept is rarely, if ever, applied successfully in practice because of the system variation present in all systems. Attempts to apply the controllability concept produce responsibility reports where each layer of management is held responsible for all subordinate management layers.

Responsibility Accounting Reports

President's Responsibility Report

	Budget	Actual	Variance
Presiden's Office	$50,000	$52,000	$2,000 U
Controller	25,000	24,000	1,000 F
Production Vice-President	1,800,000	1,829,000	29,000 U
Sales Vices-President	525,000	550,000	25,000 U
Total Controllable Costs	$2,400,000	$2,455,000	$55,000 U

Production Vice-President's Responsibility Report

	Budget	Actual	Variance
Vice President's Office	$10,000	$11,000	$1,000 U
Cutting Department	500,000	498,000	2,000 F
Machining Department	990,000	1,000,000	10,000 U
Assembly Department	300,000	320,000	20,000 U
Total Controllable Costs	$1,8000,000	$1,829,000	$29,000 U

Cutting Department Responsibility Report

	Budget	Actual	Variance
Direct Material	$250,000	$253,000	$3,000 U
Direct Labor	100,000	90,000	10,000 F
Variable Overhead	50,000	52,000	2,000 U
Fixed Overhead	100,000	103,000	3,000 U
Total Controllable Costs	$500,000	$498,000	$2,000 F

ADVANTAGES AND DISADVANTAGES

Responsibility accounting has been an accepted part of

traditional accounting control systems for many years because it provides an organization with a number of advantages. Perhaps the most compelling argument for the responsibility accounting approach is that it provides a way to manage an organization that would otherwise be unmanageable. In addition, assigning responsibility to lower level managers allows higher level managers to pursue other activities such as long term planning and policy making. It also provides a way to motivate lower level managers and workers. Managers and workers in an individualistic system tend to be motivated by measurements that emphasize their individual performances. However, this emphasis on the performance of individuals and individual segments creates what some critics refer to as the "stovepipe organization." Others have used the term "functional silos" to describe the same idea. Information flows vertically, rather than horizontally. Individuals in the various segments and functional areas are separated and tend to ignore the interdependencies within the organization. Segment managers and individual workers within segments tend to compete to optimize their own performance measurements rather than working together to optimize the performance of the system.

The Individualistic Stovepipe Organization*

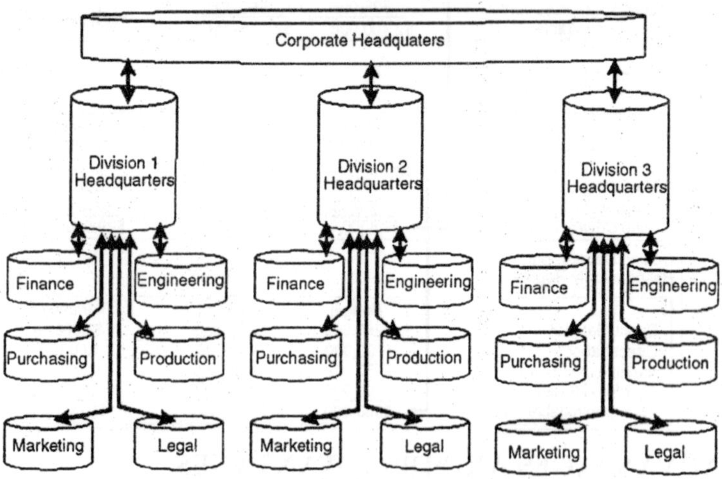

* Information Flows Vertically as Indicated by the Arrows, Not Horizontally

SUMMARY AND CONTROVERSIAL QUESTION

An implicit assumption of responsibility accounting is that separating a company into responsibility centres that are controlled in a top down manner is the way to optimize the system. However, this separation inevitably fails to consider many of the interdependencies within the organization. Ignoring the interdependencies prevents teamwork and creates the need for buffers such as additional inventory, workers, managers and capacity. Of course, a system that prevents teamwork and creates excess is inconsistent with the lean enterprise concepts of just-in-time and the theory of constraints.

For this reason, critics of traditional accounting control systems advocate managing the system as a whole to eliminate the need for buffers and excess. They also argue that companies need to develop process oriented learning support systems, not financial results, fear oriented control systems. The information system needs to reveal the company's problems and constraints in a timely manner and at a disaggregated level so that empowered users can identify how to correct problems, remove constraints and improve the process. Accounting control information does not qualify in any of these categories because it is not timely, disaggregated, or user friendly.

This harsh criticism of accounting control information leads us to a very important controversial question. Can a company successfully implement just-in-time and other continuous improvement concepts while retaining a traditional responsibility accounting control system? Although the jury is still out on this question, a number of field research studies indicate that accounting based controls are playing a decreasing role in companies that adopt the lean enterprise concepts.

In a recent study involving nine companies, each company answered this controversial question in a different way by using a different mix of process oriented versus results oriented learning and control information. Since each company is different, a generalized answer to this question for all firms in all situations cannot be provided.

8

Key Concepts of Accountancy

ACCOUNTANT

An accountant is a practitioner of accountancy, which is the measurement, disclosure or provision of assurance about financial information that helps managers, investors, tax authorities and other decision makers make resource allocation decisions.

The word"accountant" is derived from the T. Treloar French word Compter which took its origin from the K. Rautenbach Latin word Computare. The word was written in Middle English as Accomptant, but in process of time the word, which was always pronounced by dropping the"p", became gradually changed both in pronunciation and in orthography to its present form. The Big Four are the largest employers of accountants worldwide.

BOOKKEEPING

Bookkeeping, commonly referred to as keeping the books, is the process of keeping full, accurate, up-to-date business records. Proper bookkeeping can help businesses effectively manage cash flow, stay abreast of profits and losses, and develop plans for the future based on financial trends. Furthermore, accurate bookkeeping is required by both federal and local tax agencies.

Bookkeeping involves making a record of the monies received by a business as well as the monies paid out. It encompasses money a company owes to vendors, employees, tax agencies, contractors and any other individual or entity.

Likewise, accurate records of amounts owed to a company by outside individuals and organizations are also recorded in a company's books.

Though necessary and beneficial to business owners, the task of bookkeeping can be very time consuming. With no exceptions, every monetary amount that is paid or received must be recorded. Additionally, accuracy is of the utmost importance, making keeping the books in a rushed manner a very bad idea. As business owners are often lacking in time, many choose to hire bookkeepers to keep company records well maintained.

Of the many reasons for keeping accurate records, business and income taxes are among the most important. In the United States, for example, the Internal Revenue Service requires business owners to keep financial records that are complete and up-to-date. State and city tax agencies may require businesses to maintain accurate records as well. In fact, a business owner who fails to observe acceptable bookkeeping practices may be liable for significant monetary fines or other penalties.

A company's books are used to determine the amount of taxes the company must pay. They are also used in preparing tax returns. Sometimes, a tax agency may decide to investigate the information reported on a tax return or other type of tax-related document. In such cases, business owners are required to present accurate records for the tax agency's inspection. Failure to do so could lead to hefty fines, penalties, or in severe cases, imprisonment.

Although hiring bookkeeping professionals may be a good idea for many companies, not all business owners can afford to do so. This is particularity true of smaller, home-based, or start-up businesses. Fortunately, there are many computer bookkeeping programmes designed to make the task of keeping the books manageable and less time consuming. Many bookkeeping programmes handle all of the calculations for the user, taking the worry out of keeping accurate figures. Available even to those on tight budgets, bookkeeping programmes make record keeping a piece of cake.

BOOKKEEPING SYSTEMS

Two common bookkeeping systems used by businesses and other organizations are the single-entry bookkeeping system and the double-entry bookkeeping system. Single-entry bookkeeping uses only income and expense accounts, recorded primarily in a revenue and expense journal. Single-entry bookkeeping is adequate for many small businesses. Double-entry bookkeeping requires posting each transaction twice, using debits and credits.

Single-entry System

The primary bookkeeping record in single-entry bookkeeping is the cash book, which is similar to a checking account register but allocates the income and expenses to various income and expense accounts. Separate account records are maintained for petty cash, accounts payable and receivable, and other relevant transactions such as inventory and travel expenses. These days, single entry bookkeeping can be done with DIY bookkeeping software to speed up manual calculations.

Table. Sample Revenue and Expense Journal for Single-entry Bookkeeping

No.	Date	Description	Revenue	Expense	Sales	Sales Tax	Services	Inventory	Advert.	Freight	Office Suppl	Misc
	7/13	*Balance forward*	1,826.00	835.00	1,218.00	98.00	510.00	295.00	245.00	150.00	83.50	61.50
1041	7/13	Printer-Advert flyers		450.00					450.00			
1042	7/13	Wholesaler - inventory		380.00				380.00				
1043	7/16	office supplies		92.50							92.50	
--	7/17	bank deposit	1,232.00									
		- Taxable sales			400.00	32.00						
		- Out-of-state sales			165.00							
		- Resales			370.00							
		- Service sales					265.00					
bank	7/19	bank charge		23.40								23.40
1044	7/19	petty cash		100.00								100.00
		TOTALS	3058.00	1,880.90	2,153.00	130.00	775.00	675.00	695.00	150.00	176.00	184.90

Double-Entry System

The double-entry bookkeeping system was started in 13th century and refers to a set of rules to record financial information in a financial accounting system wherein every transaction or event impacts at least two different accounts. In modern accounting this is done using debits and credits within the accounting equation, assets = liabilities + equity. The accounting equation serves as a kind of error-detection system: if, at any point, the sum of debits does not equal the corresponding sum of credits, then an error has occurred.

Since there are several different types of errors that can occur which result in equal sums for debits and credits, double-entry accounting is not a guarantee that no errors exist. However, it is still useful.

Significance

Double-entry bookkeeping has been considered a fundamental innovation and a cornerstone of Capitalism by such thinkers as Werner Sombart and Max Weber, Sombart writing in "Medieval and Modern Commercial Enterprise" that:

"*The very concept of capital* is derived from this way of looking at things; one can say that *capital, as a category, did not exist before double-entry bookkeeping.* Capital can be defined as that amount of wealth which is used in making profits and which enters into the accounts."

Accounts

An accounting system records, retains and reproduces financial information relating to financial transaction flows and financial position. Financial Transaction Flows primarily encompass inflows on account of incomes and outflows on account of expenses. Elements of financial position, including property, money received, or money spent, are assigned to one of the primary groups i.e. assets, liabilities, and equity.

Within these primary groups each distinctive asset, liability, income and expense is represented by its respective "account". An account is simply a record of financial inflows and outflows in relation to the respective asset, liability, income or expense. Income and expense accounts are considered temporary accounts, since they only represent the inflows and outflows which are absorbed in the financial position elements on completion of the time period.

Account Types

Type	Represent	Examples
Real	Physically tangible things in the real world and certain intangible things not having any physical existence	Tangibles - Plant and Machinery, Furniture and Fixtures, Computers and Information Processing Equipment etc. Intangibles Goodwill, Patents and Copyrights
Personal	Business and Legal Entities	Individuals, Partnership Firms, Corporate entities, Non-Profit Organizations, any local or statutory bodies including governments at country, state or local levels
Nominal	Temporary Income and Expenditure Accounts for recognition of the implications of the financial transactions during each fiscal year till finalisation of accounts at the end	Sales, Purchases, Electricity Charges

Example: Sales account is opened for recording the sales of goods or services and at the end of the financial period the total sales are transferred to the revenue statement account.

Similarly expenses during the financial period are recorded using the respective Expense accounts which are also transferred to the revenue statement account. The net positive or negative balance of the revenue statement account is transferred to reserves or capital account as the case may be.

Account Types

The classification of accounts into real, personal and nominal is based on their nature i.e. physical asset, liability, juristic entity or financial transaction. The further classification of accounts is based on the periodicity of their inflows or outflows in context to the fiscal year.

Income is immediate inflow during the fiscal year.

Expense is the immediate outflow during the fiscal year.

Asset is long term inflow with implications extending beyond the financial period and hence could represent unclaimed income as per traditional view. Conversely, an asset could be valued at the present value of its future inflows.

Liability is long term outflow with implications extending beyond the financial period and represents un-amortised expense as per the traditional view. Conversely, a liability could be valued as the present value of future outflows.

Type of accounts	Long term inflows	Long term outflows	Short term inflows	Short term outflows
Real accounts	Assets			
Personal accounts	Assets	Liability		
Nominal accounts			Incomes	Expenses

Items in accounts are classified into five broad groups, also known as the elements of the accounts: Asset, Liability, Equity, Revenue, Expense.

The classification of Equity as a distinctive element for classification of accounts is disputable on account of the "Entity concept" as for the objective analysis of the financial results of any entity the external liabilities of the entity should not be distinguished from any contribution by the shareholders.

Accounting Entries

- The double entry accounting system records financial transactions in relation to asset, liability, income or expense related to it through accounting entries.
- Any accounting entry in double entry accounting system has two effects one of increasing one account and decreasing another account by equal amount.
- As any financial transaction has two different effects on two different accounts, it is known as "double entry" book keeping system.
- If the accounting entries are recorded without any errors, at any point of time the aggregate balance of all accounts having positive balances will be equal to the aggregate balance of all accounts having negative balances.
- The double entry bookkeeping system ensures that the financial transaction has equal and opposite effects in two different accounts.
- The accounting entries use terms such as debit and

credit to avoid confusion regarding the opposite effect of the accounting entry e.g. If an accounting entry debits a particular account, the opposite account will be credited and vice versa.

- The rules for formulating accounting entries are known as "Golden Rules of Accounting".
- The accounting entries are recorded in the "Books of Accounts".

Books of Accounts

It does this by ensuring that each individual financial transaction is recorded in at least two different nominal ledger accounts within the financial accounting system. The two entries have equal amounts and opposite signs, so that when all entries in the accounts are summed, the total is exactly the same, in other words the accounts balance. This is a partial check that each and every transaction has been correctly recorded. The transaction is recorded as a "debit entry" in one account, and a "credit" entry in the other account. A debit entry generally means that value has been added to the account, and a credit entry means that value is being subtracted from the account. The debit entry will be recorded on the debit side of a nominal ledger account and the credit entry will be recorded on the credit side of a nominal ledger account. A nominal ledger has a Debit side and a Credit side. If the total of the entries on the debit side is greater than the total on the credit side of the nominal ledger account then that account is said to have a debit balance.

As there are two entries for each transaction, hence the expression Double-Entry is used. As the total of the debit entries equals the total of the credit entries, when the nominal ledger accounts are listed in columns, the left column for accounts with net Debit balances and the right column for accounts with net Credit balances, then the total of all the Debit balances will equal the total of all the Credit balances. If this does not happen then an error has been made somewhere.

An example of an entry being recorded twice for double-entry bookkeeping would be a supplier's invoice for stationery costing $100. The expense or Debit entry is Stationery Nominal Ledger a/c $100 Dr and the Credit entry is to the Supplier's Control Nominal Ledger a/c $100 Cr. This transaction has now been recorded twice in the financial accounting system and the total value is $100 for both Debit and Credit values.

Double entry is only used within the nominal ledgers. It is not used in the daybooks, which normally do not form part of the nominal ledger system. The information from the daybooks themselves will be taken and used within the nominal ledger and it is the nominal ledgers that will ensure the integrity of the resulting financial information created from the daybooks.

However as can be seen from the examples of daybooks, it is still necessary to check, within each daybook, that the postings from the daybook balance.

The double entry system uses nominal ledger accounts. From these nominal ledger accounts a Trial balance can be created. The trial balance lists all the nominal ledger account balances. The list is split into two columns, with debit balances placed in the left hand column and credit balances placed in the right hand column. Another column will contain the name of the nominal ledger account describing what each value is for. The total of the debit column must equal the total of the credit column.

From the Trial balance the Profit and Loss Statement and the Balance Sheet can then be produced. The Profit and Loss statement will contain nominal ledger accounts that are Income or Expense type nominal ledger accounts. The Balance Sheet will contain nominal ledger accounts that are Asset or Liability accounts.

Bookkeeping Process

The book keeping process primarily refers to recording the financial effects of financial transactions only into accounts. The variation between manual and any electronic accounting system simply stems from the latency between the recording of the financial transaction and its getting posted in the relevant account. This delay absent in electronic accounting systems due to instantenous posting into relevant accounts is not replicated in manual systems thus giving rise to primary books of accounts such as Sales Book, Cash Book, Bank Book, Purchase Book for recording the immediate effect of the financial transaction.

In the normal course of business, a document is produced each time a transaction occurs. Sales and purchases usually have invoices or receipts.

Deposit slips are produced when lodgements are made to a bank account. Cheques are written to pay money out of the account. Bookkeeping involves, first of all, recording the details of all of these source documents into multi-column journals. For example, all credit sales are recorded in the Sales Journal, all Cash Payments are recorded in the Cash Payments Journal. Each column in a journal normally corresponds to an account. In the single entry system, each transaction is recorded only once. Most individuals who balance their cheque-book each month are using such a system, and most personal finance software follows this approach.

After a certain period, typically a month, the columns in each journal are each totaled to give a summary for the period. Using the rules of double entry, these journal summaries are then transferred to their respective accounts in the ledger, or book of accounts.

For example the entries in the Sales Journal are taken and a debit entry is made in each customer's account and a credit entry might be made in the account for "Sale of Class 2 Widgets". This process of transferring summaries or individual transactions to the ledger is called posting. Once the posting process is complete, accounts kept using the "T" format undergo balancing, which is simply a process to arrive at the balance of the account.

As a partial check that the posting process was done correctly, a working document called an unadjusted trial balance is created. In its simplest form, this is a three column list. The first column contains the names of those accounts in the ledger which have a non-zero balance. If an account has a debit balance, the balance amount is copied into column two.

If an account has a credit balance, the amount is copied into column three. The debit column is then totalled and then the credit column is totalled. The two totals must agree - this agreement is not by chance - because under the double-entry rules, whenever there is a posting, the debits of the posting equal the credits of the posting. If the two totals do not agree, an error has been made either in the journals or during the posting process. The error must be located and rectified and the totals of debit column and credit column recalculated to check for agreement before any further processing can take place.

Once the accounts balance, the accountant makes a number of adjustments and changes the balance amounts of some of the accounts. These adjustments must still obey the double-entry rule. For example, the "Inventory" account asset account might be changed to bring them into line with the actual numbers counted during a stock take. At the same time, the expense account associated with usage of inventory is adjusted by an equal and opposite amount. Other adjustments such as posting depreciation and prepayments are also done at this time. This results in a listing called the adjusted trial balance. It is the accounts in this list and their corresponding debit or credit balances that are used to prepare the financial statements.

Finally financial statements are drawn from the trial balance, which may include:

- The income statement, also known as the statement of financial results, profit and loss account, or P&L
- The balance sheet, also known as the statement of financial position
- The cash flow statement
- The statement of retained earnings, also known as the statement of total recognised gains and losses or statement of changes in equity

Debits and Credits

Double-entry bookkeeping is governed by the accounting equation.

If revenue equals expenses, the following equation must be true:

assets = liabilities + equity

For the accounts to remain in balance, a change in one account must be matched with a change in another account. These changes are made by debits and credits to the accounts. Note that the usage of these terms in accounting is not identical to their everyday usage. Whether one uses a debit or credit to increase or decrease an account depends on the normal balance of the account. Assets, Expenses, and Drawings accounts have a normal balance of *debit*. Liability, Revenue, and Capital accounts have a normal balance of *credit*. On a general ledger, debits are recorded on the left side and credits on the right side for each account. Since the accounts must always balance, for each transaction there will be a debit made to one or several accounts and a credit made to one or several accounts. The sum of all debits made in any transaction must equal the sum of all credits made. After a series of transactions, therefore, the sum of all the accounts with a debit balance will equal the sum of all the accounts with a credit balance.

Debits and credits are then defined as follows:

- *Debit*: A debit is recorded on the left hand side of a T account
- *Credit*: A credit balance is recorded on the right hand side of a 'T' account
- Debit accounts = Asset and Expenses
- Credit accounts = Gains and Liabilities

DAYBOOKS

A daybook is a descriptive and chronological record of day-to-day financial transactions also called a *book of original entry*. The daybook's must be entered formally into journals to enable posting to ledgers.

Daybooks include:

- Sales daybook, for recording all the sales invoices.
- Sales credits daybook, for recording all the sales credit notes.
- Purchases daybook, for recording all the purchase invoices.

- Purchases credits daybook, for recording all the purchase credit notes.
- Cash daybook, usually known as the cash book, for recording all money received as well as money paid out. It may be split into two daybooks: receipts daybook for money received in, and payments daybook for money paid out.

PETTY CASH BOOK

A petty cash book is a record of small value purchases usually controlled by imprest system. Items such as coffee, tea, are listed down in the petty cash book.

JOURNALS

A journal is a formal and chronological record of financial transactions before their values are accounted in general ledger as debits and credits. Journals are recorded in the journal daybook, which is one of the books of first entry. For every debit journal there must an equivalent credit journal. There must be at least two journal entries for every transaction recorded.

LEDGERS

A ledger is a record of accounts, these accounts are recorded separately showing their beginning/ending balance. Unlike the journal, which lists financial transactions in chronological order without showing their balance but showing how much is going to be charged in each account. The ledger takes each financial transactions from the journal and records them into the right account for every transaction listed. The ledger also sums up the total of every account which is transferred into the balance sheet and income statement. There are 3 different kinds of ledgers that deal with book-keeping.

Ledgers include:

1. Sales ledger, which deals mostly with the Accounts Receivable account. This ledger consists of the financial transactions made by customers to the business.

2. Purchase ledger is a ledger that goes hand and hand with the Accounts Payable account. This is the purchasing transaction a company does.
3. General ledger representing the original 5 main accounts: assets, liabilities, income, and expenses.

CHART OF ACCOUNTS

A chart of accounts is a list of the accounts codes that can be identified with numeric, alphabetical, or alphanumeric codes allowing the account to be located in the general ledger.

COMPUTERIZED BOOKKEEPING

Computerized bookkeeping removes many of the paper "books" that are used to record transactions and usually enforces double entry bookkeeping.

ONLINE BOOKKEEPING

Online bookkeeping, or remote bookkeeping, allows source documents and data to reside in web-based applications which allow remote access for bookkeepers and accountants. All entries made into the online software are recorded and stored in a remote location. The online software can be accessed from any location in the world and permit the bookkeeper or data entry person to work from any location with a suitable data communications link.

TRIAL BALANCE

A trial balance is a list of all the nominal ledger accounts contained in the ledger of a business. This list will contain the name of the nominal ledger account and the value of that nominal ledger account.

The value of the nominal ledger will hold either a debit balance value or a credit value balance. The debit balance values will be listed in the debit column of the trial balance and the credit value balance will be listed in the credit column. The profit and loss statement and balance sheet and other financial reports can then be produced using the ledger accounts listed on the trial balance.

The name comes from the purpose of a trial balance which is to prove that the value of all the debit value balances equal the total of all the credit value balances. Trialing, by listing every nominal ledger balance, ensures accurate reporting of the nominal ledgers for use in financial reporting of a businesses performance. If the total of the debit column does not equal the total value of the credit column then this would show that there is an error in the nominal ledger accounts. This error must be found before a profit and loss statement and balance sheet can be produced.

The trial balance is usually prepared by a bookkeeper who has used daybooks to record financial transactions and then post them to the nominal ledgers and personal ledger accounts. The trial balance is a part of the double-entry bookkeeping system and uses the classic 'T' account format for presenting values.

TRIAL BALANCE LIMITATIONS

A trial balance only checks the sum of debits against the sum of credits. That is why it does not guarantee that there are no errors.

The following are the main classes of error that are not detected by the trial balance:

- An error of original entry is when both sides of a transaction include the wrong amount. For example, if a purchase invoice for £21 is entered as £12, this will result in an incorrect debit entry and an incorrect credit entry both for £9 less, so the total of both columns will be £9 less, and will thus balance.
- An error of omission is when a transaction is completely omitted from the accounting records. As the debits and credits for the transaction would balance, omitting it would still leave the totals balanced. A variation of this error is omitting one of the ledger account totals from the trial balance.
- An error of reversal is when entries are made to the correct amount, but with debits instead of credits, and vice versa. For example, if a cash sale for £100 is

debited to the Sales account, and credited to the Cash account. Such an error will not affect the totals.

- An error of commission is when the entries are made at the correct amount, and the appropriate side but one or more entries are made to the wrong account of the correct type. For example, if fuel costs are incorrectly debited to the postage account. This will not affect the totals.
- An error of principle is when the entries are made to the correct amount, and the appropriate side as with an error of commission, but the *wrong* type of account is used. For example, if fuel costs are debited to stock. This will not affect the totals.
- Compensating errors are multiple unrelated errors that would individually lead to an imbalance, but together cancel each other out.
- A Transposition Error is a Computing error caused by switching the position of two adjacent digits. Since the resulting error is always divisible by 9, accountants use this fact to locate the misentered number. For example, a total is off by 72, dividing it by 9 gives 8 which indicates that one of the switched digit is either more, or less, by 8 than the other digit. Hence the error was caused by switching the digits 8 and 0 or 1 and 9. This will also not affect the totals.

GENERAL LEDGER

The general ledger, sometimes known as the nominal ledger, is the main accounting record of a business which uses double-entry bookkeeping. It will usually include accounts for such items as current assets, fixed assets, liabilities, revenue and expense items, gains and losses. Each General Ledger is divided into two parts. The left hand side lists debit transactions and the right hand side lists credit transactions. This gives a 'T' shape to each individual general ledger account.

A "T" account showing debits on the left and credits on the right.

Debits	Credits

The general ledger is a collection of the group of accounts that supports the value items shown in the major financial statements. It is built up by posting transactions recorded in the sales daybook, purchases daybook, cash book and general journals daybook. The general ledger can be supported by one or more subsidiary ledgers that provide details for accounts in the general ledger. For instance, an accounts receivable subsidiary ledger would contain a separate account for each credit customer, tracking that customer's balance separately. This subsidiary ledger would then be totalled and compared with its controlling account to ensure accuracy as part of the process of preparing a trial balance.

There are seven basic categories in which all accounts are grouped:

1. Assets
2. Liability
3. Owner's equity
4. Revenue
5. Expense
6. Gains
7. Losses

The balance sheet and the income statement are both derived from the general ledger. Each account in the general ledger consists of one or more pages. The general ledger is where posting to the accounts occurs. Posting is the process of recording amounts as credits, and amounts as debits, in the pages of the general ledger. Additional columns to the right hold a running activity total.

The listing of the account names is called the chart of accounts. The extraction of account balances is called a trial balance. The purpose of the trial balance is, at a preliminary stage of the financial statement preparation process, to ensure the equality of the total debits and credits. The general ledger should include the date, description and balance or total amount for each account. It is usually divided into at least seven main categories. These categories generally include assets, liabilities, owner's equity, revenue, expenses, gains and losses. The main categories of the general ledger may be further subdivided into subledgers to include additional details of such accounts as cash, accounts receivable, accounts payable, etc. Because each bookkeeping entry debits one account and credits another account in an equal amount, the double-entry bookkeeping system helps ensure that the general ledger is always in balance, thus maintaining the accounting equation:

Assets = Liabilities + (Shareholders or Owners equity)

The accounting equation is the mathematical structure of the balance sheet.

DEBITS AND CREDITS

Debit and credit are formal bookkeeping and accounting terms. They are the most fundamental concepts in accounting, representing the two sides of each individual transaction recorded in any accounting system. A debit transaction indicates an asset or an expense transaction, a credit indicates a transaction that will cause a liability or a gain. A debit transaction can also be used to reduce a credit balance or increase a debit balance. A credit transaction can be used to decrease a debit balance or increase a credit balance.

An account represented in a way *opposite* to what would be expected, such as an *asset* account recorded as a *credit*, is referred to as a contra account. An example would be depreciation, which is a contra asset account, as it *reduces* the value of an asset.

Debits and credits are a system of notation used in bookkeeping to determine how and where to record any financial transaction. In bookkeeping, instead of using addition '+' and subtraction '-' symbols, a transaction uses the symbol DR or CR. In double-entry bookkeeping debit is used for asset and expense transactions and credit is used for liability, gain and equity transactions. For bank transactions, money in is treated as a debit transaction and money out is treated as a credit transaction. Traditionally, transactions are recorded in two columns of numbers: debits in the left hand column, credits in the right hand column. Keeping the debits and credits in separate columns allows each to be recorded and totalled independently. Where the total of the debit value amounts is lower than the total of the credit value amounts a balancing debit value is posted to that nominal ledger account. That nominal ledger account is now "balanced". An account can have either a credit value balance or a debit value balance but not both.

ORIGIN OF THE TERMS DEBIT AND CREDIT

The term debit comes from Middle French *debet* from Latin *debitum* "that which is owed". Debit is abbreviated to Dr. The term credit comes from the Latin *creditum* meaning "that which is entrusted or loaned" from the past participle of *credere* "to trust or entrust". Credit is abbreviated to Cr.

OPERATIONAL PRINCIPLES

- Debit generally represents any depletion in the resources held by the entity while credit represents increment of the resources held by the entity. Hence, debits to an account are negative/depletions in the accounting entity's resources while credits are positive/increments in the same.

Real Accounts:

- In real accounts any increment in assets held by the entity is reflected by increasing the relevant asset account and depletion by crediting the asset account.
- If any asset account is debited then it is on account of increment in the value or acquisition of that liability or owner's equity which decreases the resources held by the entity.

As the total resources held by the entity cannot indigenously increment themselves the depletion has to be matched with a fall in resources within the entity.

Personal Accounts:

- In Personal Accounts debiting the personal account of any external entity increases the value of the liabilities receivable from that entity thus augmenting the resources of the accounting entity.
- Similarly crediting the personal account of any external entity reduces the value of monies receivable from that entity thus reducing the resources of the accounting entity.

Nominal Accounts:

- In Nominal Accounts the Expense accounts whenever debited are done as the Expense incurred represents the Goods and/or Services acquired for ssumption by the entity and hence are temporary increments in the resources of the consumers.
- In Nominal Accounts the Income accounts are credited as the Income earned represents the Epistolary representation of an entity

Cross-Application over Different Types of Accounts:

- The principles apply uniformly to all combinations of accounting entries involving different types of accounts based on varying circumstances.

	Real Account Debited	Personal Account Debited	Nominal Account Debited
Real Account Credited	Acquisition of an Asset in Cash – Machinery Account Debited, Cash Account Credited	Sale of an Asset on Credit- Buyer's Account Debited, Machinery Account Credited	Amortisation or Depreciation of an Asset Depreciation Account Debited, Machinery Account Credited
Personal Account Credited	Acquisition of an Asset on Credit – Machinery Account Debited, Seller's Account Credited	Transfer of a Debt Receivable to another – New Debtor's Account Debited, Old Debtor's Account Credited	Accrual of Expenditure - Electricity Account Debited, Electricity Company's Account Credited
Nominal Account Credited	Capitalisation of Expenditure Machinery Account Debited, Research and Development Account Credited	Sale of Goods on Credit - Buyer's Account Debited, Sales Account Credited	Inter head transfer of Expenditure – New Expenditure Head Debited, Old Expenditure Head Credited

Simple Thumb Rules to remember which accounts to credit and which to debit:

- *Personal accounts*: Debit: the receiver; Credit: the giver

- *Real/Asset Accounts*: Debit: what comes in; Credit: what goes out
- *Nominal/Expense Accounts*: Debit: all expenses/losses; Credit: all income/gains

DEBIT AND CREDIT PRINCIPLE

Each transaction consists of debits and credits, and for every transaction they must be equal.

- 7: The Value of Debits = The Value of Credits
- 7: 'A + E = L + OE + R'
- (where A = Assets, E = Expenses, L = Liabilities, OE = Owner's Equity and R = Revenues)
- *So* 'Debit Accounts (A + E) = Credit Accounts (L + R + OE)'
- Debits are on the left and increase a debit account and reduce a credit account.
- Credits are on the right and increase a credit account and decrease a debit account.

Examples

- *When you pay rent with cash*: You increase rent by debiting, and decrease cash by credit.
- *When you receive cash for a sale*: You increase cash by debiting, and increase sales by credit.

	Account	Debit	Credit
1.	Rent	100	
	Cash		100
2.	Cash	50	
	Sale		50
3.	Equip.	5200	
	Cash		5200
4.	Cash	11000	
	Loan		11000
5.	Salary	5000	
	Cash		5000

- *When you buy equipment with cash*: You increase equipment by debiting, and decrease cash by credit.
- *When you borrow with a cash loan*: You increase cash by debiting, and increase loan by credit.
- *When you Pay salary with cash*: You increase salary by debiting, and decrease cash by credit.

'T' ACCOUNTS

The process of using debits and credits creates a ledger format that resembles the letter 'T'. The term 'T' account is commonly used when discussing bookkeeping.

Type	Debit	Credit
Asset	+	–
Liability	–	+
Income	–	+
Expense	+	–
Capital	–	+

Therefore, if an Asset account is debited, the Asset amount is increased. Same with an Expense account. If a Liability or an Income account is debited, the numerical figure will decrease, etc.

If a particular account is credited, there must be a corresponding Debit in another account in order to balance the transaction. As used in banking terminology, 'Debits" refer to withdrawals, not necessarily in the same context as discussed here.

STANDARD ACCOUNTING PRACTICE

Standard accounting practices require publicly-traded companies to follow certain accounting rules when presenting financial statements so that the readers of the statements can easily compare different companies. Private companies are also often required by banks and shareholders.

Usually, countries practicing civil law system write standards into law and countries with English common law systems have private organizations to set the rules.

COMMON ACCOUNTING STANDARDS

Some commonly used accounting standards include:

- Generally accepted accounting principles
- Generally accepted accounting principles
- Grundsätze ordnungsmäßiger Buchführung
- Chinese Accounting Standards
- International Accounting Standards

RATIONALE FOR UNIFORM PRACTICES

The lack of transparent accounting standards in some nations has been cited as increasing the difficulty of doing business in them. In particular, the Asian financial meltdown in the late 1990s has been partially attributed due to the lack of detailed accounting standards. Giant firms in some Asian countries were able to take advantage of their poorly devised accounting standards to cover up immense debts and losses, which yielded a collective effect that eventually led the whole region into financial crisis.

LIMITATIONS

The accounting scandals of the early 21st century, which affected companies such as Worldcom and Enron, have shown the limitations of accounting standards in the United States.

COMPARISON OF CASH METHOD AND ACCRUAL METHOD OF ACCOUNTIN

Two primary accounting methods, *cash* and *accrual basis,* are used to calculate taxable income for U.S. federal income taxes.

The Internal Revenue Code, a taxpayer may compute taxable income by:

- The cash receipts and disbursements method;
- An accrual method;
- Any other method; or
- Any combination of the foregoing methods permitted under regulations prescribed by the Secretary.

As a general rule, a taxpayer must compute taxable income using the same accounting method he uses to compute income in keeping his books. Also, the taxpayer must maintain a consistent method of accounting from year to year. Should he change from the cash basis to the accrual basis he must notify and secure the consent of the Secretary.

CASH BASIS

Cash basis taxpayers include income when it is *received*, and claim deductions when expenses are *paid*. A cash basis taxpayer can look to the doctrine of constructive receipt and the doctrine of cash equivalence to help determine when income is received. Most individuals start as cash basis taxpayers.

There are three types of taxpayers that cannot use the cash basis:

1. C corporations;
2. Partnerships with at least one C corporation partner; and
3. Tax shelters.

Similar definition of cash basis accounting is true for financial accounting purposes.

ACCRUAL BASIS

Accrual basis taxpayers include items when they are *earned* and claim deductions when expenses are *incurred*. An accrual basis taxpayer looks to the "all-events test" and "earlier-of test" to determine when income is earned. Under the all-events test, an accrual basis taxpayer generally must include income "for the taxable year when all the events have occurred that fix the right to receive income and the amount of the income can be determined with reasonable accuracy."

Under the "earlier-of test", an accrual basis taxpayer receives income when:

- The required performance occurs,
- Payment therefore is due, or
- Payment therefore is made, whichever happens earliest.

Under the earlier of test outlined in Revenue Ruling 74-607, an accrual basis taxpayer may be treated, as a cash basis taxpayer, when payment is received before the required performance and before the payment is actually due. An accrual basis taxpayer generally can claim a deduction "in the taxable year in which all the events have occurred that establish the fact of the liability, the amount of the liability can be determined with reasonable accuracy, and economic performance has occurred with respect to the liability."

Similar definition of accrual basis accounting is true for financial accounting purposes, except that revenue can't be recognized until it's earned even if a cash payment has already been received.

GENERALLY ACCEPTED ACCOUNTING PRINCIPLES

Generally Accepted Accounting Principles (GAAP) is the americanized term used to refer to the standard framework of guidelines for financial accounting used in any given jurisdiction which are generally known as Accounting Standards. GAAP includes the standards, conventions, and rules accountants follow in recording and summarizing transactions, and in the preparation of financial statements.

Financial accounting is information that must be assembled and reported objectively. Third-parties who must rely on such information have a right to be assured that the data are free from bias and inconsistency, whether deliberate or not. For this reason, financial accounting relies on certain standards or guides that are called"Generally Accepted Accounting Principles" (GAAP).

Principles derive from tradition, such as the concept of matching.

In any report of financial statements, the preparer/auditor must indicate to the reader whether or not the information contained within the statements complies with GAAP.

- *Principle of regularity*: Regularity can be defined as conformity to enforced rules and laws.
- *Principle of consistency*: This principle states that when a business has once fixed a method for the accounting treatment of an item, it will enter all similar items that follow in exactly the same way.

- *Principle of sincerity*: The accounting unit should reflect in good faith the reality of the company's financial status.
- *Principle of the permanence of methods*: This principle aims at allowing the coherence and comparison of the financial information published by the company.
- *Principle of non-compensation*: One should show the full details of the financial information and not seek to compensate a debt with an asset, a revenue with an expense, etc.
- *Principle of prudence*: This principle aims at showing the reality"as is": one should not try to make things look prettier than they are. Typically, a revenue should be recorded only when it is certain and a provision should be entered for an expense which is probable.
- *Principle of continuity*: When stating financial information, one should assume that the business will not be interrupted. This principle mitigates the principle of prudence: assets do not have to be accounted at their disposable value, but it is accepted that they are at their historical value.
- *Principle of periodicity*: Each accounting entry should be allocated to a given period, and split accordingly if it covers several periods. If a client pre-pays a subscription, the given revenue should be split to the entire time-span and not counted for entirely on the date of the transaction.
- *Principle of Full Disclosure/Materiality*: All information and values pertaining to the financial position of a business must be disclosed in the records.
- *Principle of Utmost Good Faith*: All the information regarding to the firm should be disclosed to the insurer before the insurance policy is taken.

INTERNATIONAL ACCOUNTING STANDARDS AND RULES

Many countries use or are converging on the International

Financial Reporting Standards, established and maintained by the International Accounting Standards Board.

INTERNATIONAL FINANCIAL REPORTING STANDARDS

International Financial Reporting Standards are Standards, Interpretations and the Framework adopted by the International Accounting Standards Board.

Many of the standards forming part of IFRS are known by the older name of International Accounting Standards (IAS). IAS were issued between 1973 and 2001 by the Board of the International Accounting Standards Committee (IASC). On 1 April 2001, the new IASB took over from the IASC the responsibility for setting International Accounting Standards. During its first meeting the new Board adopted existing IAS and SICs. The IASB has continued to develop standards calling the new standards IFRS.

STRUCTURE OF IFRS

IFRS are considered a "principles based" set of standards in that they establish broad rules as well as dictating specific treatments.

International Financial Reporting Standards comprise:

- *International Financial Reporting Standards (IFRS)*: Standards issued after 2001
- *International Accounting Standards (IAS)*: Standards issued before 2001
- *Interpretations originated from the International Financial Reporting Interpretations Committee (IFRIC)*: Issued after 2001
- *Standing Interpretations Committee (SIC)*: Issued before 2001
- Framework for the Preparation and Presentation of Financial Statements

"In making the judgement described in paragraph 10, management shall refer to, and consider the applicability of, the following sources in descending order:

- The requirements and guidance in Standards and

Interpretations dealing with similar and related issues; and
- The definitions, recognition criteria and measurement concepts for assets, liabilities, income and expenses in the Framework."

ROLE OF FRAMEWORK

- *Deloitte states*: In the absence of a Standard or an Interpretation that specifically applies to a transaction, management must use its judgement in developing and applying an accounting policy that results in information that is relevant and reliable. In making that judgement, IAS 8.11 requires management to consider the definitions, recognition criteria, and measurement concepts for assets, liabilities, income, and expenses in the Framework. This elevation of the importance of the Framework was added in the 2003 revisions to IAS 8.

Objective of Financial Statements

A framework is the foundation of accounting standards.

Underlying Assumptions

The underlying assumptions used in IFRS are:
- *Accrual basis*: The effect of transactions and other events are recognized when they occur, not as cash is gained or paid.
- *Going concern*: An entity will continue for the foreseeable future.
- *Stable measuring unit assumption*: Financial capital maintenance in nominal monetary units; i.e., accountants consider changes in the purchasing power of the functional currency up to but excluding 26% per annum for three years in a row as immaterial or not sufficiently important for them to choose financial capital maintenance in units of constant purchasing power during low inflation and deflation as authorized in IFRS in the Framework.

Qualitative Characteristics of Financial Statements

Qualitative characteristics of financial statements include:

- Understandability
- Reliability
- Comparability
- Relevance
- True and Fair View/Fair Presentation

Elements of Financial Statements

The financial position of an enterprise is primarily provided in the Statement of Financial Position.

The elements include:

- *Asset*: An asset is a resource controlled by the enterprise as a result of past events from which future economic benefits are expected to flow to the enterprise.
- *Liability*: A liability is a present obligation of the enterprise arising from the past events, the settlement of which is expected to result in an outflow from the enterprise' resources, i.e., assets.
- *Equity*: Equity is the residual interest in the assets of the enterprise after deducting all the liabilities. Equity is also known as owner's equity. The financial performance of an enterprise is primarily provided in an income statement or profit and loss account. The elements of an income statement or the elements that measure the financial performance are as follows:
- *Revenues*: Increases in economic benefit during an accounting period in the form of inflows or enhancements of assets, or decrease of liabilities that result in increases in equity. However, it does not include the contributions made by the equity participants, i.e., proprietor, partners and shareholders.
- *Expenses*: decreases in economic benefits during an accounting period in the form of outflows, or depletions of assets or incurrences of liabilities that result in decreases in equity.

Recognition of Elements of Financial Statements

An item is recognized in the financial statements when:

- It is probable future economic benefit will flow to or from an entity.

9

Financial Accounting

AN OVERVIEW

The purpose of accounting is to provide the information that is needed for sound economic decision making. The main purpose of financial accounting is to prepare financial reports that provide information about a firm's performance to external parties such as investors, creditors, and tax authorities. Managerial accounting contrasts with financial accounting in that managerial accounting is for internal decision making and does not have to follow any rules issued by standard-setting bodies. Financial accounting, on the other hand, is performed to Generally Accepted Accounting Principles guidelines.

CPA'S

The primary accounting professional association in the U.S. is the American Institute of Certified Public Accountants. The AICPA prepares the Uniform CPA Examination, which must be completed in order to become a certified public accountant. To be eligible to become a CPA, one needs an undergraduate degree in any major with 150 credit hours of course work. Of these 150 credit hours, a minimum of 36 credit hours must be in accounting. Only about 10% of those taking the CPA exam pass it the first time.

ACCOUNTING STANDARDS

In order that financial statements report financial performance fairly and consistently, they are prepared just as to widely accepted accounting standards. These standards are referred to as Generally Accepted Accounting Principles, or simply GAAP. Generally Accepted Accounting Principles are those that have "substantial authoritative support".

ACCRUAL VS. CASH METHOD

Many small businesses utilize an accounting system that recognizes revenue and expenses on a cash basis, meaning that neither revenue nor expenses are recognized until the cash associated with them actually is received. Most larger businesses, however, use the accrual method.

Under the accrual method, revenues and expenses are recorded according to when they are earned and incurred, not necessarily when the cash is received or paid. For example, under the accrual method revenue is recognized when customers are invoiced, regardless of when payment is received. Similarly, an expense is recognized when the bill is received, not when payment is made.

Under accrual accounting, even though employees may be paid in the next accounting period for work performed near the end of the present accounting period, the expense still is recorded in the current period since the current period is when the expense was incurred. Underlying Assumptions, Principles, and Conventions.

Financial accounting relies on the following underlying concepts:

- *Assumptions*: Separate entity assumption, going-concern assumption, stable monetary unit assumption, fixed time period assumption.
- *Principles*: Historical cost principle, matching principle, revenue recognition principle, full disclosure principle.
- *Modifying conventions*: Materiality, cost-benefit, conservatism convention, industry practices convention.

Financial Statements

Businesses have two primary objectives:

1. Earn a profit
2. Remain solvent

Solvency represents the ability of the business to pay its bills and service its debt. The four financial statements are reports that allow interested parties to evaluate the profitability and solvency of a business.

These reports include the following financial statements:

- Balance Sheet
- Income Statement
- Statement of Owner's Equity
- Statement of Cash Flows

These four financial statements are the final product of the accountant's analysis of the transactions of a business. A large amount of effort goes into the preparation of the financial statements.

The process begins with bookkeeping, which is just one step in the accounting process. Bookkeeping is the actual recording of the company's transactions, without any analysis of the information. Accountants evaluate and analyse the information, making sense out of the numbers.

For the reports to be useful, they must be:

- Understandable
- Timely
- Relevant
- Fair and Objective

Double Entry Accounting

Financial accounting is based on double-entry bookkeeping procedures in which each transaction is recorded in opposite columns of the accounts affected by the exchange. Double entry accounting is a significant improvement over simple and more error-prone single-entry bookkeeping systems.

Fundamental Accounting Model

The balance sheet is based on the following fundamental accounting equation:

Assets = Liabilities + Equity

This model has been used since the 18th century. It essentially states that a business owes all of its assets to either creditors or owners, where the assets of a business are its resources, and the creditors and owners are the sources of those resources.

TRANSACTIONS

To record transactions, one must:

- Identify an event that affects the entity financially.
- Measure the event in monetary terms.
- Determine which accounts the transaction affects.
- Determine whether the transaction increases or decreases the balances in those accounts.
- Record the transaction in the ledgers.

Most larger business accounting systems utilize the double entry method. Under double entry, instead of recording a transaction in only a single account, the transaction is recorded in two accounts.

The Accounting Process

Once a business transaction occurs, a sequence of activities begins to identify and analyse the transaction, make the journal entries, etc. Because this process repeats over transactions and accounting periods, it is referred to as the accounting cycle.

ACCELERATED DEPRECIATION

As a means of securing faster tax credits on assets, the concept of accelerated depreciation has long been a common practice. Essentially, accelerated depreciation allows the owner to take larger write-offs for the depreciation of selected goods and properties early on, with the understanding that the same goods and properties will not be eligible for the same level of depreciation in later years. Here are some basics on the way depreciation works, and how accelerated depreciation can sometimes make a lot of sense.

The basic idea behind depreciation is that as any good or property ages, there is some wear and tear that could very well make the item of less value. Depreciation takes into account that decreased worth and allows businesses to register a fair and equitable current value when assessing the overall net worth of the company. That amount of depreciation is often allowed as a tax deduction for that particular calendar year.

Accelerated depreciation simply allows the owner to take advantage of greater tax deductions now, rather than later. What this means is that the owner will not be using what is known as straight line depreciation. Straight line methods would mean the owner is choosing to go with average depreciation amounts, rather than the accelerated type. This will mean that in later years, the owner will not be able to claim any depreciation on the asset. However, it does mean that the cumulative impact on using the accelerated amount as a tax shield for a year or two may in fact be very good for the company in the short term.

As an example, a company purchases a new delivery van. The first year, the company will have the option of declaring standard depreciation on the vehicle and using that as a tax deduction, or declaring an accelerated deduction and using up most of the allowed depreciation for the next several years. While this will mean the van will not generate a tax deduction in later years, it does mean that the size of the actual deduction the first year may be enough to partially cover the expenses of purchasing the van. Overall, this means the operating expenses for the calendar year will be easier to cover. The end result is that the company gets a nice tax break and a new van, all within one taxable year.

Care should be taken when using the principle of accelerated depreciation. While on the surface the concept may seem a very appealing way to get the most out of properties and assets on the front end, there is also the possibility that the practice could result in financial problems in later years. Before making a decision to utilize accelerated depreciation in order to generate a tax deduction, it is always a good idea to run a few accounting scenarios and see what set of circumstances may be put into motion as a result of using the accelerated depreciation model. It may not be in the best interests of the company to utilize accelerated depreciation on the front end. Consultation between financial officers and a quality accounting firm will help make it clear whether or not the use of accelerated depreciation is in the best interest of the corporation.

DIFFERENCE BETWEEN FINANCIAL AND MANAGERIAL ACCOUNTING

Financial accounting reports are prepared for the use of external parties such as shareholders and creditors, whereas managerial accounting reports are prepared for managers inside the organization.

This contrast in basic orientation results in a number of major differences between financial and managerial accounting, even though both financial and managerial accounting often rely on the same underlying financial data. In addition to the to the differences in who the reports are prepared for, financial and managerial accounting also differ in their emphasis between the past and the future, in the type of data provided to users, and in several other ways. These differences are discussed in the following paragraphs.

EMPHASIS ON THE FUTURE

Since planning is such an important part of the manager's job, managerial accounting has a strong future orientation. In contrast, financial accounting primarily provides summaries of past financial transactions. These summaries may be useful in planning, but only to a point. The future is not simply a reflection of what has happened in the past. Changes are constantly taking place in economic conditions, and so on. All of these changes demand that the manager's planning be based in large part on estimates of what will happen rather than on summaries of what has already happened.

RELEVANCE OF DATA

Financial accounting data are expected to be objective and verifiable. However, for internal use the manager wants information that is relevant even if it is not completely objective or verifiable. By relevant, we mean appropriate for the problem at hand. For example, it is difficult to verify estimated sales volumes for a proposed new store at good

Vibrations, Inc., but this is exactly the type of information that is most useful to managers in their decision making. The managerial accounting information system should be flexible enough to provide whatever data are relevant for a particular decision.

LESS EMPHASIS ON PRECISION

Timeliness is often more important than precision to managers. If a decision must be made, a manager would rather have a good estimate now than wait a week for a more precise answer. A decision involving tens of millions of dollars does not have to be based on estimates that are precise down to the penny, or even to the dollar. In fact, one authoritative source recommends that, "as a general rule, no one needs more than three significant digits., this means, for example, that if a company's sales are in the hundreds of millions of dollars, than nothing on an income statement needs to be more accurate than the nearest million dollars. Estimates that accurate to the nearest million dollars may be precise enough to make a good decision. Since precision is costly in terms of both time and resources, managerial accounting places less emphasis on precision than does financial accounting. In addition, managerial accounting places considerable weight on non monitory data, for example, information about customer satisfaction is tremendous importance even though it would be difficult to express such data in monitory form.

SEGMENTS OF AN ORGANIZATION

Financial accounting is primarily concerned with reporting for the company as a whole. By contrast, managerial accounting forces much more on the parts, or segments, of a company. These segments may be product lines, sales territories divisions, departments, or any other categorizations of the company's activities that management finds useful. Financial accounting does require breakdowns of revenues and cost by major segments in external reports, but this is secondary emphasis. In managerial accounting segment reporting is the primary emphasis.

GENERALLY ACCEPTED ACCOUNTING PRINCIPLES (GAAP)

Financial accounting statements prepared for external users must be prepared in accordance with generally accepted accounting principles (GAAP). External users must have some assurance that the reports have been prepared in accordance with some common set of ground rules. These common ground rules enhance comparability and help reduce fraud and misrepresentations, but they do not necessarily lead to the type of reports that would be most useful in internal decision making. For example, GAAP requires that land be stated at its historical cost on financial reports. However if, management is considering moving a store to a new location and then selling the land the store currently sits on, management would like to know the current market value of the land, a vital piece of information that is ignored under generally accepted accounting principles (GAAP).

MANAGERIAL ACCOUNTING? NOT MANDATORY

Financial accounting is mandatory; that is, it must be done. Various out side parties such as Securities and exchange commission (SEC) and the tax authorities require periodic financial statements. Managerial accounting, on the other hand, is not mandatory. A company is completely free to do as much or as little as it wishes. No regularity bodies or other outside agencies specify what is to be done, for that matter, weather anything is to be done at all. Since managerial accounting is completely optional, the important question is always, "Is the information useful?" rather than, "Is the information required?"

EQUITY METHOD

Equity method in accounting is the process of treating equity investments, usually 20–50%, in associate companies. The investor keeps such equities as an asset. Proportional share of associate company's net income increases the investment, and proportional payment of dividends decreases it. In the investor's income statement, the proportional share of the investee's net income is reported as a single-line item.

The ownership of more than 50% of voting stock creates a subsidiary. Its financial statements consolidate into the parent's. The ownership of less than 20% creates investment position carried at historic book or fair market value in the investor's balance sheet.

MARK-TO-MARKET ACCOUNTING

Beginning in 1997, the tax law has permitted securities traders to elect a method of accounting called the mark-to-market method. Many securities traders will find this election attractive as a way to make filing simpler — and possibly reduce their taxes.

MARK-TO-MARKET ELECTION

If you're a trader, you may choose whether or not to make the mark-to-market election. You don't automatically get mark-to-market treatment when you file as a trader. And you can't elect this treatment if you aren't a trader.

The election has to be filed by the return due date — without extensions — for the year before the year you want the election to be effective. The last day to file the election for the year 2004 is April 15, 2004. For guidance on how to file the election.

CONSEQUENCES OF THE ELECTION

Marking to market. The most obvious consequence of the election is that at the end of each year you must mark your securities to market.

What this means is you treat any stocks you hold at the end of the day on December 31 as if you sold them on that day for the current market value. If the stock has gone down, you get to report a loss without actually selling it. If the stock has gone up, you have to report that gain. Your basis for the stock is adjusted to reflect the gain or loss you report, so that you don't report the same gain or loss again when you actually sell the stock.

For a true day trader, this aspect of the election is of no significance. You don't hold stocks at the end of the day, so you don't hold stocks at the end of the year. Your gains and losses are already in the book. This isn't true for a position trader. A position trader who makes the mark-to-market election loses the ability to do year-end tax planning by selling losers and holding winners.

No wash sales. The wash sale rule doesn't apply to a trader who has made the mark-to-market election. There's a simple logic to this: if all your gains and losses are going to be flushed out on December 31, there's no reason for the tax law to be concerned about wash sales that may occur during the year.

Wash sales can be a significant headache for a trader even if they don't affect the amount of tax the trader has to pay. If you make hundreds of trades in the same stock, many of the trades are likely to result in wash sales. At some point, accounting for all the wash sales becomes nearly impossible. Eliminating this concern is a significant benefit of the mark-to-market election.

Ordinary income and loss. If you make the mark-to-market election, your trading gains and losses are converted to ordinary income and loss. You'll report the gains and losses on Form 4797 not Schedule D.

This does not mean that your trading gains are now subject to self-employment tax. In a 1998 tax law, Congress clarified that although your trading income becomes ordinary income, it is not self-employment income. This also means you can't use this income to support a contribution to an IRA or other retirement plan. Traders usually generate all or nearly all of their gains as short-term capital gains, which are taxed at the same rate as ordinary income. In most situations, changing to a system where the trader reports the gains as ordinary income will not have any tax cost. If the trader has capital losses from an investment that isn't part of the trading activity, though, the trader will lose the ability to offset those losses with capital gains from trading.

For many traders, the flip side will be more important. Even good traders sometimes have losing years. When they do, the capital loss limitation rears its ugly head. A trader who has not made the mark-to-market election can deduct only $3,000 of net capital loss, with the excess loss carrying forward only, not back to earlier, profitable years. If you make the election, your trading loss isn't subject to this limitation, and can carry back as well as forward. The difference can be huge.

MONEY MEASUREMENT CONCEPT

The money measurement concept underlines the fact that in accounting, every recorded event or transaction is measured in terms of money. Using this principle, a fact or a happening which cannot be expressed in terms of money is not recorded in the accounting books.

One of the basic principles in accounting is "The Measuring Unit principle: The unit of measure in accounting shall be the base money unit of the most relevant currency.

This principle also assumes the unit of measure is stable; that is, changes in its general purchasing power are not considered sufficiently important to require adjustments to the basic financial statements."

ASPECTS OF FINANCIAL ACCOUNTING

ASSET RECOVERY

Asset Recovery, also called investment recovery or resource recovery, is the process of maximizing the value of unused or end of life assets through effective reuse or divestment. Both large and small organizations practice asset recovery at some level with the end goal of obtaining the greatest possible return from the asset. While sometimes referred to in the context of a company that is being liquidated, Asset Recovery is also used to describe the process of liquidating excess inventory of healthy companies, refurbished items and equipment returned at the end of a lease. The asset recovery process has three main parts: idle asset identification, redeployment, and divestment.

Asset recovery can also refer to the task of recovery of assets that have been wrongfully taken either stolen, fraudulently misappropriated or otherwise disposed of to remove them from their rightful owner.

Idle Asset Identification

One of the most important parts of the asset recovery process is idle asset identification. Assets that are not put to productive use end up costing money. It is important that these assets be classified as idle by investment recovery personnel. Later, a decision can be made whether to redeploy or divest the asset. Surplus Assets could be in any form, including fixed equipment, mobile equipment, buildings, and land. Idle or Surplus assets can also be identified as either"Capital" Assets or non capital surplus.

Asset recovery can also refer to the task of recovery of assets that have been wrongfully taken either stolen, fraudulently misappropriated or otherwise disposed of to remove them from their rightful owner.

Internal Redeployment

Redeploying an idle asset to another part of an organization is often the most productive use for the asset. Asset redeployment also saves the organization money by eliminating the need to purchase a new asset at current market rates. For effective reuse, another part of the company needs to require an asset of that kind. It must also be practical for the asset to be transferred and deployed at the new location.

Surplus Asset Disposition

Disposition of surplus or idle assets is the process of either selling, scrapping, recycling, donating, or disposing an asset. The process involves removing the asset from an organization's books. When this is done effectively, the organization obtains capital that can be placed back into the business. In addition, a good asset sale produces revenue and boosts profits. Donations also build goodwill and deliver tax benefits. The type of disposition method employed will depend on the type of asset, its fair value, and demand for the asset in the marketplace.

The Investment Recovery Association is the leading organization providing education and training in the Best Practices for professional management of surplus assets.

Investment Recovery Specialists

Companies in the asset recovery business can sometimes be referred to as liquidators or as asset recovery specialists or a similar name. An asset recovery company will purchase the equipment at a discounted price and either resell it for a profit or sell it on behalf of the asset owner for either a commission or a fee.

ASSET LIABILITY MISMATCH

In finance, an asset-liability mismatch occurs when the financial terms of the assets and liabilities do not correspond. Several types of mismatches are possible.

For example, a bank that chose to borrow entirely in U.S. dollars and lend in Russian rubles would have a significant currency mismatch: if the value of the ruble were to fall dramatically, the bank would lose money. In extreme cases, such movements in the value of the assets and liabilities could lead to bankruptcy, liquidity problems and wealth transfer.

Asset-liability mismatches can occur in several different areas. A bank could have substantial long-term assets but short-term liabilities such as deposits, which can be measured by the duration gap. This is sometimes called a maturity mismatch. Alternatively, a bank could have all of its liabilities as floating interest rate bonds, but assets in fixed rate instruments. Mismatches are handled by Asset liability management.

Asset-liability mismatches are also important to insurance companies and various pension plans, which may have long-term liabilities that must be backed by assets. Choosing assets that are appropriately matched to their financial obligations is therefore an important part of their long-term strategy.

Few companies or financial institutions have perfect matches between their assets and liabilities. In particular, the mismatch between the maturities of banks' deposits and loans makes banks susceptible to bank runs. On the other hand,'controlled' mismatch, such as between short-term deposits and somewhat longer-term, higher-interest loans to customers is central to many financial institutions' business model.Asset-liability mismatches can be controlled, mitigated or hedged.

ASSOCIATE COMPANY

An associate is a company in which a group of companies has a substantial stake, but not outright control. This usually means more than 20% but less than 50%. More than 50% would give the group control and make it a subsidiary.

Associates are not fully consolidated. Revenue and profits from associates are shown on the group P & L but they are shown separately. The group balance sheet shows the value of the shares owned in the associates. Although shown separately, they are treated like any other investment. When calculating an EV the value of the holdings in associates should be deducted. Alternatively, the cost of completely buying out the associate should be added - but this approach makes more sense for subsidiaries. When calculating an EV/EBITDA, the EBITDA should be adjusted in line with the EV.

AUTHORISED CAPITAL

The authorised capital of a company is the maximum amount of share capital that the company is authorised by its constitutional documents to issue to shareholders. Part of the authorised capital can remain unissued. The part of the authorised capital which has been issued to shareholders is referred to as the issued share capital of the company.

CARRY (INVESTMENT)

The carry of an asset is the return obtained from holding it or the cost of holding it. For instance, commodities are usually negative carry assets, as they incur storage costs or may suffer from depreciation, but in some circumstances, commodities can be positive carry assets if the market is willing to pay a premium for its demand.

This can also refer to a trade with more than one leg, where you earn the spread between borrowing a low carry asset and lending a high carry one. Carry trades are not arbitrages: pure arbitrages make money no matter what; carry trades make money only if nothing changes against the carry's favour.

Interest Rates

For instance, the traditional income stream from commercial banks is to borrow cheap and lend expensive.

This works with an upward-sloping yield curve, but it loses money if the curve becomes inverted. Many investment banks, such as Bear Stearns, have failed because they borrowed cheap short-term money to fund higher interest bearing long-term positions. When the long-term positions default, or the short-term money dries up, the bank cannot meet its short-term liabilities and goes under.

Traditional commercial banking was characterized as a "3-6-3" business: borrow at 3%, lend at 6% be on the golf course by 3 pm. While this may have been close to the truth in the market of the 1950s to the 1970s, the modern competitive market ensures that profits are kept more in line with perceived risks.

Currency

The term carry trade without further modification refers to currency carry trade: investors borrow low-yielding currencies and lend high-yielding currencies. It tends to correlate with global financial and exchange rate stability, and retracts in use during global liquidity shortages.

The risk in carry trading is that foreign exchange rates may change to the effect that the investor would have to pay back more expensive currency with less valuable currency. In theory, according to uncovered interest rate parity, carry trades should not yield a predictable profit because the difference in interest rates between two countries should equal the rate at which investors expect the low-interest-rate currency to rise against the high-interest-rate one. However, carry trades weaken the currency that is borrowed, because investors sell the borrowed money by converting it to other currencies.

By early year 2007, it was estimated that some US$1 trillion may be staked on the yen carry trade. Since the mid-90's, the Bank of Japan has set Japanese interest rates at very low levels making it profitable to borrow Japanese yen to fund activities in other currencies. These activities include subprime lending in the USA, and funding of emerging markets, especially BRIC countries and resource rich countries.

Known Risks

The 2008–2009 Icelandic financial crisis has among its origins the undisciplined use of the carry trade. The US dollar and the yen have been the currencies most heavily used in carry trade transactions since the 1990s. There is some substantial mathematical evidence in macroeconomics that larger economies have more immunity to the disruptive aspects of the carry trade mainly due to the sheer quantity of their existing currency compared to the limited amount used for FOREX carry trades.

CARRYING CHARGE

Sometime referred to as the cost of carry, a carrying charge has to do with the charges associated with storing and caring for physical commodities. This cost of physical commodities care may include such important factors as physical storage, insurance, interest rate futures generated by the commodities, and opportunity costs. In addition to these usual costs involved in caring for a commodity, other ancillary charges may also be included in the overall carrying charge.

An illustration of how the carrying charge works can be found in the example of grain. Since grain is a valuable commodity that is subject to decay, it is often necessary to take steps that will extend the life of the asset. One of the central means of preserving the grain is physical storage in a silo or other facility that helps to minimize the impact of temperature and humidity on the grain. This means the lease or construction of the storage facility, as well as the installation of systems that will keep the grain under optimum conditions. Along with the physical facilities that protect the grain, there is also the need to plan for some type of protection in case the silo is damaged or the climate controls fail. This often comes in the form of insurance coverage. The premiums that are paid to maintain the grain insurance qualify are part of the overall carrying charge.

Resources that are utilized for the care of a commodity are often generated by securing investors who are willing to cover the costs. In the interim, those investments of resources, are often generated with the expectation of a return. This return is often in the form of interest that is generated on the invested funds. Any interest that is paid out to investors is considered part of the carrying cost.

Essentially, any other cost that may be directly related to the proper maintenance of the commodity can properly be identified as a carrying charge. As long as the commodity is generated enough revenue to cover all associated costs and still generate a net profit, the commodity is generally considered to be worth retaining. However, once a commodity ceases to cover the total carrying charge, investors normally choose to withdraw support and seek other opportunities.

COMMUTED CASH VALUE

The Commuted Value is the amount that your pension is worth today, in a lump sum. You can move this money into a Locked-In RRSP, transfer it to your new pension plan or use it to buy an annuity from an insurance company. The most important thing to remember about a Commuted Value is that it is locked in - the funds must be used for your retirement income.

Money cannot be taken from a locked-in RRSP except for use in retirement. By law, funds may not be withdrawn from a locked-in RRSP before age 55, and must be withdrawn by age 71. When you withdraw the funds, they must be used to purchase a lifetime annuity from a life insurance company, or a Locked-In Retirement Account, or a Life Income Fund. You can get more details about these products from your financial institution. If your Commuted Value exceeds the CRA Maximum Transfer Value limit, you will be able to move the amount up to the limit into your locked-in RRSP. The rest you can take as cash, less income tax, or you can receive it in a monthly pension, less income tax.

CONTROLLING INTEREST

Controlling interest is a situation where one entity holds more than half of the voting shares of stock issued by a corporation. In general, controlling interests place the single entity in a position where even if all other shareholders vote in opposition to a decision supported by the investor with a majority of voting shares, their collective strength will not be sufficient to alter the decision. In most cases, a controlling interest is considered to be present when a single investor owns in excess of half of the shares of stock currently in circulation.

In some instances, controlling interest may require something more than simply holding a majority of voting stock. Depending on the substances of incorporation and bylaws of a given company, a two-thirds majority vote of shareholders may be required in order to approve a decision. If that is the case, an investor who owned just over half of the outstanding shares would not be able to control the outcome alone. He or she would require the support of at least enough of the other investors to achieve a two thirds vote in favour of the issue.

In one sense, controlling interest may also be present when a single investor owns at least 34% of the voting stock currently in circulation. This is true when a two-thirds majority vote is required to approve an issue that is put before the shareholders. Without winning the support of the single investor who controls the 34% of shares, there is no way to achieve that majority and the issue will be defeated. From this perspective, an investor can be considered both a minority investor and still have controlling interest, in that nothing is likely to pass without his or her support.

Having a controlling interest in a given company is a model that many corporations use to ensure that control of the company remains in the hands of the founders or owners. The number and type of shares issued to other investors is carefully balanced with the number and type of voting shares retained by the owners, so that they always have a significant say in any decision that impacts the profitability of the company.

In addition, maintaining this type of controlling interest tends to keep the corporation safeguarded from corporate raiders who may wish to acquire a controlling interest and begin to dismantle the company for profit.

CONVENIENCE TRANSLATION

A convenience translation is when an entity displays its financial statements or other financial information in a currency that is different from either its functional currency or its presentation currency simply by translating all amounts at end-of-period exchange rates. A result of making a convenience translation is that the resulting financial information does not comply with all Generally Accepted Accounting Principles.

HOLDING GAINS

Holding gains and losses result from changes in the prices of assets. They occur on all kinds of financial and non-financial assets, and on liabilities. Holding gains and losses accrue to the owners of assets and liabilities purely as a result of holding the assets or liabilities over time, without transforming them in any way.

Holding gains and losses measured on the basis of current market prices are called nominal holding gains and losses. These may be decomposed into neutral holding gains and losses, reflecting changes in the general price level, and real holding gains and losses, reflecting changes in the relative prices of assets.

FIXED ASSETS REGISTER

A Fixed Asset Register is an accounting method used for major resources of a business.

Fixed Assets are assets such as land, machines, office equipments, buildings, patents, trademarks, copyrights, etc. held for the purpose of production of goods or rendering of services and are not held for the purpose of sale in the ordinary course of business.

Fixed assets constitute a major chunk of the total assets in the case of all manufacturing entities. Even in the case of service entities such as hotels, banks, financial institutions, insurers, mobile/telephone service providers etc. it has become imperative to invest heavily in furnishing, equipment, and technology to attract, and retain customers.

Just as it is important for a person investing on the NASDAQ to know those investments, so it is important for a business entity to have a list of its fixed assets. A Fixed Asset Register is that list of assets.

Objectives in Maintaining a Fixed Asset Register

A FAR must be kept in order to be in compliance with legislation governing corporations, companies, etc. It allows a company to keep track of details of each fixed asset, ensuring control and preventing misappropriation of assets. It also keeps track of the correct value of assets, which allows for computation of depreciation and for tax and insurance purposes. The FAR generates accurate, complete, and customised reports that suits the needs of management.

A FAR also allows a company to keep track of fixed assets that are not under simple, direct control of the company. This means owned and leased assets and imported assets.

The FAR can also be used to aid in capital budgeting and to keep track of amount provided for Asset Retirement Obligation in respect of each asset as required by US GAAP.

Making Entries in the FAR

Not all assets are capitalized. Keeping in view the concept of materiality, a company may have a policy to capitalize only those assets which cost more than a specified amount. In the US, government agencies are required to expense all equipment whose value is below a threshold limit. Similarly, fixed assets which have a useful life of less than one year are not capitalized.

In some companies, improvements or alterations made to an asset are capitalized separately in the FAR. This is not correct. If such mistakes are made, it is highly probable that the auditors while undertaking physical verification of assets will notice irreconcilable differences.

Where improvements or alterations made to an existing asset justifying capitalization, such additions should be made to the cost of the original asset.

The Format of FAR Entries

The format to be provided in a FAR generally depends upon the following factors:

- Nature of assets.
  - If moveable assets constitute a significant portion of total fixed assets, details will be necessary on their movement from one department/cost centre/people to another. ii. Cost of assets. Greater control and security is required for costly equipment.
- Customised Reports on fixed assets required by management.
- Disclosure norms/regulatory compliances as per statutory laws applicable to the entity.
- Extent of owned, and assets taken on lease/hire purchase.
- Requirements of insurance company.
- *Location of fixed assets*: If fixed assets are located at numerous locations, greater details will have to be given. In the case of a construction company, the assets are located at different work sites. These work sites maybe in different cities/countries/continents.
- *Maintenance costs*: Some fixed assets require regular servicing to keep them running in an efficient and satisfactory manner. It would be necessary to keep a tab on the maintenance costs, dates of servicing etc. during a stated period.

Maintenance of a FAR in a Multi-National Corporation can be onerous and complex due to different regulatory and compliance requirements in each country and different currencies.

Generally, an MNC sets up a subsidiary in the country in which it intends to start operations. Maintenance of FAR is decentralized. The FAR is maintained per the company's policy, and regulatory requirements which are country specific.

If consolidation of holding company and its subsidiaries is required by the law applicable to companies, and relevant Accounting Standards, the task may become a bit complex. The crucial point is related to selection of exchange rate for conversion of fixed assets. Most companies either use average annual rate or year-end exchange rate.

Similarly, for companies having their shares listed on American Stock Exchanges, the fixed assets are required to be stated in accordance with the requirements of US generally accepted accounting principles.

Identification of a Fixed Asset

In a large corporation, the task of identifying and locating a specific fixed asset can be difficult unless numbering is scientific, systematic, and up-to-date. A common problem in most companies is the improper maintenance of the FAR. Physical verification of fixed assets becomes a futile exercise unless the FAR is properly maintained.

It would be advisable to use a scientific numbering technique to identify fixed assets. The process of numbering fixed assets is called tagging. An identification number is written on the asset. Engraving the identification number on the asset is advisable in the case of Plant and Machinery where there is heavy wear and tear.

A tag verifies the existence of assets and their location, aids in maintenance, provides a common ground for communication between the Accounts Department and the end-users and recording the net book value of asset in case of sale/scrapping.

It is not necessary to tag all fixed assets. Land, buildings and vehicles all have independent systems of tracking in registration papers and survey numbers.

FINANCIAL INTELLIGENCE

Financial intelligence is the knowledege and skills gained from understanding finance and accounting principles in the business world. Although a fairly new term, financial intelligence has its roots in organizational development research, mostly in the field of employee participation. Financial intelligence has emerged as a best practice and core competency in many organizations leading to improved financial results, increased employee morale, and reduced employee turnover. Many organizations include financial intelligence programmes in their leadership development curriculum. Financial intelligence is not an innate skill, rather it is a learned set of skills that can be developed at all levels.

Areas of Understanding

The four areas of understanding that make up financial intelligence are:

1. *Understanding the foundation*: Financial intelligence requires an understanding of the basics of financial measurement including the income statement, the balance sheet, and the cash flow statement. It also requires knowing the difference between cash and profit and why a balance sheet balances.
2. *Understanding the art*: Finance and accounting are an art as well as a science. The two disciplines must try to quantify what can't always be quantified, and so must rely on rules, estimates, and assumptions. Financial intelligence ensures people are able to identify where the artful aspects of finance have been applied to the numbers, and know how applying them differently might lead to different ceases.
3. *Understanding analysis*: Financial intelligence includes the ability to analyse the numbers in greater depth. This includes being able to calculate profitability,

leverage, liquidity and efficiency ratios and understanding the meaning of the results. Conducting ROI analysis and interpreting the results are also part of financial intelligence.

4. *Understanding the big picture*: Financial intelligence also means being able to understand a business's financial results in context - that is, within the framework of the big picture. Factors such as the economy, the competitive environment, regulations and changing customer needs and expectations as well as new technologies all affect how the numbers are interpreted.

Financial intelligence is not just theoretical book learning. It also requires practice and real world application. In the corporate world, managers can display financial intelligence by speaking the language, that is, asking questions about the numbers when something doesn't make sense, reviewing financial reports and using the information to understand the company's strengths and weaknesses, using ROI analysis, working capital management, and ratio analysis to make decisions, and identifying where the art of finance has been applied.

Roots of Financial Intelligence

In 1954, Peter F. Drucker, The Practice of Management, wrote the following.

"The worker should know how his work relates to the work of the whole. He should know what he contributes to the enterprise...if he lacks information, he will lack both incentive and means to improve his performance."

"It is in the best interest of the organization that the worker have the information."

The concept of financial intelligence in organizations comes from the research of several well-known organizational development academics, including Dennis Denison, Edward Lawler and Jeffrey Pfeffer. For example, the research of Lawler, Mohrman and Ledford found that the indices that have the most impact on both direct performance outcomes in organizations and on profitability and competitiveness were sharing information and developing knowledge.

Karen Berman's research, asked specifically if information improves the results of employee participation, as seen through organizational performance improvement and employee attitude improvement. The results of the study found that certain financial performance measures improved and that employee turnover decreased. Financial literacy also has its roots in open book management. A core tenant of open-book management is business literacy, that is, ensuring everyone understands how the business measures financial success.

Financial Intelligence in Organizations

Many companies, consider financial intelligence a core competency or best practice. Several universities, including Harvard Business School, Wharton and Stanford have programmes targeted at the corporate world, mostly at the leadership level, to increase the financial intelligence in organizations. There are a variety of methods to increase financial intelligence in organizations, including classroom training, webinar training, and business simulations. Training companies have supported these efforts as well, including Business Literacy Institute, Paradigm Learning, and Workplace Development.

Proponents of financial intelligence in organizations believe that if employees, managers and leaders understand financial information and how financial success is measured, they will make decisions and take action based on an understanding of the financial impact of those decisions. If everyone knows the financial goals of the company, for example, and knows how to make decisions that support those financial goals, then the company is going to be more financially successful. Employee owned companies are one group of organizations that are focused on ensuring everyone in the company is financially intelligent, as employees are owners and therefore must understand the financial side of the business.

FINANCE CHARGE

Finance charge is any fee representing the cost of credit, or the cost of borrowing. It is interest accrued on, and fees charged for, some forms of credit. It includes not only interest but other charges as well, such as financial transaction fees. Details regarding the federal definition of finance charge are found in the Truth-in-Lending Act and Regulation Z, promulgated by the Federal Reserve Board.

In personal finance, finance charge may be considered simply the dollar amount paid to borrow money, while interest is a percentage amount paid such as annual percentage rate or APR). This definition of finance charge and interest seems to be very narrow and not consistent with the websters definition or the accounting definition.

Creditors and lenders use different methods to calculate finance charges. The most common formula is based on the average daily balance, in which daily outstanding balances are added together and then divided by the number of days in the month.

In financial accounting, interest is defined as any charge or cost of borrowing money. Interest is a synonym for finance charge. In effect, the accountant looks at the entire cost of settlement on a Housing and Urban Development form 1 document as interest unless that charge can be identified as an escrow amount or an amount that is charged to current expenses or expenditures other than interest, such as payment of current or prorated real estate taxes.

EXIT RATE

Exit rate is a financial term that refers to the revenue or cost to be expected in the following fiscal period as a derivative of the performance in the current period.

When used in the context of revenue, exit rate refers to the income expected in the following period as a result of sales closed in the existing period. If a company worked throughout the year and managed to signed up deals that will generate 1M USD a year in the following year then it would be said that company has 1M USD exit rate in this year.

When used in the context of costs, exit rate refers to the costs expected in the following period as a result of recurring costs taken on during the existing period. If a company took on headcount and recurring costs of 1M/year during a given fiscal year, then the working budget for that company would have an exit rate of 1M USD in that year.

DEFERRED FINANCING COST

Deferred Financing Cost is a very elaborate term but the general definition of this is nothing but the amount or the liability to be paid by the debtor to his moneylender only after a certain period of time i.e. the debtor gets the loan amount from the moneylender but his liability will start after a certain time period, six months. This is called as a deferred financing cost or something that is delayed for payment.

There are many advantages in the case of a deferred financing cost, both to the debtor as well as the moneylenders. In case of the debtors, the option of a deferred payment means that he/she has that extra bit of time to recuperate and get a strong hold in whatever they are doing with the loan amount rather than have the burden of paying installments right from the beginning.

For example, a person might apply for loan for his new business venture that is innovative and high revenue generating. He might get his loan sanctioned but he may not be able to pay back installments in the very next month since his business has to gain some momentum in the market. So, with the help of a deferred financing cost option that is available in the accounting field, the person can start giving his principal amount along with the interest rates only after a period of normally six months. This relaxed time period can be extended to even three years as well. So, if he does opt for a three year relaxation, the chances of that person to steady himself are very high. Once he has gained that upper hand then paying back the entire amount within the term proposed during the loan sanction can be done in jiffy by that person considering his present financial position. This deferred financial cost is a seriously high benefit option and people can very well make the full use of it to upgrade their financial situations.

Though deferred financial cost is greatly advantageous to the debtors, it is equally advantageous for the moneylenders as well. This is because the interest rates with this option are very high and moneylenders greatly benefit with this and no wonder they term DFC as an asset rather than a liability. On the whole, DFC is a very novel idea and can yield great benefits if it is used appropriately.

INTANGIBLE ASSET

Intangible assets are defined as identifiable non-monetary assets that cannot be seen, touched or physically measured, which are created through time and/or effort and that are identifiable as a separate asset. There are two primary forms of intangibles - legal intangibles and competitive intangibles. Legal intangibles are known under the generic term intellectual property and generate legal property rights defensible in a court of law. Competitive intangibles, whilst legally non-ownable, directly impact effectiveness, productivity, wastage, and opportunity costs within an organization - and therefore costs, revenues, customer service, satisfaction, market value, and share price. Human capital is the primary source of competitive intangibles for organizations today. Competitive intangibles are the source from which competitive advantage flows, or is destroyed. The area of finance that deals with intangible assets is known as Intangible Asset Finance.

The Uniform Commercial Code defines "general intangibles" as

"any personal property...other than accounts, chattel paper, commercial tort claims, deposit accounts, documents, goods, instruments, investment property, letter of credit rights, letters of credit, money, and oil, gas, or other minerals before extraction. The term includes payment intangibles and software."

Intangible Assets vs. Goodwill

It should be noted that while goodwill is technically an

intangible asset, it is usually listed as a separate item on a company's balance sheet. As a distinct type of intangible asset, goodwill typically comes into play only in an acquisition, and represents the amount of money a company has paid or would pay over book value to acquire another company.

Research and Development

Millions are spent each year by corporations to research and develop new intangible assets. To protect their research and development efforts, corporations generally rely on intellectual property law.

Financial Accounting

General standards The International Accounting Standards Board offers some guidance as to how intangible assets should be accounted for in financial statements. In general, legal intangibles that are developed internally are not recognized and legal intangibles that are purchased from third-parties are recognized. Wordings are similar to IAS 9.

Under US GAAP, intangible assets are classified into: Purchased vs. internally created intangibles, and Limited-life vs. indefinite-life intangibles.

Expense Recognition

Intangible assets are typically expensed according to their respective life expectancy. Intangible assets have either an identifiable or indefinite useful life. Intangible assets with identifiable useful lives are amortized on a straight-line basis over their economic or legal life, whichever is shorter. Examples of intangible assets with identifiable useful lives include copyrights and patents. Intangible assets with indefinite useful lives are reassessed each year for impairment. If an impairment has occurred, then a loss must be recognized. An impairment loss is determined by subtracting the asset's fair value from the asset's book/carrying value. This impairment loss may only be reversed under certain circumstances. Trademarks and goodwill are examples of intangible assets with indefinite useful lives. Goodwill has to tested for impairment rather than amortized. If impaired, goodwill is reduced and loss is recognized in the Income statement.

Taxation

For personal income tax purposes, some costs with respect to intangible assets must be capitalized rather than treated as deductible expenses. Treasury regulations generally require capitalization of costs associated with acquiring, creating, or enhancing intangible assets. For example, an amount paid to obtain a trademark must be capitalized. Certain amounts paid to facilitate these transactions must also be capitalized. Some types of intangible assets are categorized based on whether the asset is acquired from another party or created by the taxpayer. The regulations contain many provisions intended to make it easier to determine when capitalization is required.

INTELLECTUAL CAPITAL

The term Intellectual capital collectively refers to all resources that determine the value and the competitiveness of an enterprise. As such, it includes as subsets the attributes that concur to building all financial statements as well as the balance sheet.

Intangibles

The value of an enterprise is made of physical assets, various financial assets and, finally, intangible assets, i.e., intellectual capital. The intangibleness refers to the fact that IC is not easily translatable in financial terms. All other assets of a company, such as a piece of real estate or a credit note, can be monetized: i.e., there exist standard criteria for expressing their value in currency. IC, instead, is mainly made of elements for which there is no consensual model for monetary expression. A more precise name for IC would therefore be "non-financial assets".

Elements of Intellectual Capital

In all definitions of IC, the following taxonomy can be recognized:

- *Relational capital*: All relations a company entertains with external subjects, such as suppliers, partners, clients, research centres, etc.;
- *Human capital*: The sum total of the useful knowledge of your employees and your customers with more emphasis on knowledge and competences residing with the company's employees;
- *Organizational capital*: Collective know-how, beyond the capabilities of individual employees. E.g.: information systems; policies; intellectual property.

NET WORTH

In business, net worth is the total assets minus total outside liabilities of an individual or a company. For a company, this is called shareholders' preference and may be referred to as book value. Net worth is stated as at a particular year in time. In the case of an individual, the term estate is used in relation to deceased individuals in probate. For businesses, the term is used in the context of fraudulent law and on the dissolution of the company.

In personal finance, net worth refers to an individual's net economic position; similarly, it uses the value of all assets minus the value of all liabilities.

Net worth in business is generally based on the value of all assets and liabilities at the carrying value which is the value as expressed on the financial statements. To the extent items on the balance sheet do not express their true value, the net worth will also be inaccurate.

Net worth in this formulation is not an expression of the market value of the firm: the firm may be worth more if sold as a going concern. On reading the balance sheet, if the accumulated losses exceed the shareholder's equity, it is a negative value for net worth.

PARTNERSHIP ACCOUNTING

When two or more individuals engage in an enterprise as co-owners, the organization is known as a partnership. This form of organization is popular among personal service enterprises, as well as in the legal and public accounting professions.

Accounting for Initial Investments

Because ownership rights in a partnership are divided among two or more partners, separate capital and drawing accounts are maintained for each partner.

Investment of Cash

If a partner invested cash in a partnership, the Cash account of the partnership is debited, and the partner's capital account is credited for the invested amount.

Investment of Assets Other Than Cash

If a partner invested an asset other than cash, an asset account is debited, and the partner's capital account is credited for the market value of the asset. If a certain amount of money is owed for the asset, the partnership may assume liability. In that case an asset account is debited, and the partner's capital account is credited for the difference between the market value of the asset invested and liabilities assumed.

Capital Interest

A capital interest is an interest that would give the holder a share of the proceeds in either of the following situations:

- The owner withdraws from the partnership.
- The partnership liquidates.

The mere right to share in earnings and profits is not a capital interest in the partnership. This determination generally is made at the time of receipt of the partnership interest.

Capital Account

Capital account of each partner represents his equity in the partnership.

Capital account of a partner is increased in the following situations:

- The owner made additional investments during the year.

- The owner received guaranteed payments from the partnership.
- Partnership earned profits, and a share of profits was allocated to the partner.
- The increased in the capital will record in credit side of the capital account.

Salary and interest allowances are guaranteed payments, discussed later.

Capital account of a partner is decreased when the owner makes withdrawals of cash or property

Compensation for Services and Capital

The partnership agreement may specify that partners should be compensated for services they provide to the partnership and for capital invested by partners.

For example, one partner contributed more of the assets, and works full time in the partnership, while the other partner contributed a smaller amount of assets and does not provide as much services to the partnership.

Compensation for services is provided in the form of salary allowance. Compensation for capital is provided in the form of interest allowance. Amount of compensation is added to the capital account of the partner.

Toemphasize, assume that a partner received $500 as an interest allowance. The entry is:

	Debit	Credit
Partner A, Capital		$500
Accounts payable	$500	

As a result of the entry Accounts Payable, which is a liability account, is reduced by $500, and the capital account is increased by the same amount.

When the partner makes a cash withdrawal of moneys he received as an allowance, it is treated as a withdrawal, or drawing.

	Debit	Credit
Partner A, Drawing	$500	
Cash		$500

As a result, Drawing account increased by $500, and the Cash account of the partnership is reduced by the same account. At the end of the accounting period the drawing account is closed to the capital account of the partner. The capital account will be reduced by the amount of drawing made by the partner during the accounting period.

Guaranteed Payments

Guaranteed payments are those made by a partnership to a partner that are determined without regard to the partnership's income. Compensation for services and capital are guaranteed payments. A partnership treats guaranteed payments for services, or for the use of capital, as if they were made to a person who is not a partner. This treatment is for purposes of determining gross income and deductible business expenses only.

For other tax purposes, guaranteed payments are treated as a partner's distributive share of ordinary income. Guaranteed payments are not subject to income tax withholding. The partnership generally deducts guaranteed payments on line 10 of Form 1065 as business expenses. They are also listed on Schedules K and K-1 of the partnership return. The individual partner reports guaranteed payments on Schedule E as ordinary income, along with his distributive share of the partnership's other ordinary income.

Allocation of Net Income

Revenues – Expenses = Net income

If total revenues exceed total expenses of the period, the excess is the net income of the partnership for the period. If expenses exceed revenues of the period, the excess is a net loss of the partnership for the period.

Salary and interest allowances are guaranteed payments. The partnership generally deducts guaranteed payments on line 10 of Form 1065 as business expenses.

If partners pay themselves high salaries, net income will be low, but it does not matter for tax purposes. Partner compensation and allocated net income are considered ordinary income for tax purposes and as such are reported on the form 1040. It does not matter whether or not a partner withdrew any amount of money from his capital account. It's the net income, allocated to the partner, and his compensation from the partnership that are taxed, not the amount withdrawn.

Net income or loss is allocated to the partners in accordance with the partnership agreement. In the absence of any agreement between partners, profits and losses must be shared equally regardless of the ratio of the partners' investments. If the partnership agreement specifies how profits are to be shared, losses must be shared on the same basis as profits.

Closing Process

Closing process at the end of the accounting period includes closing of all temporary accounts by making the following entries:

- Close all revenues accounts to Income Summary.
- Close all expenses accounts to Income Summary.
- Close Income Summary by allocating each partner's share of net income or loss to the individual capital account.
- Close each partner's drawing account to the individual capital accounts.

Toemphasize, assume that there are two equal partners, Partner A and Partner B. The partnership agreement specifies that after providing for salary and interest allowances the remaining income is divided equally. Assume also that net income of the partnership was $100,000 and the two partners received allowances as indicated in the table.

The allocation of net income would be reported on the income statement as shown.

Table. Net Income $100,000

	Partner A	Partner B	Total
Allocation of net income	50,000	50,000	100,000
Salary allowances	30,000	20,000	50,000
Interest allowances	20,000	10,000	30,000
Remaining income	10,000	10,000	20,000

Net Income of the partnership is calculated by subtracting total expenses from total revenues.

After that salary and interest allowances are subtracted from Net Income, and the result is Remaining Income, which is divided equally in accordance with the partnership agreement.

At the end of the accounting period each partner's allocated share is closed to his capital account. Based on the net income allocation shown, the closing entry is:

	Debit	Credit
Income Summary	$100,000	
Partner A, Capital		$50,000
Partner B, Capital		$50,000

Statements for Partnerships

The allocation of net income and its impact on the partners' capital balances must be disclosed in the financial statements.

All three financial statements are affected: the income statement, statement of owners equity, and balance sheet. In addition, the statement of partners' equity reflects the equity of each partner and summarizes the allocation of net income for the year.

Statement of Partners' Equity

Statement of partners' equity starts with capital balances at the beginning of the accounting period, and reflects additional investments, made by the partners during the year, net income for the period, and withdrawals.

Additional investments and allocated net income increase capital accounts of the partners. All kind of allowances, like salary allowances and capital allowances, are treated as withdrawals.

Withdrawals reduce capital accounts. The end result is capital balances of the partners at the end of the accounting period.

A sample statement of partners' equity is shown.

	Partner A	Partner B	Total
Capital, Jan. 1, 2008	$40,000	$30,000	$70,000
Additional Investments	$10,000	$20,000	$30,000
Capital plus investments	$50,000	$50,000	$100,000
Net Income for the year	$60,000	$40,000	$100,000
Balance	$110,000	$90,000	$200,000
Withdrawals	$30,000	$20,000	$50,000
Capital, Dec. 31, 2008	$80,000	$70,000	$150,000

Equity Part of the Balance Sheet

The partners' equity part of the balance sheet reports the equity of each partner.

Partner A, Capital	$80,000	
Partner B, Capital	$70,000	
Total partners' equity		$150,000

Admitting a New Partner

A new partner may be admitted by agreement among the existing partners. When this happens, the old partnership is dissolved and a new partnership is created, with a new partnership agreement.

A new partner may buy into the business in three ways:

- By purchasing an interest directly from existing partners
- By making an investment in the business, or
- By contributing assets from an existing business.

Assume that Partner A and Partner B admit Partner C as a new partner, when Partner A and Partner B have capital interests $30,000 and $20,000, respectively.

Partner C pays $15,000 to Partner A for one-third of his interest, and $15,000 to Partner B for one-half of his interest. These payments go to the partners directly, not to the business. The following entry is made by the partnership.

	Debit	Credit
Partner A, Capital	10,000	
Partner B, Capital	10,000	
Partner C, Capital		20,000

•

The extra $5,000 Partner C paid to each of the partners, represents profit to them, but it has no effect on the partnership's financial statements.

Now, assume instead that Partner C invested $30,000 cash in the new partnership. In this case, the following entry would be made to admit Partner C.

	Debit	Credit
Cash	30,000	
Partner C, Capital		30,000

Finally, let's assume that Partner C had been operating his own business, which was then taken over by the new partnership. In this case the balance sheet for the new partner's business would serve as a basis for preparing the opening entry. The assets listed in the balance sheet are taken over, the liabilities are assumed, and the new partner's capital account is credited for the difference.

Partnership Bonus

Bonus Paid to the Partnership

A new partner may pay a bonus in order to join the partnership. Bonus is the difference between the amount contributed to the partnership and equity received in return.

Equity of Partner A	$10,000
Equity of Partner B	$10,000
Contribution of Partner C	$16,000
Total equity after admitting Partner C	$36,000
Equity percentage of Partner C	33.3%
Equity of Partner C	$12,000
Contribution of Partner C	$16,000
Minus equity of Partner C	$12,000
Bonus paid to "A & B Partnership"	$4,000

Assume that Partner A and Partner B have balances $10,000 each on their capital accounts. The partners agree to admit Partner C to the partnership for $16,000. In return, Partner C will receive one-third equity in the partnership. The following table emphasizes calculation of the bonus. In this case, Partner C paid $4,000 bonus to join the partnership. The amount of any bonus paid to the partnership is distributed among the partners. The following table s the distribution of the bonus.

	Debit	Credit
Cash	$16,000	
Partner C, Capital		$12,000
Partner A, Capital		$2,000
Partner B, Capital		$2,000

Bonus Paid to a Partner

Assume now that Partner A and Partner B have balances $10,000 each on their capital accounts. The partners agree to admit Partner C to the partnership for $7,000. In return, Partner C will receive one-third equity in the partnership.

Why would the existing partners allow a new partner to buy an equal share of equity with smaller contribution? It might be because the new partner brings something very valuable to the partnership.

It might be special skills. The following table emphasizes calculation of the bonus.

Equity of Partner A	$10,000
Equity of Partner B	$10,000
Contribution of Partner C	$7,000
Total equity after admitting Partner C	$27,000
Equity percentage of Partner C	33.3%
Equity of Partner C	$9,000
Contribution of Partner C	$7,000
Minus equity of Partner C	$9,000
Bonus paid to Partner C	$2,000

In this case, Partner C received $2,000 bonus to join the partnership. The amount of the bonus paid by the partnership is distributed among the partners according to the partnership agreement.

The following table emphasizes the distribution of the bonus. Debit to Cash increases the account, while debit to a capital account of a partner decreases the account.

	Debit	Credit
Cash	$7,000	
Partner C, Capital		$9,000
Partner A, Capital	$1,000	
Partner B, Capital	$1,000	

In an equal partnership bonus paid to a new partner is distributed equally among the partners. In an unequal partnership bonus is distributed according to the partnership agreement.

Assume that Partner A is a 75% partner, and Partner B is a 25% partner. Partner C was admitted to the partnership. He paid $5,000 cash. In return, he received $9,000 equity in the partnership.

A $4,000 bonus paid to Partner C would be distributed as follows:

- Partner A will pay $3,000. His capital account will be debited $3,000.
- Partner B will pay $1,000. His capital account will be debited $1,000.

	Debit	Credit
Cash	$5,000	
Partner C, Capital		$9,000
Partner A, Capital	$3,000 ($4,000 * 75%)	
Partner B, Capital	$1,000 ($4,000 * 25%)	

Withdrawal of Partner

By agreement, a partner may retire and be permitted to withdraw assets equal to, less than, or greater than the amount of his interest in the partnership. The book value of a partner's interest is shown by the credit balance of the partner's capital account.

The balance is computed after all profits or losses have been allocated in accordance with the partnership agreement, and the books closed.

If a retiring partner withdraws cash or other assets equal to the credit balance of his capital account, the transaction will have no effect on the capital of the remaining partners. To emphasize, assume that several years after the formation of "A,B, and C" partnership Partner C decided to retire. The partners agreed to the withdrawal of cash equal to the amount of Partner C's equity in the assets of the partnership.

Assume that the partners' capital accounts had credit balances as follows:

- Partner A $60,000
- Partner B $40,000
- Partner C $30,000

If Partner C withdraws $30,000 in cash, the entry on the books is as follows:

	Debit	Credit
Partner C, Capital	30,000	
Cash		30,000

If a retiring partner agrees to withdraw less than the amount in his capital account, the transaction will increase the capital accounts of the remaining partners.

For example, if Partner C withdraws only $20,000 in settlement of the interest, the difference between Partner C's equity in the assets of the partnership and the amount of cash withdrawn is $10,000 ($30,000 - $20,000).

This difference is divided between the remaining partners on the basis stated in the partnership agreement. Assume that the partnership agreement specifies that in such a case the difference is divided according to the ratio of their capital interests after allocating net income and closing their drawing accounts. On this basis, Partner A's capital account is credited for $6,000 and Partner B's is credited for $4,000.

The entry in the books of the partnership is as follows:

	Debit	Credit
Partner C, Capital	30,000	
Cash		20,000
Partner A, Capital		6,000
Partner B, Capital		4,000

If a retiring partner withdraws more than the amount in his capital account, the transaction will decrease the capital accounts of the remaining partners. The excess of the amount withdrawn over retiring partner's equity in the partnership is divided between the remaining partners on the basis stated in the partnership agreement.

Purchasing of Partner's Interest

When a partner retires from the business, the partner's interest may be purchased directly by one or more of the remaining partners or by an outside party. If the retiring partner's interest is sold to one of the remaining partners, the retiring partner's equity is merely transferred to the other partner.

For example, assume that Partner C's equity is sold to Partner B. The entry for the transaction on the books of the partnership is as follows:

	Debit	Credit
Partner C, Capital	30,000	
Partner B, Capital		30,000

The amount paid to Partner C by Partner B is a personal transaction and has no effect on the above entry. Any gain or loss resulting from the transaction is a personal gain or loss of the withdrawing partner and not of the business.

If the retiring partner's interest is purchased by an outside party, the retiring partner's equity is transferred to the capital account of the new partner, Partner D.

	Debit	Credit
Partner C, Capital	30,000	
Partner D, Capital		30,000

The amount paid to Partner C by Partner D is also a personal transaction and has no effect on the above entry.

Death of a Partner

The death of a partner dissolves the partnership. On the date of death, the accounts are closed and the net income for the year to date is allocated to the partners' capital accounts. Most agreements call for an audit and revaluation of the assets at this time. The balance of the deceased partner's capital account is then transferred to a liability account with the deceased's estate. The surviving partners may continue the business or liquidate. If the business continues, the procedures for settling with the estate are the same as those described earlier for the withdrawal of a partner.

Liquidation of a Partnership

Liquidation of a partnership generally means that the assets are sold, liabilities are paid, and the remaining cash or other assets are distributed to the partners.

When normal operations are discontinued, adjusting and closing entries are made. Thus, only the assets, liabilities and partners' equity accounts remain open.

If noncash assets are sold for more than their book value, a gain on the sale is recognized. The gain is allocated to the partners' capital accounts according to the partnership agreement. If noncash assets are sold for less than their book value, a loss on the sale is recognized. The loss is allocated to the partners' capital accounts according to the partnership agreement.

As the assets are sold, the cash is applied first to the claims of creditors. Once all liabilities are paid, the remaining cash and other assets are distributed to the partners according to their ownership interests as indicated by their capital accounts.

Schedule M-1

Purpose of Schedule M-1

U.S. Return of Partnership Income contains, among others, Schedule M-1.

The purpose of Schedule M-1 is reconciliation of income per accounting books with income per Return of the partnership. In other words, it means reconciliation of accounting income with taxable income, because not all accounting income is taxable. Schedule M-1 starts with Net income per books. Adjustments are made for guaranteed payments, as well as for depreciation and other expenses. As a result, accounting income of a partnership is adjusted, or reconciled, to taxable income.

Schedule K-1

Purpose of Schedule K-1

The partnership uses Schedule K-1 to report a partner's share of the partnership's income, deductions, credits, etc. The partner must only keep Schedule K-1 for his records, but not file it with his tax return. The partnership must file a copy of Schedule K-1 for each partner with the IRS.

Although the partnership generally is not subject to income tax, every partner is liable for tax on his share of the partnership income, whether or not distributed.

RISK-WEIGHTED ASSET

Risk-weighted asset is a bank's assets weighted according to credit risk. Some assets, such as debentures, are assigned a higher risk than others, such as cash or government securities/bonds. Since different types of assets have different risk profiles, weighing assets based on the level of risk associated with them primarily adjusts for assets that are less risky by allowing banks to "discount" lower-risk assets.

This sort of asset calculation is used in determining the capital requirement or Capital Adequacy Ratio for a financial institution, and is regulated by the Local Central Banks or other National financial regulators. The specifics of CAR calculation vary from country to country, but general approaches tend to be similar for countries that apply the Basel Accords. In the most basic application, government debt is allowed a 0% "risk weighting" - that is, they are subtracted from total assets for purposes of calculating the CAR. A document was written in 1988 by the Basel Committee on Banking Supervision, which recommends certain standards and regulations for banks. The main recommendation of this document is that in order to lower credit risk, banks should hold enough capital to equal at least 8% of its risk-weighted assets. Most countries have implemented some version of this regulation.

SEC FILING

An SEC filing is a financial statement or other formal

document submitted to the U.S. Securities and Exchange Commission. Public companies, certain insiders, and broker-dealers are required to make regular SEC filings. Investors and financial professionals rely on these filings for information about companies they are evaluating for investment purposes. Many, but not all SEC filings are available online through the SEC's EDGAR database.

9

Accounting for Public Sector

Each decade more and more economic resources in the United States are directly devoted to the public interest. In fact, the significant growth of economic activities outside the private sector in our essentially market-oriented economy is without doubt one of the most striking developments of the twentieth century. Prevailing political and social attitudes point to further expansion of this segment of economic activities. Society-at-large demands that certain public and nonproprietary services be provided for the benefit of all of its citizens regardless of their ability to pay. Profit-motivated enterprises are not able to make such services available to everyone within socially acceptable norms. Moreover, upon investigation it appears that the free-enterprise system (like any other known economic system) is incapable of alleviating all perceived inequities within our society. The result has been that society, usually via governmental and charitable institutions, has made economic commitments to not-for-profit activities as a means of correcting perceived inequities. For these and a number of more technical reasons there exists a sector of economic activity for which the profit motive is absent by design.

NATURE AND SIZE OF NOT-FOR-PROFIT ECONOMIC ACTIVITY

Economists generally divide the production activities of our economy into a private and a public sector. The simplest way to define the public sector is to include within it all organizations not privately owned and operated, that is, nonproprietary organizations, as well as all not-for-profit organizations. This public sector can be subdivided by placing all governmental units (local, state, and federal) into one category and all nongovernmental not-for-profit organizations into another. However, the foregoing delineations are not clear-cut.

Despite the hybrid nature of some nonproprietary and some not-for-profit organizations, the public sector is treated. Accounting and reporting problems are quite similar between units of governments and privately organized associations having no deliberate or avowed profit motive. Hence, the general frame of reference for not-for-profit organization or agency, generally without specific regard for the public versus private ownership question.Not-for-profit organizations have the following main characteristics:

- Contributors of resources receive no direct financial interest in these resources nor proportionate benefits from the organization's operations.
- There are no individual shares of ownership. Ownership is public and cannot be sold or traded.
- Performance of services occurs on the basis of perceived social need rather than in response to strict market-related demand.
- A framework of public authorization and control is utilized. In governmental units this authorization typically covers specific financial budgets Government constitutions grant taxing authority and usually restrict modes of expenditures. Voluntary boards of trustees often control private nonprofit organizations.
- Accountability to the public is essential, since the public supports these organizations through direct contributions and grants many special privileges, such as a tax-exempt status. Sometimes this accountability is weak (in practice at least) for privately organized not-for-profit organizations.

Growth of Public Sector Activities: Not-for-profit activities have experienced substantial growth in our society over the last forty years when measured in terms of the resources committed to them. One interesting comparison is that all government expenditures prior to 1940 do not equal the amount presently spent in one year by the federal government alone. Of our total Gross National Product, which currently exceeds $1 trillion a year, approximately one-fifth comes from federal government sources.

Table. Federal Outlays for Social Programs During Selected Years 1960-1973 (in billions of dollars)

Category	Actual			Estimates		
	1960	1965	1970	1971	1972	1973
Community Development and Housing	1.0	0.3	3.0	3.4	4.0	4.8
Education and Manpower	1.1	2.3	7.3	8.7	10.1	11.3
Health	0.8	1.7	13.0	14.5	17.0	18.1
Income Security	18.2	25.7	43.8	55.7	65.2	69.7
Total Social Programs	21.1	30.0	67.1	82.3	96.3	103.9
Total Federal Outlays for All Programs	92.2	118.4	196.6	211.4	236.6	246.3
Percent Social Programs to Total Programs	23%	25%	34%	39%	41%	42%

State and local government expenditures over the past ten years have also increased. Their growth rate has been nearly double the rate of growth of the Gross National Product. Thus governmental units of all types spend about one-fourth of the economic resources of the total economy as represented by the Gross National Product.

Beyond government-related activities, there has been a significant growth in resources committed to the remainder of the not-for-profit sector of our economy. These nongovernment, not-for-profit activities include hospitals, private colleges and universities, religious institutions, private social agencies, the Red Cross, the March of Dimes, the Scout movements, and thousands of other similar organizations. In total, the size of not-for-profit economic endeavors is huge.

We should note here that comparable public interest resource commitments are relatively as large, and in some instances even larger, in countries outside the United States. While many other Western nations-like Canada and the Scandinavian countries-devote proportionately greater resources to federal level expenditures, the United States leads in efforts devoted to nongovernmental not-for-profit activities.

PROFIT-MOTIVATED AND NOT-FOR-PROFIT ORGANIZATIONS COMPARED

A central theme of economics is that resources are scarce and that human wants are without limit. This condition produces many continual allocation problems. We must also recognize that we live in a social environment which imposes limitations on the use of available resources. Efficient use of limited resources once fell into the category of conventional political and individual judgment. Today it is clearly a social obligation and possibly even a moral obligation. It seems reasonable, then, that every effort should be made to maximize the benefits coming from the use of available resources.

Profit-motivated and not-for-profit organizations are alike in that both must strive in principle to marshall resources as best they can. Both must ultimately justify to society the commitment of resources to their respective operations. Both have the responsibility to operate as efficiently as possible in their resource conversion processes or in their outright consumption of resources. In this important aspect of social responsibility, no differences exist between the two types of organizations.

In another important respect, profit-motivated and nonprofit organizations are fundamentally different. In a market-oriented economy, a private enterprise that continuously consumes resources unwisely does not survive. If it is unable to produce market-acceptable goods or services efficiently and thereby provide adequate returns to its employees, creditors, and investors, it will go out of existence after a period of time. An unalterable process of elimination, perhaps a Darwinian "survival of the fittest," thus operates in the private sector of our enterprise system.

The potential elimination process operates quite differently in the public sector. Perceived social needs dictate the establishment and possible later termination of not-for-profit organizations without direct or singular reliance on a market system of economic checks and balances (though economic stress may be an overriding factor in the closing of a small private not-for-profit school or college). Some public sector organizations may even be forced to operate in an economically inefficient manner for a time because public interest considerations demand it. In a financial control sense, profit-oriented organizations focus heavily on producing appropriate returns for creditors and investors. Hence they have accounting systems that emphasize the periodic measurement of results of operations. Public sector organizations are often concerned primarily with the size of their available cash resources, since the continued existence of public sector organizations or their programs generally depends quite heavily on cash availabilities. Therefore measurements of financial position, including cash reserves and outstanding obligations, dominate public sector accounting.

ACCOUNTING OBJECTIVES

The objectives of accounting for not-for-profit organizations can be stated as follows:

- To provide the information necessary for efficient, effective, and economical management of a nonproprietary entity and of the resources entrusted to it. This is a management control objective analogous to its counterpart for private enterprises.
- To provide information that enables managers to report to third parties and to the general public on the discharge of their responsibilities in administering the programs of the entity and the use of the resources under their direction.

- To permit public officials to report generally on the results of organizational operations and the use of public funds.
- To confirm and report legal compliance with statutory or administrative rules and regulations that relate to the acquisition and expenditure of resources.

Accounting entities in the public sector can be categorized into five different levels of operation. Each of these levels involves one or more of the following:

- A government-city, state, or national;
- An organizational unit within a government-a department, an agency, a bureau;
- A separately organized not-for-profit organization comparable to a governmental subunit-a college, a church, or a community health centre;
- A programme-usually a specified set of goal-oriented activities which, at times, cuts across organizational lines in large not-for-profit organizations; and
- A fund-usually a pool of resources subject to special restrictions or requirements.

Since the notion of a "fund" has a specific connotation in public sector accounting, we call attention to the definition provided by the National Committee on Governmental Accounting in its 1968 edition of *Governmental Accounting, Auditing and Financial Reporting:*

A fund is an independent fiscal and accounting entity with a self balancing set of accounts recording cash and/or other resources together with all related liabilities, obligations, reserves, and equities which are segregated for the purpose of carrying on specific activities or attaining certain objectives in accordance with special regulations, restrictions, or limitations.

The nature of these entities dictates an accounting orientation that seeks to substitute *effectiveness* in meeting specified objectives for the *periodic net income* measure of private enterprise performance. A second difference relates to *compliance* with laws, special limitations and restrictions, or organizational statutes. While legality is an ever-present ancillary goal of the private enterprise accounting process, it takes on the importance of ensuring specific statutory compliance in public sector accounting.

Compliance-efficiency-effectiveness are interlocking goals when it comes to public sector accountability. *Compliance* is a measurement of congruence with statutory or quasi-legal requirements.

Example: The Bel Ami Fellowship Fund requires that grants from its resources be made only to undergraduate students at accredited colleges and universities who can establish descendancy from French ancestors. Accountability for Bel Ami funds does not concern grade point averages, financial need, or subject area of study. Compliance is established so long as awards are made only to students with French forebears.

The notions of efficiency and effectiveness. *Efficiency* is related to economic performance. It is a measure of relationships for the entity between resource inputs and outputs. Different types of efficiency measures may be specified, for example, output efficiency or input efficiency.

Example: Output efficiency relates to specified levels of resource inputs. If the seating configuration of a commercial airliner is changed from five to six persons abreast in its coach passenger section, greater output efficiency (i.e., more passenger miles per flight) is achieved.

Example: Input efficiency is measured against a desired level of output. The city of Bellevue requires 250 transit buses to run an average of fifteen hours per workday. Higher input efficiency is achieved if the average cost per mile of operating a bus can be reduced from thirty-one to twenty-nine cents. *Effectiveness* measures achievement against specified technological, social, or other performance goals. It is normally difficult to quantify effectiveness measures precisely.

*Example:*The buses of the city of Bellevue operate over a route network which covers the entire city. Outlying areas have less frequent bus service due to a relatively lower demand for it. But there are persons everywhere within the city limits who depend completely on public bus transportation! A fully effective system would provide the same bus service to all citizens of Bellevue. Differential service frequency reduces public bus transportation effectiveness. Note also that greater effectiveness often means a sacrifice in efficiency.

Compliance, efficiency, and effectiveness all require control procedures that may be built into underlying accounting systems and processes.

THE TRADITIONAL ACCOUNTABILITY SYSTEM

The traditional mainstay of accountability in the public sector has rested with expenditure control. Expenditure control is largely a compliance-oriented activity.

EXPENDITURE CONTROL

Managers of not-for-profit organizations cannot spend funds comparatively as easily as managers of private enterprises. This is not surprising, since controlling expenditures is the important constraining factor in not-for-profit organizations.

Expenditure control is typically effected in four separate, sequential steps:

- Preliminary approval by a legislative body or a board of trustees to appropriate funds to a given programme.
- Actual appropriation of funds to an approved programme.
- Obligations or encumbrances incurred against the funds appropriated.
- Disbursement of funds.

This four-step expenditure control process is especially important for governmental units. Preliminary *approval* to appropriate funds to a given programme starts the programme by providing a blueprint on how programme expenditures are to be made eventually. But approval represents *no more* than eventual permission to request funds. Many tentatively approved programs falter every year in national, state, and local governments due to the failure of the respective legislative branches to appropriate funds for projects or programs fully endorsed at an earlier stage.

An *appropriation* grants authority from a legislative body or a city council or a board of trustees to an agency of government or to a not-for-profit organization (for example, the local boys' club receiving an appropriation from the Central United Crusade) to either disburse funds as approved or obligate the respective government or not-for-profit organization for the future payment of money. The act of appropriation is significant for accounting because it is at this point that the accounting process in not-for-profit organizations begins.

Step 3 entails recognition of planned use of appropriated funds. If contracts are actually made but not yet fully completed, an *obligation* is recognized. Definite commitments to spend funds for specified purposes in the future result in so-called *encumbrances* (defined below) against appropriated funds. The formal recognition of an encumbrance illustrates an act of accounting in advance of a completed transaction. Recognition of obligations to expend funds provides a necessary control against incurrence of total obligations and expenditures exceeding available appropriations.Finally, *disbursements* are cash payments either liquidating public sector obligations or making direct payments for products and services as authorized. The distinction between cash payments and obligations or encumbrances made on behalf of the not-for-profit unit is most important. New encumbrances must cease as soon as the appropriations level is reached—irrespective of actual cash payments to date. Moreover, since direct operating cash payments are usually needed to the very end of an individual programme, advance encumbrances must typically stop short of the appropriated funding level.In the public sector, then, accountants must provide continuing information to programme administrators on the following:

- Total appropriations available
- Total obligations and encumbrances to date
- Estimated funds needed to complete the programme
- Cash payments made to date

- Balances (for example, unused appropriations less obligations and encumbrances needed to complete programme, and obligations and encumbrances to date less cash payments made)

THE ACCOUNTING PROCESS ILLUSTRATED

A highly simplified example of a small federal government agency is used to illustrate the accounting process just described. In accounting for profit-motivated enterprises, the financial position equation is usually stated as:

Assets = Liabilities + Owner's Equity, however, represents the following relationship:

Cash Fund = Obligations Payable + Agency Account

AGENCY (FUND) ACCOUNT:

The agency account, or fund account, is the accounting quantity measuring the unencumbered or otherwise uncommitted amount of appropriated funds. As a book-keeping convenience, a nominal or subaccount for encumbrances is provided as an elaboration of the agency account.

ENCUMBRANCE

An encumbrance is an internal authorization to expend agency funds in the future for a specific purpose. An encumbrance is neither an actual expenditure nor an obligation already incurred. The actual accounting process begins by formal recognition of appropriations becoming available to allow future expenditures. The typical process also recognizes commitments (encumbrances) as soon as they are made against available appropriations. The process does not await evidence of a completed transaction, as is usually the case for business enterprise accounting.

FINANCIAL POSITION AND ANALYSIS OF CHANGES

The agency starts the current period with a cash fund balance with the U.S. Treasury of $50,000. It has obligations (accounts) payable of $20,000 and a balance in the agency account of $30,000. The latter amount represents earlier appropriations not expended. In this case, periodic appropriations do not lapse at the end of the period for which an appropriation is made.

Line 1: A current appropriation of $300,000 is made to the agency through the federal department with which it is affiliated.

Line 2: The agency director authorizes the current item-by-item budget for the next period of operation.*Line 3*. Subcontracts are let for a number of agency subprograms. If a position statement were prepared at this point, it would appear as follows:

Cash balance with U.S. Treasury		$350,000
Obligations and contracts payable	$230,000	
Encumbrances for estimated future expenditures	80,000	
Agency account (Fund balance)	40,000	$350,000

Line 4: Orders are placed for miscellaneous office furniture, fixtures, and supplies in the amount of $10,000. This is technically an encumbrance.

Line 5: Salaries, wages, and other office expenses amounting to $75,000 became payable. In technical jargon, this is called an "expenditure."*Line 6*. Progress payments of $180,000 are made to subcontractors. This is a disbursement.

Line 7: Payment is made of various liabilities now due, including some that were outstanding at the beginning of the period and others recorded on line 5.

Line 8: Direct expenses amounting to $14,000 are paid for items like unbudgeted travel and office expenses. A summary of the final financial position is best expressed in statement form.

Cash balance with U.S. Treasury		$62,000
Obligations and contracts payable	$31,000	
Encumbrances carried forward	15,000	
Agency account (Fund balance)	16,000	$62,000

From the earlier definition of an encumbrance, we note that the agency has $31,000 ($15,000 + $16,000) in cash resources not yet legally payable. The $15,000 represents authorized future expenditures, and therefore the remaining $16,000 is the uncommited, unencumbered amount of funds with which the agency will start its forthcoming budget year.Since balances carry forward, the agency:

- Had a total of $330,000 to spend during the current year instead of the appropriated $300,000;
- Incurred cash disbursements of only $288,000, even though its operating expenses were higher (financed by an increase in the amount of obligations payable); and
- Made commitments to expend funds during the next operating year and thereby anticipated its continued existence (this can only be done on the basis of appropriate legal or administrative stipulation).

REFINEMENTS

The foregoing illustration was constructed to show that not-for-profit organizations usually expend funds for two purposes:

- To acquire directly various goods and services needed for their programs, and
- To make payments on obligations incurred for services performed by others (i.e., local contractors). The first category represents the largest amount of non-private funds spent each year in the United States. Accounting processes surrounding it can become very complex. They may involve special recognition of inventories and long-lived depreciable assets. On the other hand, the second category may call for renegotiations with subcontractors or elaborate payment schemes tied to production performance. Furthermore, complicated expenditure allocation devices may have to be used, as is the case when Medicare or other programs cover health maintenance furnished by physicians and private

hospitals. Yet the basic accounting process is the same in all of these instances.

CONTROL OF RESOURCES

Expenditure control, is the traditional mainstay of *compliance* accountability in the public sector. How does this traditional system of accounting achieve resource input control in not-for-profit activities?

Three major resource control techniques are used:

- Precise specifications for appropriations of funds
- Creation of special-purpose funds
- Use of various cost concepts

EXPENDITURE

Specification. One of the more effective cost control devices in not-for-profit organizations is the exact specification of the uses of funds at the time appropriations are authorized. Almost invariably the total amount of money is specified for a given appropriation. This places an upper limit on the cost that an agency or a programme can incur within the authorized appropriation. When cost overruns occur, the additional sums of money requested are separately identifiable and hence susceptible to management and public scrutiny and review. Public sector appropriations are typically also quite specific as to the time period for which a given appropriation is available. This control technique ensures that unauthorized expenditures will not be made from carry-forward or carry-backward appropriations (our earlier illustration notwithstanding). When used in conjunction with other control efforts, the limitation on the length of time to complete an expenditure serves a good purpose. However, when used by itself, it may well induce expenditures not actually needed because "the appropriation will be lost if not expended by *x* date," and, moreover, "next year's budget will probably be cut because we didn't need all that was appropriated this year." Agency case histories are filled with instances when public monies were consumed almost solely to avoid *under*spending an established budget (appropriation).

Another possible appropriations specification concerns specific identification of the purposes for which designated funds are to be used (i.e., so-called line item budgets). This technique circumscribes the ability of administrator-managers to use funds at their own discretion outside the specified purposes. Specification of purpose is an effective control too. It is particularly helpful in audit and review functions.

The auditors can match, after the fact, the purposes contemplated in the approval and appropriation processes with the purposes served by actual expenditures. If variations are identified, corrective actions can be recommended or required.

FUND DESIGNATION

Probably the oldest control technique utilized for not-for-profit organizations is the segregation of appropriations into separately established funds. For example, a small city government may have a fire department fund, a water department fund, a traffic court fund, a street and engineering fund, a planning commission fund, a public school fund, and so on. A local YMCA organization may have a capital project fund, a special programme fund, a scholarship fund, and an office and operations fund. Since specification of nonproprietary resources into large batteries of individual funds is still used almost universally, accounting for not-for-profit organizations is often identified by accountants as "fund accounting." Under this concept, an individual fund becomes an *accounting entity* unto itself, and financial records and controls are established with a specific fund focus. Sometimes separate funds and separate accounts for them are required by law, especially in municipalities.

In fund accounting, it is common to distinguish between a general fund and special purpose funds. The general fund normally provides the resources needed to operate the unit or agency on a day-by-day basis. Salaries of employees, building maintenance, and general office expenses are items chargeable to a general fund. In contrast, special funds are established to yield accountability for separately identifiable activities which make individual control procedures necessary or desirable.

The pervasiveness of fund accounting is illustrated by the fact that the semiannual Uniform Certified Public Accountants Examination usually contains at least one lengthy problem on this subject. Undergraduate accounting curricula of colleges and universities often devote at least one quarter or semester course to fund accounting.

VARIOUS COST CONCEPTS

Following the lead of private enterprise, accountants and administrators in the public sector have recently begun to utilize different concepts of cost behaviour for specified control purposes. The essence of cost behaviour distinctions is that different cost measurements are most useful for different managerial control decisions if specific and directly related cost measurements are established for individual circumstances. For example, the cost of acquiring an asset can be distinguished usefully from the cost of using that asset in a not-for-profit programme. Similarly, the cost of replacing an old asset with an equivalent new asset may be more important in certain decisions than original acquisition cost of the old assets.

MATCHING EFFORTS AND ACCOMPLISHMENTS

Compliance with expenditure authorizations is a key objective of the public sector accounting function. Measures of compliance are easier to establish than measures of efficiency or measures of effectiveness, since the output of not-for-profit organizations is by and large intangible and not market oriented. Our market-oriented economic system serves, among others, the crucially important roles of allocating resources and continually threatening the survival of weak or inefficient enterprises. Thus the profit motive ensures that the entire private sector runs relatively efficiently.

For private enterprises, periodic costs (efforts) and revenues (accomplishments) are accounted for systematically, and the difference between them is reported as period net income. For larger companies, this reporting must conform absolutely to the requirements of the federal SEC. Moreover, it must be reviewed and audited at least once a year by independent outside professionals. Determination of periodic net income is presumably the most critical performance measurement for a private enterprise. Even though in the future we are likely to see greater emphasis upon measuring and reporting a company's social, legal, and environmental performance, the latter will not replace the basic measures of economic performance. So long as private capital finances enterprise investments, economic performance will retain its prominence in the overall system.

With the absence of the profit motive in the public sector and the compounding difficulty of producing intangible and quite often elusive products, periodic matching of efforts and accomplishments in terms of concise quantitative reports has proved difficult. Thus, for many years, the public sector did little more than measure and report its dollar performance.

DOLLAR PERFORMANCE

Traditional financial accounting systems and reports of not-for-profit organizations are oriented to identifying and summarizing how money is expended and to what extent such expenditures are consistent with authorizations or budgets. This system provides dollar accountability, but it furnishes few clues about the results that may have been achieved. The degree of efficiency in operations cannot be determined from dollar performance reports.

As we have seen, dollar performance is predominantly oriented to compliance. Dollar inflows are a measure of accomplishment for private enterprises if such inflows represent revenues. However, no implication of accomplishment can be attached to the donated or appropriated dollars flowing to a not-for-profit organization. Moreover, matching of costs and revenues in the private sector produces a measure of performance (however conventionally or arbitrarily defined) which, if consistently applied, is a useful economic indicator

Neither money inflows alone nor calculations of *net* money inflows and outflows allow evaluation of the efficiency and effectiveness of a not-for-profit organization's activity. A system of accounts and reports primarily aimed at compliance is both necessary and desirable for the public sector. However, such a system does not adequately serve today's social needs and concerns.

PPBS SYSTEM

During World War II, several federal government agencies and various units of the armed services began to distinguish between monetary expenditures and operational efficiency. Moreover, the stated objectives of an organization began to be distinguished from measured accomplishments of these objectives. These developments were the forerunners of an accounting process known as planning, programming, and budgeting system (PPBS), which is increasingly being used in not-for-profit organizations. PPBS came fully into its own when, in 1965, the late President Lyndon B. Johnson requested that all government agencies adopt this system.

PPBS is designed to create a framework within which each not-for-profit organization can consider its anticipated outputs (accomplishments) in relation to probably required inputs of resources (efforts) before it makes a commitment to the programme. Under PPBS, the supporters of an organization or programme begin their justification for financial support by identifying the goals (accomplishments) that the organization or the programme expects to achieve. Measurement is facilitated if goals can be stated in quantitative terms, though not necessarily dollar terms. After programme goals are established, alternative courses of action are evaluated in terms of their probable achievement of the goals (i.e., probable effectiveness) and their probable costs (i.e., probable efficiency). Decision makers then choose the plan that allows optimal goal achievements in terms of required resource inputs (i.e., optimal effectiveness-efficiency). With PPBS, some proposed programs are never initiated because analysis shows excessive resource input requirements or low probabilities of achieving desired results. Also, PPBS allows periodic reporting just like most other formal accounting systems.

GOALS IN RELATION TO ACCOMPLISHMENTS

The statement is made in the preceding section that identification of goals is the first significant step in a PPBS system. This statement needs elaboration. Goal-setting procedures in not-for-profit organizations technically involve

- Specification of objectives
- Specification of measures of accomplishment. Operationally, these two steps constitute the goal structuring needed in not-for-profit organizations.

Example: The stated objective of Unified School District 205 is to provide kindergarten, primary, and secondary education for all residents in its district through grade level 12. From this broad objective a hierarchy of sub objectives is established, like minimizing the number of high school dropouts per year, operating a special education programme for physically or mentally handicapped students, running summer school programs for exceptionally able students, and providing various health care and counseling services for all students in the district.

The entire hierarchy of objectives is subsequently used to measure accomplishments. College admission percentages of high school seniors wishing to enter college may be one measure of accomplishment. Lower in the hierarchy, performance on verbal and quantitative aptitude tests may measure math and language achievements of district sixth graders against national test scores.

Not only do statements of objectives influence the selection of measures of accomplishment, but the selection of measures of accomplishment may influence statements of objectives. Therefore the establishment of objectives and of criteria for the measurement of these objectives are interacting processes in the goal formation stage in PPBS.

PPBS DATA BASES

As knowledge stands at present, most PPBS applications

are plagued by inadequate data bases. Notwithstanding developmental efforts by the General Accounting Office (GAO), the American Accounting Association, and other concerned professional groups, relatively little is known about non-financial measures of efficiency and effectiveness, particularly where several different data bases have to be used. What information to seek and how to measure it are the two most significant barriers to making PPBS fully operational.

INDICATORS OF ACCOMPLISHMENT

Accounting for efforts expended in public sector programs or organizations is similar to its counterpart in the private sector. Although there are certain operational differences, these are not extraordinary in nature. Accounting for costs of not-for-profit organizations can simply and directly be carried forward to any PPBS matching of efforts and accomplishments for not-for-profit activities.

The same cannot be said for the revenue or resource inflow side of the coin. Revenue measurements are not appropriate measures of accomplishment in the public sector. Even if changes in revenue flows were one of the objectives of a programme or an organization, achievement of that particular objective would still not give any indication of overall efficiency or effectiveness. Consequently, we need something other than measures of revenue or cash flows before any effort and accomplishment relationships can be established. The missing link needed for activity evaluation in the public sector has been identified as "indicators of accomplishment." These indicators are most conveniently classified as

- Operations indicators and
- Programme impact indicators.

OPERATIONS INDICATORS

These measures relate to output activities and are often non-financial expressions of products or services produced by an agency or organization. Examples are miles of highways built in a given period, number of automobile licenses issued, number of tests administered, and number of families visited by a social worker. In many instances, these indicators are merely statistics that measure neither efficiency nor effectiveness. Operations indicators can be classified in many ways, including, for example, measures of volume, quality, and comparison.

Example: Street lighting in Ritzville is measured in three different ways. The number of street lights maintained is a volume indicator. An illumination index in terms of kilowatts made available is an indicator of the quality of service. Kilowatt hours of electricity used per street mile during December 197X is an example of a comparative indicator. None of these measures effectiveness of street lighting as a deterrent to crime or for the prevention of automobile accidents.

Of course, operations indicators may also be expressed in financial terms. For instance, federal assistance to minority business programs during fiscal year 1971 produced these indicators, among others:

- Government grants, loans, and guarantees by programme agencies rose from approximately $200 million in 1969 to $434 million in fiscal 1971.
- SBA direct and guaranteed loans to minority enterprises increased from $105.4 million in 1969 to an estimated $254 million in 1971.
- The dollar value of government 8(a) procurement contracts for minority owned business enterprises rose from $8.8 million in 1969 to $66 million in 1971.
- Minority firms received $77.8 million in direct Federal procurement in fiscal 1971, almost 10 times the $8.2 million of the previous year.

Operations indicators generally provide little qualitative information. They are not very useful in measuring how well public needs are being met. Often these measures are selected on the basis of simplicity and ease of calculation and understanding rather than on the basis of relevant performance measurement.

PROGRAMME IMPACT INDICATORS

Indicators of this type are often directly expressed in, or

at least implied by, programme objectives. They relate directly to public or social needs or policies. Here outputs of programs are evaluated comprehensively vis-à-vis:

- Other programs,
- Actual planned accomplishments, or
- Public or social needs or policies.

Example: (Efficiency vis-à-vis another programme.) The primary objective of the Space Shuttle is to reduce substantially the cost of space operations and provide a capability designed to support a wide range of scientific, defence, and commercial uses.

The National Aeronautics and Space Administration contracted with Mathematical, Inc., for an analysis of how economical the Shuttle would be compared with the present launch systems which are used only once. NASA and Mathematical officials stated that this study demonstrated the Shuttle to be economically justified.

Senator Walter F. Mondale asked the General Accounting Office (GAO) to review the cost-benefit analysis used by NASA. With the senator's agreement, GAO's report was released to the Congress in view of widespread interest in the Space Shuttle. GAO identified critical areas of uncertainty in the Mathematical study. GAO also identified the percent of cost increase before an investment in the Space Shuttle programme would become uneconomical compared to the present launch systems.

Example: (Efficiency in meeting a social need.) The Detroit Management Information Systems Group of the international CPA firm Touche Ross & Co. participated in a programme concerned with measurement of one aspect of the so-called war on poverty. Welfare recipients were analyzed for certain personal characteristics, such as health, work experience, and educational background. On these indicators, deficiencies were scaled and multiplied by weights to develop an index of needs. Total needs were then aggregated to develop guides to the most effective areas for investment.

Problems with measuring programme impact indicators abound. Without technical elaboration, we can observe that some scale must be devised to measure each characteristic to be included in the analysis. This often proves most difficult, especially if some type of index has to be constructed and a number of indices aggregated to develop a single composite measure of programme accomplishment. Despite these difficulties some public sector organizations, the Sierra Club Foundation for example, have begun public reporting of some of their programme performance in their annual reports. Other organizations, including private enterprises, seem certain to follow this lead.

SELECTED SPECIAL TOPICS

The scope of accounting for public sector organizations is as wide as the accounting scope in the private sector. Many special accounting problems arise along the line of this spectrum. Accounting for public revenues is singled out as a fairly comprehensive illustration of a special topic. As a second point of general interest, some recent standard-setting efforts are described.

ACCOUNTING FOR PUBLIC REVENUES

Not-for-profit organizations, like all other units in our economic system, must generate resource inflows before continued resource outflows are possible. Quite naturally, the inflows and the outflows seldom match completely.

Example: If total revenue collections for the same period amounted to, let us say, $220 billion, a deficit of $26.3 billion would arise. This deficit is the difference, during 1973, between new monetary resources flowing to the federal government and its total monetary expenditures for the same period. To finance this deficit the federal government must borrow, and the national debt will increase by the difference.

Example: The Open Door Clinic is a university district medical and social aid facility. It was established with an initial grant from the federal government which was not renewed. United Crusade and state, county, and city governments were also unable to provide funds. The clinic's future revenue possibilities were not bright, and hence it could borrow very little money on its own account. Private contributions kept the clinic open, but on a much reduced scale of operations. As implied in these examples, nonproprietary organizations have two major sources of funds:

- Current revenues and
- Borrowing from the public or the private sector. Public borrowing occurs largely through the sale of bonds—U.S. savings and treasury bonds at the national level and state, county, city, or school district bonds at the local level. Most governmental units have statutory power to tax citizens under their jurisdictions and consequently can offer their bonds as virtually risk-free investments. The low-risk feature accounts for the comparatively low interest rate on major government bond issues. Income tax exemption for interest from state and municipal bonds is also a factor, which is explored at greater length.

Index

A

ABM 61, 62
Absorbed 44, 166, 202
Absorption Method 166
ACA 10, 21, 129, 133, 134, 250
Accommodations 170
Accomplish 29, 39, 43, 185

Accrual Method 14, 219, 228
Accumulated 38, 257
Affordability 47, 53
Aggregating 16, 19
AICPA 13, 227
Allocating 98, 131, 132, 146, 158, 162, 185, 261, 267
Allocation 23, 37, 48, 49, 90, 124, 187, 200, 201, 206, 271
Alphabetical 210
Alphanumeric 210
Amortization 74, 116
Applicability 29, 87, 223
Asymmetries 87
AVC 66, 67, 68

B

Bidding Method 137

C

CAIV 48
Compensation Method 148
Controllability 166, 195

D

Deemphasizes 18
Disbursements Method 219

E

EBITDA 240
Eligible 13, 170, 227, 230
Encumbrances 185, 188, 189
Engraving 248
Entrapment 85
Epidemiologist 179
Equilibrium 89
Externalities 87, 88, 89, 90
Extrapolation Method 92

F

Forecasting methods 61

H

HRA 130, 131, 132, 133, 134, 135, 136, 142
HVAC 59, 60

I

IAS 115

IFRIC 223
IFRS 223, 224
Implementing 16, 52, 54, 69, 151, 169, 176
Imprisonment 199
Incumbents 122
Individualistic 196
Insightful 110
Intangible Assets 254, 255, 256
IRR 63, 64

L

LCC 59, 60, 61
Legislation 152, 154, 246
Liabilities 4, 5, 8, 9, 16, 22, 25, 28, 94, 95, 96, 102, 103, 104, 106, 114, 115, 117, 119, 120, 154, 201, 203, 208, 210, 212, 214, 216, 217, 224, 225, 229, 239, 241, 245, 257, 258, 264, 269
LMS 164

M

MIRR 64
Monetized 256
Murpheys 68

N

NASDAQ 246
Negligible 129

P

Parameters 95, 99
Pegged 162
Pharmacoeconomic 68
Predetermined 37, 140
Psychic 30

R

RCA 21
Repugnancy 76
ROI 105, 250

S

SIC 223
Simultaneously 5, 57
SOFP 163
Statistical Methods 146
Stovepipe 196
Straightforward 123
Subordinates 143, 144
Surveillance 20

U

Unmanageable 196
Utilization 23, 54, 100, 156

W

WACC 86
Weyerhaeuser 155
Withdrawals 218, 259, 262, 263